FIGURE SKATING COMPETITION HANDBOOK

WHO WON WHAT AT ALL THE MAJOR COMPETITIONS FROM 1891 to PRESENT DAY

FIGURE SKATING COMPETITION HANDBOOK

WHO WON WHAT AT ALL THE MAJOR COMPETITIONS FROM 1891 to PRESENT DAY

GREG FOX

SUGAR MAPLE PRESS

Sugar Maple Press

www.sugarmaplepress.com

e-mail: sugarmaplepress@yahoo.com

Sugar Maple Press edition: Copyright © 2017 by Greg Fox

All rights reserved. No part of this book may be reproduced in any form or by any means without prior written consent of the Publisher, excepting brief quotes used in reviews.

All Sugar Maple Press titles are available at special quantity discounts for bulk purchases, for sales promotions, premiums, fund-raising, educational or institutional use.
Contact us at sugarmaplepress@yahoo.com for details.

ISBN-13: 978-0-9995984-0-5
ISBN-10: 0999598406

First Sugar Maple Press Trade Paperback Printing: Fall, 2017

PHOTO CREDITS:
All stock photos in this book are licensed through Shutterstock (shutterstock.com), and are credited individually. All other photos in this book, (the ones that are uncredited), are public domain.
All interior illustrations are by Greg Fox ©2017
FRONT COVER : Illustration and design by Greg Fox ©2017
BACK COVER: Illustration and design by Greg Fox ©2017

*F*or Eleanor & Sheila

and

*F*or all those figure skaters who never
won any medals, but whose artistry & athleticism
brought joy & beauty to the world.

ACKNOWLEDGMENTS

I am deeply grateful to the following people for their valuable input:

- Elaine Hooper, Historian and Archivist, National Ice Skating Association of Great Britain , for generously providing me with access to the records of the British National Championships database, and thus ensuring that this book would have what may be the most comprehensive and accurate record of British National Championships medallists ever published.

- Ryan Stevens, whose keen insights guided me to making this a much more accurate and comprehensive book, particularly in regards to the Canadian National Championships. Please check out his wonderful **Skate Guard** blog, "the ultimate archive of figure skating's fascinating and fabulous history."
http://skateguard1.blogspot.ca
and on Facebook at:
http://www.facebook.com/SkateGuard

Table of Contents

11.....Country Abbreviations

13.....Introduction

17.....A Brief History of Competitive Figure Skating

31.....US National Championships

59.....Canadian National Championships

83.....British Figure Skating Championships

101.....European Championships

129.....Grand Prix Events
        133.....Skate America
        144.....Skate Canada International
        156.....NHK Trophy
        168.....Cup of China
        172.....Trophée de France / Internationaux de France
        181.....Cup of Russia / Rostelecom Cup
        186.....Bofrost Cup On Ice
        193.....Grand Prix of Figure Skating Finals

199.....ISU Challenger Series
        201.....Nebelhorn Trophy
        215.....Ondrej Nepela Trophy
        221.....Finlandia Trophy

227.....Four Continents Championships

237.....World Championships

267.....World Junior Championships

283.....Olympics

294.....Figure Skating Resources Online

ABBREVIATIONS OF COUNTRIES

AND	Andorra	ITA	Italy
ARG	Argentina	JPN	Japan
ARM	Armenia	KAZ	Kazakhstan
AUS	Australia	KOR	Korea
AUT	Austria	LAT	Latvia
AZE	Azerbaijan	LTU	Lithuania
BEL	Belgium	LUX	Luxemborg
BER	Bermuda	MEX	Mexico
BIH	Bosnia and Herzegovina	MNE	Montenegro
BLR	Belarus	MON	Monaco
BRA	Brazil	NED	The Netherlands
BUL	Bulgaria	NOR	Norway
CAN	Canada	NZL	New Zealand
CHN	China	PHI	Philippines
CRO	Croatia	POL	Poland
CZE	Czech Republic	POR	Portugal
DEN	Denkark	PRK	North Korea
ESP	Spain	PUR	Puerto Rico
EST	Estonia	ROM	Romania
EUA	United Team of Germany	ROU	Romania
EUN	The Unified Team	RSA	South Africa
FIN	Finland	RUS	Russia
FRA	France	SIN	Singapore
FRG	West Germany	SLO	Slovenia
GBR	Great Britain	SRB	Serbia
GDR	East Germany	SUI	Switzerland
GEO	Georgia	SVK	Slovakia
GER	Germany	SWE	Sweden
GER/FIN	Germany/Finland	THA	Thailand
GRE	Greece	TPE	Chinese Taipei
HKG	Hong Kong	TUR	Turkey
HUN	Hungary	UKR	Ukraine
IND	India	URS	Soviet Union
IRL	Ireland	USA	United States
ISL	Iceland	UZB	Uzbekistan
ISR	Israel	YUG	Yugoslavia

Greg Fox

Introduction

Like many of us, for me, it began with the Olympics.

Actually, no... it began on the frozen ponds and ice rinks around my suburban neighborhood on Long Island, New York. Many hours as a little kid spent gliding across sheets of ice in freezing weather. Often by myself, just enjoying the thrill of it, without a thought of competing for medals or landing a perfect triple axel.

And then there was Innsbruck. Winter of 1976. Dorothy Hamill captivated the world with her stellar, gold medal-winning performance. I hadn't known much about the Olympics before then, (aside from Mark Spitz winning a record number of gold medals in the 1972 Summer games in his stars & stripes Speedo, which I was barely old enough to stay up & watch). But after watching Dorothy skate, and seeing the other skaters, too, I was now hooked on figure skating as a **sport**.

And yes, it *is* a sport. Real athletes who work extremely hard to pull off incredible physical feats on, (and often above), the ice.

But, let's be honest... it's also a bit of a circus. The costumes. The hairstyles. The "kiss & cry", and all of the bouquets of flowers and stuffed animals tossed on to the ice by the adoring fans. Add to that the *drama* that always seems to be swirling around the sport.... the judging scandals... Nancy & Tonya.... battle of the Brians.... dueling Carmens... Johnny Weir! Yes, it *is* a sport... but it's a heck of a colorful, sometimes crazy one, unlike any other!

Opposite Page: **Johnny Weir** and **Tara Lipinski** both had illustrious competitive careers in figure skating. Weir is a 3-time US National Champion, a bronze medallist in World Championships, and he's won numerous medals in the Grand Prix Series of events. Lipinski is the 1998 Olympic gold medallist, (the youngest competitor in the ladies' event to ever win the title), the 1997 World Champion, and the 1997 US Nationals Champion. She also is a 2-time winner of the Grand Prix of Figure Skating Final. In 2014, Weir & Lipinski teamed up to do some commentary at the Sochi Olympics for NBC Sports. They were so well-received that NBC promoted the duo, (along with Terry Gannon), to be the primary commentators of all figure skating events aired on the network.

As mentioned, it was the Olympics that drew me in to watching competitive figure skating, but I was soon to discover the annual figure skating competitions that kick off every year in the Fall and continue through until late March. The ISU Challenger Series, the Grand Prix Series, the US, Canadian and British Nationals, the European Championships, the 4 Continents Championships, and then the biggest one of the year.... the World Championships. The Olympics do seem to get the lion's share of the spotlight, (the fact that they're only held once every four years makes them even more special... and sometimes more heartbreaking, as mistakes made at the Olympics cannot be undone the following season). But, as any true figure skating fan knows, the other competitions can be equally captivating and, at times, more important.

And it was through many years of watching these various competitions that the idea for this book arose. Often, I'd be watching a particular competition, and wonder about who'd won the previous one.... who'd gotten the silver.... and perhaps who'd been left off of the medal platform in prior years. There didn't seem to be any one reference book to incorporate ALL of the medal winners from the history of figure skating, in all of the competitions, (including the Olympics). Wouldn't it be great to have a reference book to pick up and see who won the gold, silver, and bronze in Pairs skating in, say, the 1968 European Championships? Or to find out who won the gold medal in Men's figure skating at the World Championships in 1994 after Alexei Urmanov's unexpected gold medal win at the Olympics that same year? (Hint: it wasn't Alexei Urmanov!).

Well, I do have some experience in the world of publishing, so I figured.... why don't I write that book? Little did I know the amount of time it would take to compile *all* of the competition records that would ultimately be included in this volume. But it was time well spent, and I'm especially proud that this may be the first and only book to feature not only the medal-winners of the most well-known events, (Olympics, World Championships, US, Canadian, British and European Championships), but also the 4 Continents Championship, the entire Grand Prix series of events, the key ISU Challenger series events, and the Junior Worlds, too.

One quirk that I found in my research was that for some competitions, especially in the early years, complete records were not always kept. I was very fortunate in my research to come across Elaine Hooper of the National Ice Skating Association of Great Britain, who was kind enough to provide me with far more accurate records of the British National Championships than, I believe, have ever been published elsewhere. (Just compare what's on Wikipedia for the British National Championships to the far more inclusive listings in this book and you'll see what I mean). Also, Ryan Stevens of the Skate Guard blog was tremendously helpful in pointing me in the right direction for a more inclusive historical listing of the Canadian National Championships. Still, in certain cases, in some of the early decades, a number of silver and bronze medal winners in selected competitions simply are not known, (thankfully, these instances are not widespread... but it is still disappointing to know that some medal winners names are lost to history. Perhaps some of those names will surface at some point, and future editions of this book will be able to include them. If you happen to know of any medal winners not included here, please do contact me at gregfox727@gmail.com).

And one other thing before we proceed. While this book is a compendium of medal winners... I'd also like to offer a huge salute to all those competitive figure skaters who have never won a medal, and whose names did not make it into this book. Winning a medal is wonderful, but there are thousands of dedicated, talented skaters who, for a variety of reasons, have never won a medal...but whose artistry & athleticism have still inspired many, and who are worthy of great acknowledgement for what they have given the sport. It is to them that I dedicate this book.

A Brief History of Competitive Figure Skating

Greg Fox

ABOVE: **Jackson Haines**...a revolutionary, groundbreaking American skater who many consider to be the father of modern figure skating. Generally unappreciated at the time in the USA, he was embraced in Europe and would go on to create the "International Style" of skating, influencing generations of figure skaters.

Ice skating has existed for many centuries, tracing back to the earliest skaters in northern Europe, Siberia, and China. Bones, walrus tusks, and even cornstalks were used to enable skaters to glide across the ice. Steel blades appeared in the Netherlands sometime around the Renaissance era, allowing skaters to move more gracefully on the ice's surface. As the Dutch population embraced this form of winter activity throughout the 17th & 18th centuries, it spread across the continent to France, Italy and beyond, as well as across the channel to Great Britain, (the first official skating club being established in Edinburgh, Scotland in 1742). More skating clubs and man-made rinks appeared throughout the 1800s.

During this time skating as a competitive sport began to grow in popularity, mainly consisting of racing, (both long and short distance), a precursor of modern speed skating. References to figure skating, as a separate discipline, appear as early as the 1700s. "Figure skating" originally was very much focused on tracing precise "figures" on the ice... circles and figure eights. However, it was not until the late 1800s that figure skating as we know it today was born, thanks to the boldly inventive styles of US figure skater Jackson Haines, (born 1840 in New York City). A trained ballet master, Haines brought the beauty and dynamic qualities of ballet to the ice, while inventing some of figure skating's classic moves, such as the sit spin, the spiral, and the spread eagle, as well as an early version of the camel spin. He also had the brilliant idea to screw the figure skating blades directly to his boots, creating much more stability and enabling him to do jumps and athletic moves. (Up to that point, it was common practice to strap or tie blades to a boot).

Dazzling and groundbreaking as he was, Haines was not embraced in his home country. At the time, American skaters emulated British skaters and skated rigidly and precisely, arms locked, without much dynamic quality, (in what was known as "the English style"). Their focus was more about tracing the established patterns on the ice than on the dancing and showmanship that Haines specialized in. Still, Haines managed to win some competition medals during his time in America, (including, according to some sources, the "Championships of America" title circa 1863-64). While this wouldn't have been an officially sanctioned competition, (the first official US National Figure Skating Championships would not be held until 1914), it certainly showed that Haines knew how to command attention... both on, and off, the ice.

He had much more success on the European continent, becoming a star in such countries as Austria, Hungary, Germany and Russia. Becoming especially beloved in Vienna, Haines would influence an entirely new generation of figure skaters who would go on to transform and establish the sport into what it is today. Although he died at the age of 35, Haines' followers in Vienna, (known as the Vienna school), founded the International Skating Union in 1892.

By the late 19th century, some of the official competitions that exist to this day were established. In 1891, the first European Figure Skating Championships were held, and in 1896, the first World Figure Skating Championships.

At the dawn of the 20th century, figure skating had a new blazing star, Ulrich Salchow, (born 1877). who would go on to become a ten-time World Figure Skating Champion. The Swedish superstar, like Haines, revolutionized ice skates... in his case, by introducing a slightly serrated blade that allowed for longer jumps. In fact, what he remains most known for today is the jump named in his honor, the Salchow, (a jump launched from the back inside edge of the skating blade).

The first woman to compete in an officially sanctioned competition

ABOVE: **Ulrich Salchow**, 10-time winner of the World Figure Skating Championships, 9-time European Championships winner, and also the first-ever Olympic gold medallist in figure skating. And, yes... the Salchow jump is named after him, (after winning all those medals, don't you think he deserves it?).

RIGHT: **Madge Syers,** who won silver in the previously all-male World Championships event in 1902, which led to women being banned from the competition immediately afterwards! (By 1906, a separate ladies competition was added to the World Championships, which Syers would go on to win for the next 2 years). Syers won the gold medal in the ladies competition at the 1908 Olympics, the (first to feature figure skating), as well as the bronze medal in the pairs competition, in which she competed with her husband Edgar.

was Madge Syers, who placed an impressive second place at the 1902 World competition, (since there were no other women competing, she was competing against the men). Unfortunately, the ISU promptly banned women from competing against men in international competitions, but by 1906. had introduced a separate "ladies" competition. (And, to this day, most figure skating competitions use the "ladies" term as opposed to "women's". [Aside from Canada, which uses the term "women's".] One wonders why the men's competition was not referred to as the "gentlemen's"!). Happily, Madge Syers would go on to win gold in the first two British Figure Skating Championships in 1903 and 1904, (again competing against the men), and at the 1906 and 1907 World competitions, and also gold at the 1908 Olympics, the first Olympic games to feature figure skating competition.

Canada's first national competition occurred in 1905, (although, 1914 was considered to be the first *official* Canadian Figure Skating Championships). Figure skating premiered at the Olympics at the 1908 Summer Olympics in London, (the first winter sport to become a part of the

Olympics). The first official US National Figure Skating Championships were held in 1914, but would take a break from 1915-1917 due to World War One.

Pairs skating, (a team consisting of one man and one woman), appeared in most competitions quite soon after these first official events began. Pairs made their debut at the World Championships in 1908, and later that year at the 1908 Olympics.

In 1924, the first Winter Olympics were held at Chamonix, France, featuring an 11-year old Sonja Henie who came in last place in the ladies' figure skating competition. Henie, (born 1912 in Oslo, Norway), would go on the win the gold medal in the next three Winter Olympics, as well as become a ten-time World Champion, a six-time European Champion, and a Hollywood superstar, (possibly being the biggest star figure skating has ever produced).

International competitions were put on hold due to World War 2, and in the post-war era, the United States emerged as a figure skating powerhouse with World and Olympic champions such as Dick Button, Tenley Albright, Hayes Alan Jenkins, David Jenkins, and Carol Heiss. Canada also produced such champions as Barbara Ann Scott and Donald Jackson. It would be later on in the 1950s that the Russians emerged as a formidable force, especially in Pairs skating, where, starting in 1964, they began an unmatched 40-year gold medal streak.

Ice dancing entered the world stage as its own event in 1952, debuting that year at the World Championships for the first time. Unlike pairs skating, with its high-lifts, throws, and multi-spin jumps, ice dancing is derived more from a ballroom dance style. It would take several more decades, though, for ice dancing to make it to the Olympics; it appeared as a "demonstration event" at the 1968 Winter Olympics in

---

OPPOSITE PAGE: Diagrams of "special figures", a separate event in itself at the 1908 Olympics. Unlike compulsory figures, special figures were more elaborate, complex figures of the skaters' own design. While compulsory figures would continue to be a part of competitions well into the 20th century, special figures would be phased out of major competitions in the earlier part of the century. (Image from *"A Handbook of Figure Skating Arranged for Use on the Ice"* by George Henry Browne, 1907).

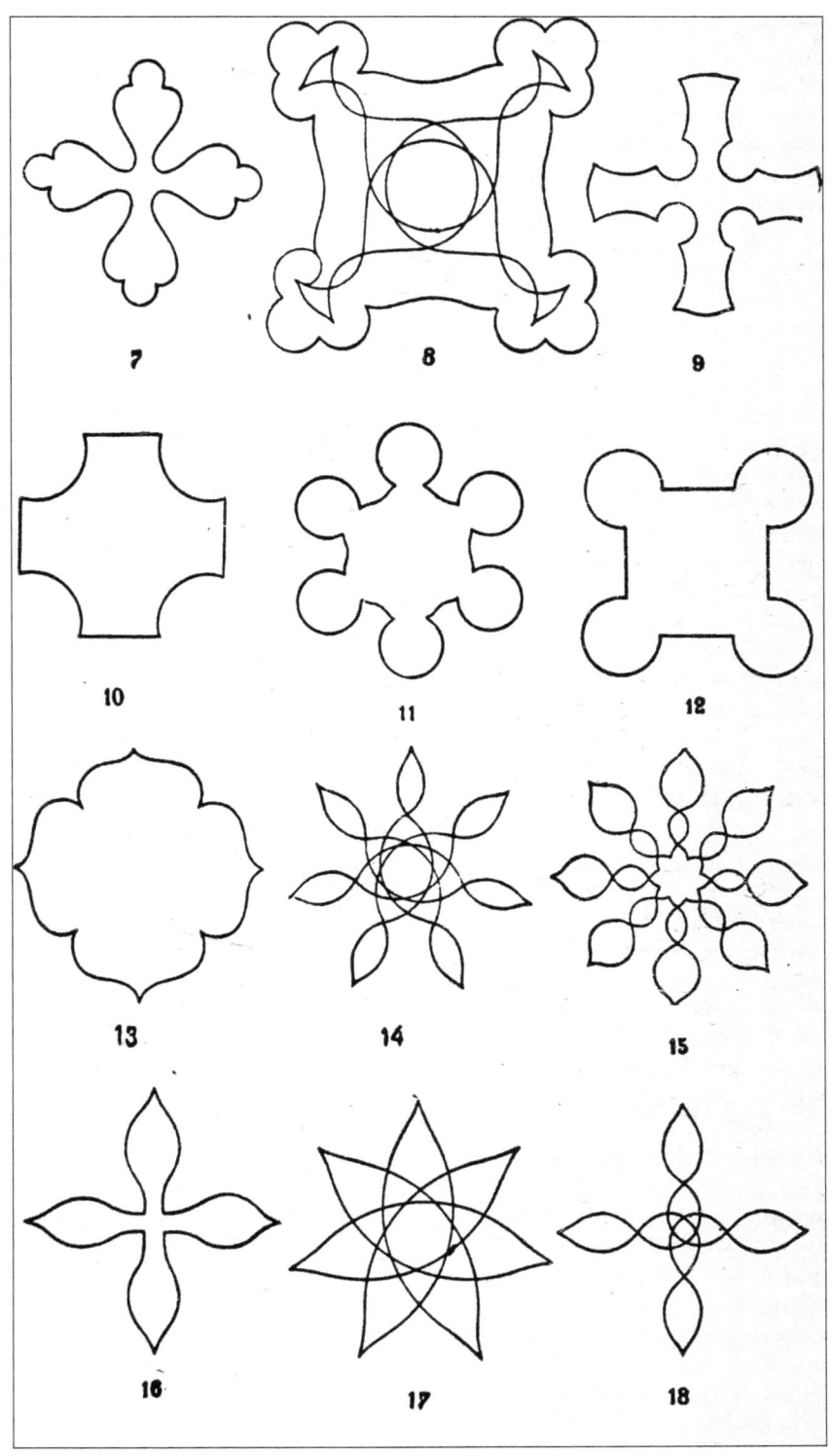

Greg Fox

Grenoble, and finally was added as an official event at the 1976 games at Innsbruck.

The figure skating world, in particular US figure skating, received a devastating blow on February 15, 1961 when a 707 jet, carrying the entire US figure skating team, crashed in Belgium, killing all 72 people on board, (and one person on the ground). The jet was on its way to the 1961 World Figure Skating Championships in Prague, Czechoslovakia, but in the wake of this profound tragedy, the event was cancelled.

The US Figure Skating program would, understandably, take several years to recover; Scott Allen's bronze medal win at the 1964 Olympics was an encouraging sign, and at the 1968 Grenoble, France Olympics, Peggy Fleming's gold medal win in the ladies' competition, and Tim Wood's silver medal win in the men's showed the US team was back in top form.

From the beginning, an important aspect of figure skating competition was Compulsory Figures, (the art of accurately carving a series of specific patterns into the ice). Indeed, this accounted for 60% of a skater's score up until 1968. At that point, things changed. Due to the pressure of televised competitions, (which rarely showed the somewhat tedious Compulsory Figures portion of the event), the weight of the figures dropped to 50% of the score, and a new portion of the competition was added, the Short Program. While the Free Skate, (or Long Program), accounted for the highest percentage of the score, over the years the Compulsory Figures dropped from 40%, to 30%, to 20% of the skater's score. By 1990, they had been dropped completely from most international competitions, (although they continued to be a part of the US National competitions through 1998).

As the Compulsory Figures portion of figure skating competition was disappearing, an increasing focus on athleticism emerged in the 1980s. Although triple jumps, (three revolutions in the air, and three and a half for the Axel jump), had existed in competition since 1952, (first achieved by Dick Button), by the 1980s the new frontier for male skaters was the quad jump, (four revolutions in the air). After a series of failed quad attempts throughout the 1980s by various skaters, Kurt

Browning of Canada landed the first ratified quad jump, a quad toe loop, at the 1988 World Championships. While it would take a while for the quad to become a regular occurrence at competitions, by the late 1990s it was becoming practically a required element for male skaters, (to the point where it became controversial when a male skater would win a competition *without* a quad jump in his program, such as Jeffrey Buttle's 2008 World Championship win and Evan Lysacek's 2010 Olympic win).

While quad jumps were the new frontier for male skaters, some female skaters were breaking new boundaries by attempting triple axel jumps. The technically challenging three-and-a-half rotation

Above: American figure skater **Tenley Albright**, who won silver at the 1952 Olympics and gold in 1956. She also won World Championships in 1953 & 1955, and was US Champion for five years in a row, from 1952—1956.

jump was first successfully completed by a female skater when Midori Ito of Japan included one in her program at the 1988 NHK Trophy. (Ito holds some other important records, too, being the first woman to complete a triple/triple jump combination, and also the first to land seven triple jumps in a free program). Triple axel jumps have not become the nearly required element for female skaters that the quad jump has become for men; since Midori Ito's first successful landing in 1988, only 8 other female skaters have successfully landed any in competition, (most recently by American skater Mirai Nagasu at the start of the 2017/2018 season). Perhaps the triple axel will become a more commonplace element amongst female skaters' programs in the coming decades. For the record, several female skaters have attempted quad jumps, too.... Surya Bonaly of France had several close, but under-rotated, quad jump attempts in the early 90s, and Sasha Cohen of the USA landed a quad Salchow in warm-up practice at Skate America in

2001. To date, the only successfully completed quad jump by a female skater in competition was achieved by Miki Ando of Japan at the 2002 Junior Grand Prix Final.

Throughout the years, various figure skating stars have emerged to engage viewers and bring in new fans of the sport. Peggy Fleming's 1968 Olympic gold medal win made her the first figure skating star of the "color TV era". Dorothy Hamill followed in 1976, and the 1988 Winter Olympics brought figure skating to new heights of viewership with the "Battle of the Brians", (Boitano and Orser), and the "Dueling Carmens", (Katarina Witt and Debi Thomas).

This only set the stage for 1990s, though, when figure skating viewership reached an all-time high in the wake of the Tonya Harding/Nancy Kerrigan debacle surrounding the 1994 US Nationals and the Winter Olympics of that same year. Tonya Harding's then-husband, Jeff Gillooly was implicated as having orchestrated a club attack on Nancy Kerrigan around the time of the US Nationals in Detroit. All hell broke loose in the US media as details emerged in the ensuing weeks, including revelations that Tonya Harding may have assisted in covering up the incident. The United States Olympic Committee attempted to remove Harding from the Olympic team, but backed down after Harding threatened legal action. By the time of the Olympics in Lillehammer, Norway the following month, international media were following Harding and Kerrigan's every move, and the Olympic competition became a media circus, (also generating staggering TV ratings). Kerrigan would win the silver medal, and Harding placed eighth. But figure skating as a sport had now reached unprecedented heights in public consciousness.

Eight years later, when echoes of the Harding/Kerrigan cataclysm had just begun to fade, a new scandal emerged to once again propel figure skating into the media and tabloid glare. This time at the 2002 Winter Olympics in Salt Lake City, Utah. Canadian pairs skaters Jamie Salé and David Pelletier, following the short program, were in a very close second place, behind first place Russian skaters Elena Berezhnaya and Anton Sikharulidze. For the longer, (and more important, scoringwise), free skate program, Salé and Pelletier skated flawlessly, while Berezhnaya and Sikharulidze had an obvious technical error when Sik-

Above: **Jason Brown**, American skater who ratcheted up a number of medal wins at the Junior level, and has consistently been a crowd favorite since his Senior debut in 2013. He's also won a number of Senior level medals, including 3 gold medals in various ISU Challenger Series competitions, a gold, silver, and bronze each in the US National Championships, and a bronze medal in the Team event at the 2014 Olympics. He has struggled with the quad jump over the years, but excels in virtually every other jump and is a powerhouse artistically.

harulidze stepped out of a double axel landing. Most observers felt the Canadians had clearly won, however, when the judges scores were revealed, the Russians had won gold, and the Canadians silver.

Salé and Pelletier were gracious in their acceptance of the silver medal, but almost immediately, there was outcry in the media. Suspicions of a judging fix were focused on the French judge, but after the medals were awarded, it seemed as if that would be the final word. If the International Olympic Committee, (IOC), thought the controversy would blow over in a few days, though, they were wrong; throughout the following week, accusations of wrongdoing and foul play reached a fever pitch, and threatened to cast a dark cloud over the entire Olympics. And then, when unconfirmed reports surfaced that the French judge, Marie-Reine Le Gougne, may have indeed been pressured to vote for the Russians in a deal to gain the Russian judge's vote in the ice-dancing competition, the International Olympic Committee, (IOC), finally decided to take action.

International Skating Union (ISU) President Ottavio Cinquanta announced to the press that an internal review would be conducted by the ISU on the matter, at its next council meeting. Unsatisfied with this casual dismissal, the press, (and millions of fans), went into overdrive. Within five days of the controversial decision, Cinquanta and IOC president, feeling the mounting pressure, held a joint press conference to announce that, Salé and Pelletier's medals would be upgraded to gold, while Berezhnaya and Sikharulidze would also retain their gold medals. A second medals ceremony was held, Salé and Pelletier wound up on the covers of Time AND Newsweek in the same week, and figure skating judging would never be the same.

Throughout the history of figure skating competition, judging has been fraught with controversies and questionable decisions. Unlike, say, downhill skiing or swimming, where the winners are clearly determined by the fastest competitor.... figure skating takes into account a whole host of factors in determining placement in competitions. While landing difficult jumps is clearly an important aspect of a skater's program, there are other elements to consider in scoring. Spins, footwork, presentation and even musical choice and costuming can play a role in how a skater is judged.

Prior to 2004, skaters were judged on a system that used marks ranging from 0.0 to 6.0. Judges focused on required elements in the short program and technical merit in the free skate, and presentation in both programs. Criticism often arose due to the subjective nature of judges' marks, and in the wake of the 2002 judging scandal at the Salt Lake City Olympics, the ISU set out to develop a new judging system.

That new system, (officially known as the ISU Judging System), debuted in 2004 as a way of addressing the previous problems. The new system is far more exacting in codifying every possible component in a program with its own score range. It also sought to alleviate judge tampering by, with a panel of 9 judges, discarding the highest and lowest marks and averaging the remaining 7. The judges marks would also remain anonymous. While some have applauded the new system, criticisms have arisen over the complexity and also the judges' anonymity, (which some believe prevents detection of cheating). In the US, in fact, judges do not remain anonymous and all 9 scores are used. While many in the figure skating world long for the old "6.0" system, it appears the new system is here to stay for a while.

And what does the future of figure skating competition hold? Will the focus increasingly become about quad jumps for the men, and possibly triple axels for the ladies? Or will there be a shift back to an emphasis on artistry? Jason Brown, the 2015 US Nationals Men's champion, won the title without a quad in his program, (however, after sitting out much of the 2016 season due to injury, he added a quad to his program for the 2017 season). It would seem, with the emergence of skaters like American skater Nathan Chen, who scored a record 7 cleanly-landed quads in one competition at the 2017 US National Championships, that quad-packed programs are where things are headed in men's skating.. (Chen also has the distinction of being the only skater with five different types of quad jumps in his program: toe loop, Salchow, loop, Lutz and flip). And American female skater Mirai Nagasu kicked off the 2017/2018 season by landing two triple axels, one in each program, at the U.S. International Figure

Skating Classic, (the first American female skater to land *two* triple axels in the same competition since Tonya Harding in 1991, [however, American skater Kimmie Meissner did land *one* triple axel at the 2005 US National Championships]). While some may lament the emphasis on jumping over artistry in present-day competition, one thing can be counted on...the drama, excitement, and pure spectacle of competitive figure skating will continue to dazzle & thrill us for many years to come!

A Note About Years: The competition results in this book go up to and include the 2016/2017 season. However, while this book was in the last stages of production, the 2017/2018 season kicked off, so I was able to include some results from that season. Specifically, in three ISU Challenger Series events: the **Nebelhorn Trophy**, the **Ondrej Nepela Trophy** and the **Finlandia Trophy**. For those three events, the medal results listed here include the 2017/2018 season.

A Note About Sequencing of Events: Within each of the competition chapters in this book, I have chosen to present the events in the following order: Men, Pairs, Ladies, and Ice Dancing. The reason for this is that it follows the historical establishment of each event. The first official figure skating competitions were Men, (starting in the late 1800s). followed by Pairs, (generally in the 1910s), followed by the Ladies, (in the 1920s), and finally Ice Dancing, (in the 1940s thru 1970s).

United States Figure Skating Championships

ABOVE: **Irving Brokaw** won first place in 1906 and 1908 at the unofficial US National competitions that preceded the first official one in 1914. Brokaw would go on to represent the USA at the 1908 Olympics, (the first to feature figure skating), where he placed 6th. After winning an international competition in Switzerland, he is credited as being the one to bring the "international style" of skating back to America. In 1910, he published his book "The Art of Skating", which was considered a hugely influential figure skating manual for many years. He was later elected as an honorary president of the UFSA, (United States Figure Skating Association).

The US Figure Skating Championships, (known as "the Nationals" within the USA), is the annual competition to determine the national champion of the United States. As with most other figure skating competitions around the world, medals are awarded in four categories: men's singles, ladies' singles, pairs and ice dancing. Although most other figure skating competitions award only the top three competitors, the US Figure Skating Championships honor the top *four*: gold (first), silver (second), bronze (third), and pewter (fourth).

The medalists in each year's US Nationals generally go on to represent the US at the World Championships, World Junior Championships, Four Continents Championships, and the Winter Olympics. (Although, in a number of circumstances, other criteria have been used to make those determinations).

While a number of national US figure skating competitions had existed back in the mid to late 19th century, the first official competition was held in 1914. (The United States Figure Skating Association, or USFA, would be established in 1921). the US Figure Skating Championships have been held every year since 1914 except for 1915-1917, (due to World War I), 1919, and 1944-1945, (due to World War II).

Prior to the event, US skaters compete in a number of smaller, regional competitions to work their way up to qualify for the national championships. However, certain skaters can also earn the right to compete at the US Championships without competing at a sectional competition. Skaters who have placed first through fifth at the previous nationals, skaters who have won a medal at the last year's World Championships, and skaters who gave won a medal at the most recent Olympic Winter Games all qualify for a "bye", (a direct invitation that eliminates the need to compete in the sectional qualifications).

* **Note** - as with many of the other figure skating competitions, records of some of the very early silver, bronze and pewter medallists in this competition were unfortunately not recorded or have simply been lost to history.

U.S. Figure Skating Championships - MEN

Year	Gold	Silver	Bronze	Pewter
1914	Norman M. Scott	Edward Howland	Nathaniel Niles	
1915-1917	NO COMPETITION HELD W. W. 1			
1918	Nathaniel Niles	Karl Engel	Edward Howland	
1919	NO COMPETITION HELD			
1920	Sherwin Badger	Nathaniel Niles	Petros Wahlman	
1921	Sherwin Badger	Nathaniel Niles	Edward Howland	
1922	Sherwin Badger	Nathaniel Niles		
1923	Sherwin Badger	Chris Christenson	Julius Nelson	
1924	Sherwin Badger	Nathaniel Niles	Chris Christenson	
1925	Nathaniel Niles	George Braakman	Carl Engel	
1926	Chris Christenson	Nathaniel Niles	Ferrier Martin	
1927	Nathaniel Niles	Roger Turner	George Braakman	
1928	Roger Turner	Fredrick Goodridge	Dr. Walter Langer	
1929	Roger Turner	Fredrick Goodridge	J. Lester Madden	
1930	Roger Turner	J. Lester Madden	George Hill	
1931	Roger Turner	J. Lester Madden	George Hill	
1932	Roger Turner	J. Lester Madden	George Borden	

Year	Gold	Silver	Bronze	Pewter
1933	Roger Turner	J. Lester Madden	Robin Lee	
1934	Roger Turner	Robin Lee	George Hill	
1935	Robin Lee	Roger Turner	J. Lester Madden	
1936	Robin Lee	Erle Reiter	George Hill	
1937	Robin Lee	Erle Reiter	William Nagle	
1938	Robin Lee	Erle Reiter	Ollie Haupt Jr.	
1939	Robin Lee	Ollie Haupt Jr.	Eugene Turner	
1940	Eugene Turner	Ollie Haupt Jr.	Skippy Baxter	
1941	Eugene Turner	Arthur Vaughn Jr.	William Nagle	
1942	Bobby Specht	William Grimditch	Arthur Vaughn Jr.	
1943	Arthur Vaughn Jr.	Arthur Preusch	William Nagle	
1944-1945	NO COMPETITION HELD - WW 2			
1946	Richard Button	James Lochead	Johm Tuckerman	
1947	Richard Button	John Lettengarver	James Grogan	
1948	Richard Button	James Grogan	John Lettengarver	
1949	Richard Button	James Grogan	Hayes Alan Jenkins	
1950	Richard Button	Hayes Alan Jenkins	Richard Dwyer	
1951	Richard Button	James Grogan	Hayes Alan Jenkins	
1952	Richard Button	James Grogan	Hayes Alan Jenkins	
1953	Hayes Alan Jenkins	Ronald Robertson	Dudley Richards	
1954	Hayes Alan Jenkins	David Jenkins	Ronald Robertson	
1955	Hayes Alan Jenkins	David Jenkins	Hugh Graham	

Year	Gold	Silver	Bronze	Pewter
1956	Hayes Alan Jenkins	Ronald Robertson	David Jenkins	
1957	David Jenkins	Tim Brown	Tom Moore	
1958	David Jenkins	Tim Brown	Tom Moore	
1959	David Jenkins	Tim Brown	Robert Brewer	Bradley Lord
1960	David Jenkins	Tim Brown	Robert Brewer	Bradley Lord
1961	Bradley Lord	Gregory Kelley	Tim Brown	Douglas Ramsay
1962	Monty Hoyt	Scott Allen	David Edwards	James Short
1963	Thomas Litz	Scott Allen	Monty Hoyt	
1964	Scott Allen	Thomas Litz	Monty Hoyt	
1965	Gary Visconti	Scott Allen	Tim Wood	Duane Maki
1966	Scott Allen	Gary Visconti	Billy Chapel	Tim Wood
1967	Gary Visconti	Scott Allen	Tim Wood	John Misha Petkevich
1968	Tim Wood	Gary Visconti	John Misha Petkevich	
1969	Tim Wood	John Misha Petkevich	Gary Visconti	
1970	Tim Wood	John Misha Petkevich	Kenneth Shelley	Roger Bass
1971	John Misha Petkevich	Kenneth Shelley	Gordon McKellen, Jr.	James Demogines
1972	Kenneth Shelley	John Misha Petkevich	Gordon McKellen, Jr.	John Baldwin
1973	Gordon McKellen, Jr.	Robert Bradshaw	David Santee	
1974	Gordon McKellen, Jr.	Terry Kubicka	Charles Tickner	
1975	Gordon McKellen, Jr.	Terry Kubicka	Charles Tickner	Ken Newfield
1976	Terry Kubicka	David Santee	Scott Cramer	Charles Tickner
1977	Charles Tickner	Scott Cramer	David Santee	John Carlow Jr.
1978	Charles Tickner	David Santee	Scott Hamilton	
1979	Charles Tickner	Scott Cramer	David Santee	Scott Hamilton

Year	Gold	Silver	Bronze	Pewter
1980	Charles Tickner	David Santee	Scott Hamilton	Scott Cramer
1981	Scott Hamilton	David Santee	Robert Wagenhoffer	
1982	Scott Hamilton	Robert Wagenhoffer	David Santee	Brian Boitano
1983	Scott Hamilton	Brian Boitano	Mark Cockerell	Bobby Beauchamp
1984	Scott Hamilton	Brian Boitano	Mark Cockerell	Paul Wylie
1985	Brian Boitano	Mark Cockerell	Scott Williams	Christopher Bowman
1986	Brian Boitano	Scott Williams	Daniel Doran	Angelo D'Agostino
1987	Brian Boitano	Christopher Bowman	Scott Williams	Daniel Doran
1988	Brian Boitano	Paul Wylie	Christopher Bowman	Daniel Doran
1989	Christopher Bowman	Daniel Doran	Paul Wylie	Erik Larson
1990	Todd Eldredge	Paul Wylie	Mark Mitchell	Erik Larson
1991	Todd Eldredge	Christopher Bowman	Paul Wylie	Mark Mitchell
1992	Christopher Bowman	Paul Wylie	Mark Mitchell	Scott Davis
1993	Scott Davis	Mark Mitchell	Michael Chack	Aren Nielsen
1994	Scott Davis	Brian Boitano	Aren Nielsen	Todd Eldredge
1995	Todd Eldredge	Scott Davis	Aren Nielsen	Damon Allen
1996	Rudy Galindo	Todd Eldredge	Daniel Hollander	Scott Davis
1997	Todd Eldredge	Michael Weiss	Daniel Hollander	Scott Davis
1998	Todd Eldredge	Michael Weiss	Scott Davis	Shepherd Clark
1999	Michael Weiss	Trifun Zivanovic	Timothy Goebel	Matthew Savoie
2000	Michael Weiss	Timothy Goebel	Trifun Zivanovic	Matthew Savoie
2001	Timothy Goebel	Todd Eldredge	Matthew Savoie	Michael Weiss
2002	Todd Eldredge	Timothy Goebel	Michael Weiss	Matthew Savoie

Year	Gold	Silver	Bronze	Pewter
2003	Michael Weiss	Timothy Goebel	Ryan Jahnke	Scott Smith
2004	Johnny Weir	Michael Weiss	Matthew Savoie	Ryan Jahnke
2005	Johnny Weir	Timothy Goebel	Evan Lysacek	Matthew Savoie
2006	Johnny Weir	Evan Lysacek	Matthew Savoie	Michael Weiss
2007	Evan Lysacek	Ryan Bradley	Johnny Weir	Jeremy Abbott
2008	Evan Lysacek	Johnny Weir	Stephen Carriere	Jeremy Abbott
2009	Jeremy Abbott	Brandon Mroz	Evan Lysacek	Ryan Bradley
2010	Jeremy Abbott	Evan Lysacek	Johnny Weir	Ryan Bradley
2011	Ryan Bradley	Richard Dornbush	Ross Miner	Jeremy Abbott
2012	Jeremy Abbott	Adam Rippon	Ross Miner	Armin Mahbanoo-zadeh
2013	Max Aaron	Ross Miner	Jeremy Abbott	Joshua Farris
2014	Jeremy Abbott	Jason Brown	Max Aaron	Joshua Farris
2015	Jason Brown	Adam Rippon	Joshua Farris	Max Aaron
2016	Adam Rippon	Max Aaron	Nathan Chen	Grant Hochstein
2017	Nathan Chen	Vincent Zhou	Jason Brown	Grant Hochstein

U.S. Figure Skating Championships - PAIRS

Year	Gold	Silver	Bronze	Pewter
1914	Jeanne Chevalier / Norman M. Scott	Theresa Weld / Nathaniel Niles	Eleanor Crocker / Edward Howland	
1915-1917	NO COMPETITION HELD W.W. 1			
1918	Theresa Weld / Nathaniel Niles	Clara Frothingham / Sherwin Badger		
1919	NO COMPETITION HELD			
1920	Theresa Weld / Nathaniel Niles	Edith Rotch / Sherwin Badger		
1921	Theresa Weld Blanchard / Nathaniel Niles	Mrs. Edward Howland / Edward Howland	Clara Frothingham / Charles Rotch	
1922	Theresa Weld Blanchard / Nathaniel Niles	Mrs. Edward Howland / Edward Howland	Edith Rotch / Francis Munroe	
1923	Theresa Weld Blanchard / Nathaniel Niles			
1924	Theresa Weld Blanchard / Nathaniel Niles	Grace Munstock / Joel Liberman		
1925	Theresa Weld Blanchard / Nathaniel Niles	Ada Bauman / George Braakman	Grace Munstock / Joel Liberman	
1926	Theresa Weld Blanchard / Nathaniel Niles	Sydney Goode / James Greene	Grace Munstock / Joel Liberman	
1927	Theresa Weld Blanchard / Nathaniel Niles	Beatrix Loughran / Raymond Harvey	Ada Bauman / George Braakman	
1928	Maribel Vinson / Thornton Coolidge	Theresa Weld Blanchard / Nathaniel Niles	Ada Bauman / George Braakman	

Greg Fox

Year	Gold	Silver	Bronze	Pewter
1929	Maribel Vinson / Thornton Coolidge	Theresa Weld Blanchard / Nathaniel Niles	Edith Second / Joseph Savage	
1930	Beatrix Loughran / Sherwin Badger	Maribel Vinson / George Hill	Edith Second / Joseph Savage	
1931	Beatrix Loughran / Sherwin Badger	Maribel Vinson / George Hill	Grace Madden / J. Lester Madden	
1932	Beatrix Loughran / Sherwin Badger	Maribel Vinson / George Hill	Gertrude Meredith / Joseph Savage	
1933	Maribel Vinson / George Hill	Grace Madden / J. Lester Madden	Gertrude Meredith / Joseph Savage	
1934	Grace Maden / J. Lester Madden	Eva Schwerdt / William Bruns		
1935	Maribel Vinson / George Hill	Grace Madden / J. Lester Madden	Eva Schwerdt / William Bruns	
1936	Maribel Vinson / George Hill	Polly Blodgett / Roger Turner	Marjorie Parker / Howard Meredith	
1937	Maribel Vinson / George Hill	Grace Madden / J. Lester Madden	Joan Tozzer / Bernard Fox	
1938	Joan Tozzer / Bernard Fox	Grace Madden / J. Lester Madden	Ardelle Sanderson / Roland Janson	
1939	Joan Tozzer / Bernard Fox	Annah M. Hall / William Hall	Eva Schwerdt Bruns / William Bruns	
1940	Joan Tozzer / Bernard Fox	Hedy Stenuf / Skippy Baxter	Eva Schwerdt Bruns / William Bruns	
1941	Donna Atwood / Eugene Turner	Patricia Vaeth / Jack Might	Joan Mitchell / Bobby Specht	
1942	Doris Schubach / Walter Noffke	Janette Ahrens / Robert Uppgren	Margaret Field / Jack Might	

Figure Skating Competition Handbook

Year	Gold	Silver	Bronze	Pewter
1943	Doris Schubach / Walter Noffke	Janette Ahrens / Robert Uppgren	Dorothy Goos / Edward LeMaire	
1944	Doris Schubach / Walter Noffke	Janette Ahrens / Arthur Preusch	Marcella May / James Lochead	
1945	Donna J. Pospisil / Jean Pierre Brunet	Ann McGean / Michael McGean	Marcella May Willis / James Lochead	
1946	Donna J. Pospisil / Jean Pierre Brunet	Karol Kennedy / Peter Kennedy	Patty Sonnekson / Charles Brinkman	
1947	Yvonne Sherman / Robert Swenning	Karol Kennedy / Peter Kennedy	Carolyn Welch / Charles Brinkman	
1948	Karol Kennedy / Peter Kennedy	Yvonne Sherman / Robert Swenning	Harriet Sutton / Lyman Wakefield	
1949	Karol Kennedy / Peter Kennedy	Irene Maguire / Walter Muehlbronner	Anne Davies / Carleton Hoffner	
1950	Karol Kennedy / Peter Kennedy	Irene Maguire / Walter Muehlbronner	Anne Davies / Carleton Hoffner	
1951	Karol Kennedy / Peter Kennedy	Janet Gerhauser / John Nightingale	Anne Holt / Austin Holt	
1952	Karol Kennedy / Peter Kennedy	Janet Gerhauser / John Nightingale		
1953	Carole Ormaca / Robin Greiner	Margaret A. Graham / Hugh C. Graham	Kay Servatius / Sully Kothman	
1954	Carole Ormaca / Robin Greiner	Margaret A. Graham / Hugh C. Graham	Lucille Ash / Sully Kothman	
1955	Carole Ormaca / Robin Greiner	Lucille Ash / Sully Kothman	Agnes Tyson / Robert Swenning	
1956	Carole Ormaca / Robin Greiner	Lucille Ash / Sully Kothman	Maribel Owen / Charles Foster	
1957	Nancy Rouillard / Ronald Ludington	Mary J. Watson / John Jarmon	Anita Tefkin / James Barlow	
1958	Nancy Rouillard Ludington / Ronald Ludington	Sheila Wells / Robin Greiner	Maribel Owen / Dudley Richards	

Year	Gold	Silver	Bronze	Pewter
1959	Nancy Ludington / Ronald Ludington	Gayle Freed / Karl Freed	Maribel Owen / Dudley Richards	Ila Ray Hadley / Ray Hadley, Jr.
1960	Nancy Ludington / Ronald Ludington	Maribel Owen / Dudley Richards	Ila Ray Hadley / Ray Hadley, Jr.	Gayle Freed / Karl Freed
1961	Maribel Owen / Dudley Richards	Ila Ray Hadley / Ray Hadley, Jr.	Laurie Hickox / William Hickox	Janet Browning / Jim Browning
1962	Dorothyann Nelson / Pieter Kollen	Judianne Fotheringill / Jerry Fotheringill	Vivian Joseph / Ronald Joseph	Janet Browning / Jim Browning
1963	Judianne Fotheringill / Jerry Fotheringill	Vivian Joseph / Ronald Joseph	Patti Gustafson / Pieter Kollen	
1964	Judianne Fotheringill / Jerry Fotheringill	Vivian Joseph / Ronald Joseph	Cynthia Kauffman / Ronald Kauffman	
1965	Vivian Joseph / Ronald Joseph	Cynthia Kauffman / Ronald Kauffman	Joanne Heckart / Gary Clark	Barbara Yaggi / Gene Floyd
1966	Cynthia Kauffman / Ronald Kauffman	Susan Berens / Roy Wagelein	Page Paulsen / Larry Duisch	
1967	Cynthia Kauffman / Ronald Kauffman	Susan Berens / Roy Wagelein	Betty Lewis / Richard Gilbert	
1968	Cynthia Kauffman / Ronald Kauffman	Sandi Sweitzer / Roy Wagelein	JoJo Starbuck / Kenneth Shelley	Betty Lewis / Richard Gilbert
1969	Cynthia Kauffman / Ronald Kauffman	JoJo Starbuck / Kenneth Shelley	Melissa Militano / Mark Miltano	Sheri Thrapp / Larry Duisch
1970	JoJo Starbuck / Kenneth Shelley	Melissa Militano / Mark Miltano	Sheri Thrapp / Larry Duisch	Kathy Normile / Gregory Taylor

Year	Gold	Silver	Bronze	Pewter
1971	JoJo Starbuck / Kenneth Shelley	Melissa Militano / Mark Miltano	Barbara Brown / Doug Berndt	Sheri Thrapp / Larry Duisch
1972	JoJo Starbuck / Kenneth Shelley	Melissa Militano / Mark Miltano	Barbara Brown / Doug Berndt	Cozette Cady / Jack Courtney
1973	Melissa Militano / Mark Miltano	Gale Fuhrman / Joel Fuhrman	Emily Benenson / Johnny Johns	Debbie Hughes / Philip Grout
1974	Melissa Militano / Johnny Johns	Tai Babilonia / Randy Gardner	Erica Susman / Thomas Huff	
1975	Melissa Militano / Johnny Johns	Tai Babilonia / Randy Gardner	Emily Benenson / Jack Courtney	Erica Susman / Thomas Huff
1976	Tai Babilonia / Randy Gardner	Alice Cook / William Fauver	Emily Benenson / Jack Courtney	
1977	Tai Babilonia / Randy Gardner	Gail Hamula / Frank Sweiding	Sheryl Franks / Michael Boticelli	Lorene Mitchell Donald Mitchell
1978	Tai Babilonia / Randy Gardner	Gail Hamula / Frank Sweiding	Sheryl Franks / Michael Boticelli	Vicki Heasley / Robert Waggenhoffer
1979	Tai Babilonia / Randy Gardner	Vicki Heasley / Robert Wagenhoffer	Sheryl Franks / Michael Boticelli	Tracey Prussack / Scott Prussack
1980	Tai Babilonia / Randy Gardner	Caitlin "Kitty" Carruthers / Peter Carruthers	Sheryl Franks / Michael Boticelli	Vicki Heasley / Robert Waggenhoffer
1981	Caitlin "Kitty" Carruthers / Peter Carruthers	Lee Ann Miller / William Fauver	Beth Flora / Ken Flora	Maria DiDomenico / Burt Lancon
1982	Caitlin "Kitty" Carruthers / Peter Carruthers	Maria DiDomenico / Burt Lancon	Lee Ann Miller / William Fauver	Vicki Heasley / Peter Oppegard

Year	Gold	Silver	Bronze	Pewter
1983	Caitlin "Kitty" Carruthers / Peter Carruthers	Lee Ann Miller / William Fauver	Jill Watson / Burt Lancon	Gillian Wachsman / Robert Daw
1984	Caitlin "Kitty" Carruthers / Peter Carruthers	Lee Ann Miller / William Fauver	Jill Watson / Burt Lancon	Gillian Wachsman / Robert Daw
1985	Jill Watson / Peter Oppegard	Natalie Seybold / Wayne Seybold	Gillian Wachsman / Todd Waggoner	Susan Dungjen / Jason Dungjen
1986	Gillian Wachsman / Todd Waggoner	Jill Watson / Peter Oppegard	Natalie Seybold / Wayne Seybold	Katy Keeley / Joseph Mero
1987	Jill Watson / Peter Oppegard	Gillian Wachsman / Todd Waggoner	Katy Keeley / Joseph Mero	Natalie Seybold / Wayne Seybold
1988	Jill Watson / Peter Oppegard	Gillian Wachsman / Todd Waggoner	Natalie Seybold / Wayne Seybold	Katy Keeley / Joseph Mero
1989	Kristi Yamaguchi / Rudy Galindo	Natalie Seybold / Wayne Seybold	Katy Keeley / Joseph Mero	
1990	Kristi Yamaguchi / Rudy Galindo	Natasha Kuchiki / Todd Sand	Sharon Carz / Doug Williams	Calla Urbanski / Mark Naylor
1991	Natasha Kuchiki / Todd Sand	Calla Urbanski / Rocky Marval	Jenni Meno / Scott Wendland	Sharon Carz / Doug Williams
1992	Calla Urbanski / Rocky Marval	Jenni Meno / Scott Wendland	Natasha Kuchiki / Todd Sand	Karen Courtland / Todd Reynolds
1993	Calla Urbanski / Rocky Marval	Jenni Meno / Todd Sand	Karen Courtland / Todd Reynolds	Katie Wood / Joel McKeever
1994	Jenni Meno / Todd Sand	Kyoko Ina / Jason Dungjen	Karen Courtland / Todd Reynolds	Natasha Kuchiki / Rocky Marval

Year	Gold	Silver	Bronze	Pewter
1995	Jenni Meno / Todd Sand	Kyoko Ina / Jason Dungjen	Stephanie Stiegler / Lance Travis	Shelby Lyons / Brian Wells
1996	Jenni Meno / Todd Sand	Kyoko Ina / Jason Dungjen	Shelby Lyons / Brian Wells	Stephanie Stiegler / John Zimmerman
1997	Kyoko Ina / Jason Dungjen	Jenni Meno / Todd Sand	Stephanie Stiegler / John Zimmerman	Shelby Lyons / Brian Wells
1998	Kyoko Ina / Jason Dungjen	Shelby Lyons / Brian Wells	Danielle Hartsell / Steve Hartsell	Tiffany Stiegler / Johnnie Stiegler
1999	Danielle Hartsell / Steve Hartsell	Kyoko Ina / John Zimmerman	Laura Lynn Handy / J. Paul Binnebose	Tiffany Stiegler / Johnnie Stiegler
2000	Kyoko Ina / John Zimmerman	Tiffany Scott / Philip Dulebohn	Larisa Spielberg / Craig Joeright	Amanda Magarian / Jered Guzman
2001	Kyoko Ina / John Zimmerman	Tiffany Scott / Philip Dulebohn	Danielle Hartsell / Steve Hartsell	Stephanie Kalesavich / Aaron Parchem
2002	Kyoko Ina / John Zimmerman	Tiffany Scott / Philip Dulebohn	Stephanie Kalesavich / Aaron Parchem	Rena Inoue / John Baldwin
2003	Tiffany Scott / Philip Dulebohn	Katie Orscher / Garrett Lucash	Rena Inoue / John Baldwin	Larisa Spielberg / Craig Joeright
2004	Rena Inoue / John Baldwin	Katie Orscher / Garrett Lucash	Tiffany Scott / Philip Dulebohn	Jennifer Don / Jonathon Hunt
2005	Katie Orscher / Garrett Lucash	Rena Inoue / John Baldwin	Marcy Hinzmann / Aaron Parchem	Tiffany Scott / Philip Dulebohn
2006	Rena Inoue / John Baldwin	Marcy Hinzmann / Aaron Parchem	Katie Orscher / Garrett Lucash	Tiffany Scott / Rusty Fein

Year	Gold	Silver	Bronze	Pewter
2007	Brooke Castile / Benjamin	Rena Inoue / John Baldwin	Naomi Nari Nam / Themisto-	Amanda Evora / Mark
2008	Keauna McLaughlin /	Rena Inoue / John Baldwin	Brooke Castile / Benjamin Okolski	Tiffany Vise / Derek Trent
2009	Keauna McLaughlin /	Caydee Denney / Jeremy Barrett	Rena Inoue / John Baldwin	Amanda Evora / Mark
2010	Caydee Denney / Jeremy	Amanda Evora / Mark Ladwig	Rena Inoue / John Baldwin	Rena Inoue / John
2011	Caitlin Yankowskas /	Amanda Evora / Mark Ladwig	Caydee Denney / Jeremy Barrett	Mary Beth Marley /
2012	Caydee Denney / John Coughlin	Mary Beth Marley / Rockne Brubaker	Amanda Evora / Mark Ladwig	Gretchen Donlan / Andrew
2013	Marissa Castelli / Simon Shnapir	Alexa Scimeca / Christopher Knierim	Felicia Zhang / Nathan Bartholomay	Lindsay Davis / Mark Ladwig
2014	Marissa Castelli / Simon Shnapir	Felicia Zhang / Nathan Bartholomay	Caydee Denney / John Coughlin	Alexa Scimeca / Christopher
2015	Alexa Scimeca / Christopher Knierim	Haven Denney / Brandon Frazier	Tarah Kayne / Danny O'Shea	Madeline Aaron / Max Settlage
2016	Tarah Kayne / Danny O'Shea	Alexa Scimeca / Christopher Knierim	Marissa Castelli / Mervin Tran	Madeline Aaron / Max Settlage
2017	Haven Denney / Brandon Frazier	Marissa Castelli / Mervin Tran	Ashley Cain / Timothy LeDuc	Deanna Stellato / Nathan Bartholomay

U.S. Figure Skating Championships - LADIES

Year	Gold	Silver	Bronze	Pewter
1914	Theresa Weld	Edith Rotch	Raynham Townshend	
1915 - 1917	NO	COMPETITION	HELD	
1918	Rosemary Beresford	Theresa Weld		
1919	NO	COMPETITION	HELD	
1920	Theresa Weld	Martha Brown	Lilian Cramer	
1921	Theresa Weld Blanchard	Lilian Cramer		
1922	Theresa Weld Blanchard	Beatrix Loughran		
1923	Theresa Weld Blanchard	Beatrix Loughran	Lilian Cramer	
1924	Theresa Weld Blanchard	Rosalie Knapp		
1925	Beatrix Loughran	Theresa Weld Blanchard	Rosalie Knapp	
1926	Beatrix Loughran	Theresa Weld Blanchard	Maribel Vinson	
1927	Beatrix Loughran	Maribel Vinson	Theresa Weld Blanchard	
1928	Maribel Vinson	Suzanne Davis		
1929	Maribel Vinson	Edith Secord	Suzanne Davis	
1930	Maribel Vinson	Edith Secord	Suzanne Davis	
1931	Maribel Vinson	Edith Secord	Hulda Berger	
1932	Maribel Vinson	Margaret Bennett	Louise Weigel	
1933	Maribel Vinson	Suzanne Davis	Louise Weigel	
1934	Suzanne Davis	Louise Weigel	Estelle Weigel	
1935	Maribel Vinson	Suzanne Davis	Louise Weigel	
1936	Maribel Vinson	Louise Weigel	Audrey Peppe	
1937	Maribel Vinson	Polly Blodgett	Katherine Durbrow	

Year	Gold	Silver	Bronze	Pewter
1938	Joan Tozzer	Audrey Peppe	Polly Blodgett	Jane Vaughn
1939	Joan Tozzer	Audrey Peppe	Charlotte Walther	
1940	Joan Tozzer	Hedy Stenuf	Jane Vaughn	
1941	Jane Vaughn	Gretchen Merrill	Charlotte Walther	
1942	Jane Vaughn Sullivan	Gretchen Merrill	Phebe Tucker	
1943	Gretchen Merrill	Dorothy Goos	Janette Ahrens	
1944	Gretchen Merrill	Dorothy Goos	Ramona Allen	
1945	Gretchen Merrill	Janette Ahrens	Madelon Olson	
1946	Gretchen Merrill	Janette Ahrens	Madelon Olson	
1947	Gretchen Merrill	Janette Ahrens	Eileen Seigh	
1948	Gretchen Merrill	Yvonne C. Sherman	Helen Uhl	
1949	Yvonne C. Sherman	Gretchen Merrill	Virginia Baxter	
1950	Yvonne C. Sherman	Sonya Klopfer	Virginia Baxter	
1951	Sonya Klopfer	Tenley Albright	Virginia Baxter	
1952	Tenley Albright	Frances Dorsey	Helen Geekie	
1953	Tenley Albright	Carol Heiss	Margaret Graham	Margaret Dean
1954	Tenley Albright	Carol Heiss	Frances Dorsey	Margaret Graham
1955	Tenley Albright	Carol Heiss	Catherine Machado	Patricia Firth
1956	Tenley Albright	Carol Heiss	Catherine Machado	Mary Anne Dorsey
1957	Carol Heiss	Joan Schenke	Claralynn Lewis	Nancy Heiss
1958	Carol Heiss	Carol Wanek	Lynn Finnegan	Nancy Heiss
1959	Carol Heiss	Nancy Heiss	Barbara Roles	Lynn Finnegan
1960	Carol Heiss	Barbara Roles	Laurence Owen	Stephanie Westerfeld
1961	Laurence Owen	Stephanie Westerfeld	Rhode Lee Michelson	

Year	Gold	Silver	Bronze	Pewter
1962	Barbara Roles Pursley	Lorraine Hanlon	Victoria Fisher	Frances Gold
1963	Lorraine Hanlon	Christina Haigler	Karen Howland	
1964	Peggy Fleming	Albertina Noyes	Christina Haigler	
1965	Peggy Fleming	Christina Haigler	Albertina Noyes	
1966	Peggy Fleming	Albertina Noyes	Pamela Schneider	
1967	Peggy Fleming	Albertina Noyes	Jennie Walsh	Janet Lynn
1968	Peggy Fleming	Albertina Noyes	Janet Lynn	
1969	Janet Lynn	Julie Lynn Holmes	Albertina Noyes	Dawn Glab
1970	Janet Lynn	Julie Lynn Holmes	Dawn Glab	Jennie Walsh
1971	Janet Lynn	Julie Lynn Holmes	Suna Murray	Dawn Glab
1972	Janet Lynn	Julie Lynn Holmes	Suna Murray	Dorothy Hamill
1973	Janet Lynn	Dorothy Hamill	Juli McKinstry	
1974	Dorothy Hamill	Juli McKinstry	Kath Malmberg	
1975	Dorothy Hamill	Wendy Burge	Kath Malmberg	Barbie Smith
1976	Dorothy Hamill	Linda Fratianne	Wendy Burge	
1977	Linda Fratianne	Barbie Smith	Wendy Burge	
1978	Linda Fratianne	Lisa-Marie Allen	Priscilla Hill	Carrie Rugh
1979	Linda Fratianne	Lisa-Marie Allen	Carrie Rugh	
1980	Linda Fratianne	Lisa-Marie Allen	Sandy Lenz	Elaine Zayak
1981	Elaine Zayak	Priscilla Hill	Lisa-Marie Allen	Rosalynn Sumners
1982	Rosalynn Sumners	Vikki de Vries	Elaine Zayak	Jackie Farrell
1983	Rosalynn Sumners	Elaine Zayak	Tiffany Chin	Vikki de Vries
1984	Rosalynn Sumners	Tiffany Chin	Elaine Zayak	Jill Frost

Greg Fox

Year	Gold	Silver	Bronze	Pewter
1985	Tiffany Chin	Debi Thomas	Caryn Kadavy	Kathryn Adams
1986	Debi Thomas	Caryn Kadavy	Tiffany Chin	Tracey Damigella
1987	Jill Trenary	Debi Thomas	Caryn Kadavy	Tiffany Chin
1988	Debi Thomas	Jill Trenary	Caryn Kadavy	Jeri Campbell
1989	Jill Trenary	Kristi Yamaguchi	Tonya Harding	Holly Cook
1990	Jill Trenary	Kristi Yamaguchi	Holly Cook	Nancy Kerrigan
1991	Tonya Harding	Kristi Yamaguchi	Nancy Kerrigan	Tonia Kwiatkowski
1992	Kristi Yamaguchi	Nancy Kerrigan	Tonya Harding	Lisa Ervin
1993	Nancy Kerrigan	Lisa Ervin	Tonia Kwiatkowski	Tonya Harding
1994	[none] †	Michelle Kwan	Nicole Bobek	Elaine Zayak
1995	Nicole Bobek	Michelle Kwan	Tonia Kwiatkowski	Kyoko Ina
1996	Michelle Kwan	Tonia Kwiatkowski	Tara Lipinski	Sydne Vogel
1997	Tara Lipinski	Michelle Kwan	Nicole Bobek	Angela Nikodinov
1998	Michelle Kwan	Tara Lipinski	Nicole Bobek	Tonia Kwiatkowski
1999	Michelle Kwan	Naomi Nari Nam	Angela Nikodinov	Sarah Hughes
2000	Michelle Kwan	Sasha Cohen	Sarah Hughes	Angela Nikodinov
2001	Michelle Kwan	Sarah Hughes	Angela Nikodinov	Jennifer Kirk
2002	Michelle Kwan	Sasha Cohen	Sarah Hughes	Angela Nikodinov
2003	Michelle Kwan	Sarah Hughes	Sasha Cohen	Ann Patrice McDonough
2004	Michelle Kwan	Sasha Cohen	Jennifer Kirk	Amber Corwin
2005	Michelle Kwan	Sasha Cohen	Kimmie Meissner	Jennifer Kirk

† The 1994 gold medal winner, Tonya Harding, was officially stripped of her title by the United States Figure Skating Association in June, 1994.

Year	Gold	Silver	Bronze	Pewter
2006	Sasha Cohen	Kimmie Meissner	Emily Hughes	Katy Taylor
2007	Kimmie Meissner	Emily Hughes	Alissa Czisny	Beatrisa Liang
2008	Mirai Nagasu	Rachael Flatt	Ashley Wagner	Caroline Zhang
2009	Alissa Czisny	Rachael Flatt	Caroline Zhang	Ashley Wagner
2010	Rachael Flatt	Mirai Nagasu	Ashley Wagner	Sasha Cohen
2011	Alissa Czisny	Rachael Flatt	Mirai Nagasu	Agnes Zawadzki
2012	Ashley Wagner	Alissa Czisny	Agnes Zawadzki	Caroline Zhang
2013	Ashley Wagner	Gracie Gold	Agnes Zawadzki	Courtney Hicks
2014	Gracie Gold	Polina Edmunds	Mirai Nagasu	Ashley Wagner
2015	Ashley Wagner	Gracie Gold	Karen Chen	Polina Edmunds
2016	Gracie Gold	Polina Edmunds	Ashley Wagner	Mirai Nagasu
2017	Karen Chen	Ashley Wagner	Mariah Bell	Mirai Nagasu

U.S. Figure Skating Championships - ICE DANCING

Year	Gold	Silver	Bronze	Pewter
1936	Marjorie Parker / Joseph Savage	Nettie Prantell / Harold Hartshorne	Clara Frothingham / Ashton Parmeter	
1937	Nettie Prantell / Harold Hartshorne	Marjorie Parker / Joseph Savage	Ardelle Kloss / Roland Jansea	
1938	Nettie Prantell / Harold Hartshorne	Katherine Durbrow / Joseph Savage	Louise W. Atwell / Otto Dallmayr	Marjorie Parker / George Boltres
1939	Sandy MacDonald / Harold Hartshorne	Nettie Prantell / Joseph Savage	Marjorie Parker / George Boltres	
1940	Sandy MacDonald / Harold Hartshorne	Nettie Prantell / George Boltres	Vernafay Thysell / Paul Harrington	
1941	Sandy MacDonald / Harold Hartshorne	Elizabeth Kennedy / Eugene Turner	Edith Whetstone / A.L. Richards	
1942	Edith Whetstone / A.L. Richards	Sandy MacDonald / Harold Hartshorne	Ramona Allen / Herman Torrano	
1943	Marcella May / James Lochead	Marjorie Parker Smith / Joseph Savage	Nettie Prantell / Harold Hartshorne	
1944	Marcella May / James Lochead	Kathe Mehl / Harold Hartshorne	Mary Anderson / Jack Anderson	
1945	Kathe Mehl Williams / Robert Swenning	Marcella May Willis / James Lochead	Anne Davies / Carleton Hoffner	
1946	Anne Davies / Carleton Hoffner	Lois Waring / Walter Bainbridge	Carmel Waterbury / Edward Bodel	
1947	Lois Waring / Walter Bainbridge	Anne Davies / Carleton Hoffner	Marcella Willis / Frank Davenport	

Year	Gold	Silver	Bronze	Pewter
1948	Lois Waring / Walter Bainbridge	Anne Davies / Carleton Hoffner	Irene Maguire / Frank Davenport	
1949	Lois Waring / Walter Bainbridge	Irene Maguire / Walter Muehlbronner	Carmel Bodel / Edward Bodel	
1950	Lois Waring / Michael McGean	Irene Maguire / Walter Muehlbronner	Anne Davies / Carleton Hoffner	
1951	Carmel Bodel / Edward Bodel	Virginia Hoyns / Donald Jacoby	Carol Ann Peters / Daniel Ryan	
1952	Lois Waring / Michael McGean	Carol Ann Peters / Daniel Ryan	Carmel Bodel / Edward Bodel	
1953	Carol Ann Peters / Daniel Ryan	Virginia Hoyns / Donald Jacoby	Carmel Bodel / Edward Bodel	
1954	Carmel Bodel / Edward Bodel	Phyllis Forney / Martin Forney	Patsy Reidel / Roland Junso	
1955	Carmel Bodel / Edward Bodel	Joan Zamboni / Roland Junso	Phyllis Forney / Martin Forney	
1956	Joan Zamboni / Roland Junso	Carmel Bodel / Edward Bodel	Sidney Arnold / Franklin Nelson	
1957	Sharon McKenzie / Bert Wright	Andree Anderson / Donald Jacoby	Joan Zamboni / Roland Junso	
1958	Andree Anderson / Donald Jacoby	Claire O'Neil / John Bejshak, Jr.	Susan Sebo / Tim Brown	
1959	Andree Anderson Jacoby / Donald Jacoby	Margie Ackles / Charles Phillips	Judy Ann Lamar / Ronald Ludington	
1960	Margie Ackles / Charles Phillips	Marilyn Meeker / Larry Pierce	Yvonne Littlefield / Roger Campbell	
1961	Diane Sherbloom / Larry Pierce	Dona Lee Carrier / Roger Campbell	Patricia Dineen / Robert Dineen	Jan Jacobsen / Marshall Campbell

Year	Gold	Silver	Bronze	Pewter
1962	Yvonne Littlefield / Peter Betts	Dorothyann Nelson / Pieter Kollen	Lorna Dyer / King Cole	Rosemary McEvoy / Ralph Owen
1963	Sally Schantz / Stanley Urban	Yvonne Littlefield / Peter Betts	Lorna Dyer / John Carrell	
1964	Darleen Streich / Charles Fetter	Carole MacSween / Robert Munz	Lorna Dyer / John Carrell	
1965	Kristin Fortune / Dennis Sveum	Lorna Dyer / John Carrell	Susan Urban / Stanley Urban	
1966	Kristin Fortune / Dennis Sveum	Lorna Dyer / John Carrell	Susan Urban / Stanley Urban	
1967	Lorna Dyer / John Carrell	Alma Davenport / Roger Berry	Judy Schwomeyer / James Sladky	Dolly Rodenbaugh / Tom Lescinski
1968	Judy Schwomeyer / James Sladky	Vicki Camper / Eugene Heffron	Debbie Gerken / Raymond Tiedemann	
1969	Judy Schwomeyer / James Sladky	Joan Bitterman / Brad Hislop	Debbie Gerken / Raymond Tiedemann	
1970	Judy Schwomeyer / James Sladky	Anne Millier / Harvey Millier	Debbie Ganson / Brad Hislop	
1971	Judy Schwomeyer / James Sladky	Anne Millier / Harvey Millier	Mary Campbell / Johnny Johns	
1972	Judy Schwomeyer / James Sladky	Anne Millier / Harvey Millier	Mary Campbell / Johnny Johns	Debbie Ganson / Brad Hislop
1973	Mary Campbell / Johnny Johns	Anne Millier / Harvey Millier	Jane Pankey / Richard Horne	
1974	Colleen O'Connor / Jim Millns	Anne Millier / Harvey Millier	Michelle Ford / Glenn Patterson	

Year	Gold	Silver	Bronze	Pewter
1975	Colleen O'Connor / Jim Millns	Judi Genovese / Kent Weigle	Michelle Ford / Glenn Patterson	Anne Millier / Harvey Millier
1976	Colleen O'Connor / Jim Millns	Judi Genovese / Kent Weigle	Susan Kelley / Andrew Stroukoff	
1977	Judi Genovese / Kent Weigle	Susan Kelley / Andrew Stroukoff	Michelle Ford / Glenn Patterson	Stacey Smith / John Summers
1978	Stacey Smith / John Summers	Carol Fox / Richard Dalley	Susan Kelley / Andrew Stroukoff	Kim Krohn / Barry Hagan
1979	Stacey Smith / John Summers	Carol Fox / Richard Dalley	Judy Blumberg / Michael Seibert	
1980	Stacey Smith / John Summers	Judy Blumberg / Michael Seibert	Carol Fox / Richard Dalley	Kim Krohn / Barry Hagan
1981	Judy Blumberg / Michael Seibert	Carol Fox / Richard Dalley	Kim Krohn / Barry Hagan	
1982	Judy Blumberg / Michael Seibert	Carol Fox / Richard Dalley	Elisa Spitz / Scott Gregory	Kim Krohn / Barry Hagan
1983	Judy Blumberg / Michael Seibert	Elisa Spitz / Scott Gregory	Carol Fox / Richard Dalley	
1984	Judy Blumberg / Michael Seibert	Carol Fox / Richard Dalley	Elisa Spitz / Scott Gregory	
1985	Judy Blumberg / Michael Seibert	Renee Roca / Donald Adair	Suzanne Semanick / Scott Gregory	Lois Luciani / Russ Witherby
1986	Renee Roca / Donald Adair	Suzanne Semanick / Scott Gregory	Lois Luciani / Russ Witherby	Susan Wynne / Joseph Druar
1987	Suzanne Semanick / Scott Gregory	Renee Roca / Donald Adair	Susan Wynne / Joseph Druar	April Sargent / Russ Witherby
1988	Suzanne Semanick / Scott Gregory	Susan Wynne / Joseph Druar	April Sargent / Russ Witherby	Renee Roca / James Yorke

Year	Gold	Silver	Bronze	Pewter
1989	Susan Wynne / Joseph Druar	April Sargent / Russ Witherby	Suzanne Semanick / Ron Kravette	Jeanne Miley / Michael Verlich
1990	Susan Wynne / Joseph Druar	April Sargent / Russ Witherby	Suzanne Semanick / Ron Kravette	Jeanne Miley / Michael Verlich
1991	Elizabeth Punsalan / Jerod Swallow	April Sargent / Russ Witherby	Jeanne Miley / Michael Verlich	Elizabeth McLean / Ron Kravette
1992	April Sargent Thomas / Russ Witherby	Rachel Mayer / Peter Breen	Elizabeth Punsalan / Jerod Swallow	Jeanne Miley / Michael Verlich
1993	Renee Roca / Gorsha Sur	Susan Wynne / Russ Witherby	Elizabeth Punsalan / Jerod Swallow	Amy Webster / Ron Kravette
1994	Elizabeth Punsalan / Jerod Swallow	Susan Wynne / Russ Witherby	Amy Webster / Ron Kravette	Wendy Millette / Jason Tebo
1995	Renee Roca / Gorsha Sur	Elizabeth Punsalan / Jerod Swallow	Amy Webster / Ron Kravette	Kate Robinson / Peter Breen
1996	Elizabeth Punsalan / Jerod Swallow	Renee Roca / Gorsha Sur	Eve Chalom / Mathew Gates	Kate Robinson / Peter Breen
1997	Elizabeth Punsalan / Jerod Swallow	Eve Chalom / Mathew Gates	Kate Robinson / Peter Breen	Amy Webster / Ron Kravette
1998	Elizabeth Punsalan / Jerod Swallow	Jessica Joseph / Charles Butler	Naomi Lang / Peter Tchernyshev	Eve Chalom / Mathew Gates
1999	Naomi Lang / Peter Tchernyshev	Eve Chalom / Mathew Gates	Deborah Koegel / Oleg Fediukov	Beata Handra / Charles Sinek
2000	Naomi Lang / Peter Tchernyshev	Jamie Silverstein / Justin Pekarek	Deborah Koegel / Oleg Fediukov	Beata Handra / Charles Sinek
2001	Naomi Lang / Peter Tchernyshev	Tanith Belbin / Benjamin Agosto	Jessica Joseph / Brandon Forsyth	Beata Handra / Charles Sinek
2002	Naomi Lang / Peter Tchernyshev	Tanith Belbin / Benjamin Agosto	Melissa Gregory / Denis Petukhov	Beata Handra / Charles Sinek

Year	Gold	Silver	Bronze	Pewter
2003	Naomi Lang / Peter Tchernyshev	Tanith Belbin / Benjamin Agosto	Melissa Gregory / Denis Petukhov	Loren Galler-Rabinowitz / David Mitchell
2004	Tanith Belbin / Benjamin Agosto	Melissa Gregory / Denis Petukhov	Loren Galler-Rabinowitz / David Mitchell	Kendra Goodwin / Brent Bommentre
2005	Tanith Belbin / Benjamin Agosto	Melissa Gregory / Denis Petukhov	Lydia Manon / Ryan O'Meara	Tiffany Stiegler / Sergey Magerovskiy
2006	Tanith Belbin / Benjamin Agosto	Melissa Gregory / Denis Petukhov	Jamie Silverstein / Ryan O'Meara	Morgan Matthews / Maxim Zavozin
2007	Tanith Belbin / Benjamin Agosto	Melissa Gregory / Denis Petukhov	Meryl Davis / Charlie White	Kimberly Navarro / Brent Bommentre
2008	Tanith Belbin / Benjamin Agosto	Meryl Davis / Charlie White	Kimberly Navarro / Brent Bommentre	Emily Samuelson / Evan Bates
2009	Meryl Davis / Charlie White	Emily Samuelson / Evan Bates	Kimberly Navarro / Brent Bommentre	Madison Hubbell / Keiffer Hubbell
2010	Meryl Davis / Charlie White	Tanith Belbin / Benjamin Agosto	Emily Samuelson / Evan Bates	Kimberly Navarro / Brent Bommentre
2011	Meryl Davis / Charlie White	Maia Shibutani / Alex Shibutani	Madison Chock / Greg Zuerlein	Madison Hubbell / Keiffer Hubbell
2012	Meryl Davis / Charlie White	Maia Shibutani / Alex Shibutani	Madison Hubbell / Zachary Donohue	Lynn Kriengkrairut / Logan Giulietti-Schmitt

Year	Gold	Silver	Bronze	Pewter
2013	Meryl Davis / Charlie White	Madison Chock / Evan Bates	Maia Shibutani / Alex Shibutani	Madison Hubbell / Zachary Donohue
2014	Meryl Davis / Charlie White	Madison Chock / Evan Bates	Maia Shibutani / Alex Shibutani	Madison Hubbell / Zachary Donohue
2015	Madison Chock / Evan Bates	Maia Shibutani / Alex Shibutani	Madison Hubbell / Zachary Donohue	Kaitlin Hawayek / Jean-Luc Baker
2016	Maia Shibtani / Alex Shibutani	Madison Chock / Evan Bates	Madison Hubbell / Zachary Donohue	Anastasia Cannuscio / Colin McManus
2017	Maia Shibtani / Alex Shibutani	Madison Chock / Evan Bates	Madison Hubbell / Zachary Donohue	Elliana Pogrebinsky / Alex Benoit

Canadian Figure Skating Championships

Greg Fox

Above: **Patrick Chan**, Canadian men's figure skater, is a nine-time gold medal winner in the Canadian National Championships (2008–2014, 2016–2017). He's also excelled elsewhere: A silver medallist in the men's and team events at the 2014 Olympics, a three-time World Champion (2011, 2012, 2013), a two-time Grand Prix Final champion (2010 and 2011), and a three-time Four Continents champion. Plus, a number of gold, silver and bronze medals in various Grand Prix, (6 gold medals alone at Skate Canada!), and ISU Challenger series events. And he's still going strong!

The Canadian Figure Skating Championships have been held since 1905, although they were not considered official until the 1914 event, at which time The Figure Skating Department of the Amateur Skating Association of Canada came into existence. (That organization was subsequently renamed "Canadian Figure Skating Association" (CFSA) in 1939, and renamed again as "Skate Canada" in 2000).

Competitions were not held in 1907, (when the Minto Skating Club rink was destoyed by fire), in 1909, and from 1915-1919 due to World War I. Senior level competition was not held in 1943 due to World War II. (Yet ladies singles competition did return in 1944, but men's singles and pairs did not resume until 1945).

The Canadian Figure Skating Championships help to establish each year's Canadian teams for the World Figure Skating Championships, the World Junior Figure Skating Championships, and the Four Continents Figure Skating Championships.

* <u>Note</u>- as with many of the other competitions, records of some of the very early silver and bronze medallists in this competition were unfortunately not recorded or have simply been lost to history.
(Thanks again to Ryan Stevens of **Skate Guard** for pointing me in the direction of more accurate historical records of these competitions).

Canadian Figure Skating Championships - MEN

Year	Gold	Silver	Bronze
1905	Ormond B. Haycock		
1906	Ormond B. Haycock		
1907	NO COMPETITION HELD - Minto Club Rink destroyed by fire.		
1908	Ormond B. Haycock		
1909	NO COMPETITION HELD		
1910	Douglas H. Nelles		
1911	Ormond B. Haycock	J. Cecil McDougall	
1912	Douglas H. Nelles		
1913	Philip Chrysler	Norman Scott	

Year	Gold	Silver	Bronze
1914	Norman Scott	Philip Chrysler	
1915 - 1919 W. W. 1 - NO COMPETITION HELD			
1920	Duncan Hodgson	John Machado	Melville Rogers
1921	Norman Scott	Duncan Hodgson	Melville Rogers
1922	Duncan Hodgson	Melville Rogers	John Machado
1923	Melville Rogers	John Machado	Norman Gregory
1924	John Machado	Montgomery Wilson	Norman Gregory
1925	Melville Rogers	John Machado	Montgomery Wilson
1926	Melville Rogers	Montgomery Wilson	
1927	Melville Rogers	Montgomery Wilson	Jack Eastwood
1928	Melville Rogers		
1929	Montgomery Wilson	Stewart Reburn	Jack Eastwood
1930	Montgomery Wilson	Lewis Elkin	
1931	Montgomery Wilson	Stewart Reburn	Lewis Elkin
1932	Montgomery Wilson	Guy Owen	Hubert Sprott
1933	Montgomery Wilson	Guy Owen	Rupert Whitehead
1934	Montgomery Wilson	Guy Owen	Rupert Whitehead
1935	Montgomery Wilson	Osborne Colson	Guy Owen
1936	Osborne Colson	Wingate Snaith	Philip Lee
1937	Osborne Colson	Wingate Snaith	Philip Lee
1938	Montgomery Wilson	Ralph McCreath	Wingate Snaith
1939	Montgomery Wilson	Ralph McCreath	Wingate Snaith
1940	Ralph McCreath	Donald Gilchrist	Wingate Snaith
1941	Ralph McCreath	Donald Gilchrist	Jack Vigeon
1942	Michael Kirby	Donald Gilchrist	
1943- 1944 W.W. 2 - NO COMPETITION HELD			
1945	Nigel Stephens	Frank Sellers	
1946	Ralph McCreath	Norris Bowden	Roger Wickson
1947	Norris Bowden	Wallace Diestelmeyer	Gerrard Blair
1948	Wallace Diestelmeyer	Roger Wickson	
1949	Roger Wickson	William Lewis	Donald Tobin

Year	Gold	Silver	Bronze
1950	Roger Wickson	Donald Tobin	William Lewis
1951	Peter Firstbrook	Roger Wickson	William Lewis
1952	Peter Firstbrook	William Lewis	Peter Dunfield
1953	Peter Firstbrook	Charles Snelling	Peter Dunfield
1954	Charles Snelling	Douglas Court	Paul Tatton
1955	Charles Snelling	Douglas Court	
1956	Charles Snelling	Donald Jackson	Douglas Court
1957	Charles Snelling	Donald Jackson	Edward Collins
1958	Charles Snelling	Donald Jackson	Edward Collins
1959	Donald Jackson	Edward Collins	
1960	Donald Jackson	Donald McPherson	Louis Stong
1961	Donald Jackson	Donald McPherson	Bradley Black
1962	Donald Jackson	Donald McPherson	Donald Knight
1963	Donald McPherson	Donald Knight	Bill Neale
1964	Charles Snelling	Donald Knight	Jay Humphry
1965	Donald Knight	Charles Snelling	Jay Humphry
1966	Donald Knight	Charles Snelling	Jay Humphry
1967	Donald Knight	Jay Humphry	Charles Snelling
1968	Jay Humphry	David McGillivray	Steve Hutchinson
1969	Jay Humphry	David McGillivray	Toller Cranston
1970	David McGillivray	Toller Cranston	Ron Shaver
1971	Toller Cranston	Paul Bonenfant	Kenneth Polk
1972	Toller Cranston	Paul Bonenfant	Kenneth Polk
1973	Toller Cranston	Ron Shaver	Robert Rubens
1974	Toller Cranston	Ron Shaver	Robert Rubens
1975	Toller Cranston	Robert Rubens	Stan Bohonek
1976	Toller Cranston	Ron Shaver	Stan Bohonek
1977	Ron Shaver	Brian Pockar	Vern Taylor
1978	Brian Pockar	Vern Taylor	Jim Szabo
1979	Brian Pockar	Vern Taylor	Gordon Forbes
1980	Brian Pockar	Gordon Forbes	Gary Beacom
1981	Brian Orser	Brian Pockar	Gordon Forbes
1982	Brian Orser	Brian Pockar	Dennis Coi
1983	Brian Orser	Gary Beacom	Gordon Forbes
1984	Brian Orser	Gary Beacom	Gordon Forbes

Greg Fox

Year	Gold	Silver	Bronze
1985	Brian Orser	Neil Paterson	Gordon Forbes
1986	Brian Orser	Neil Paterson	Jaimee Eggleton
1987	Brian Orser	Kurt Browning	Michael Slipchuk
1988	Brian Orser	Kurt Browning	Neil Paterson
1989	Kurt Browning	Michael Slipchuk	Matthew Hall
1990	Kurt Browning	Elvis Stojko	Michael Slipchuk
1991	Kurt Browning	Elvis Stojko	Michael Slipchuk
1992	Michael Slipchuk	Elvis Stojko	Sébastien Britten
1993	Kurt Browning	Elvis Stojko	Marcus Christensen
1994	Elvis Stojko	Kurt Browning	Sébastien Britten
1995	Sébastien Britten	Marcus Christensen	Ravi Walia
1996	Elvis Stojko	Sébastien Britten	Marcus Christensen
1997	Elvis Stojko	Jeff Langdon	Sébastien Britten
1998	Elvis Stojko	Emanuel Sandhu	Jeff Langdon
1999	Elvis Stojko	Emanuel Sandhu	Jean-Francois Hebert
2000	Elvis Stojko	Emanuel Sandhu	Ben Ferreira
2001	Emanuel Sandhu	Jayson Dénommée	Ben Ferreira
2002	Elvis Stojko	Emanuel Sandhu	Jeffrey Buttle
2003	Emanuel Sandhu	Jeffrey Buttle	Fedor Andreev
2004	Emanuel Sandhu	Ben Ferreira	Jeffrey Buttle
2005	Jeffrey Buttle	Emanuel Sandhu	Shawn Sawyer
2006	Jeffrey Buttle	Emanuel Sandhu	Shawn Sawyer
2007	Jeffrey Buttle	Christopher Mabee	Emanuel Sandhu
2008	Patrick Chan	Jeffrey Buttle	Shawn Sawyer
2009	Patrick Chan	Vaughn Chipeur	Jeremy Ten
2010	Patrick Chan	Vaughn Chipeur	Kevin Reynolds
2011	Patrick Chan	Shawn Sawyer	Joey Russell
2012	Patrick Chan	Kevin Reynolds	Jeremy Ten
2013	Patrick Chan	Kevin Reynolds	Andrei Rogozine
2014	Patrick Chan	Kevin Reynolds	Liam Firus
2015	Nam Nguyen	Jeremy Ten	Liam Firus
2016	Patrick Chan	Liam Firus	Kevin Reynolds
2017	Patrick Chan	Kevin Reynolds	Nam Nguyen

Canadian Figure Skating Championships - PAIRS

Year	Gold	Silver	Bronze
1905	Katherine Haycock & Ormond Haycock		
1906	Katherine Haycock & Ormond Haycock		
1907	NO COMPETITION HELD - Minto Rink destroyed by fire.		
1908	Aimee Haycock & Ormond Haycock		
1909	NO COMPETITION HELD		
1910	Lady Evelyn Grey & Ormond Haycock		
1911	Lady Evelyn Grey & Ormond Haycock	Eleanor Kingsford & Philip Chrysler	
1912	Eleanor Kingsford & Douglas Nelles		
1913	Muriel Burrows & Gordon McLennan	Jeanne Chevalier & Norman Scott	
1914	Jeanne Chevalier & Norman Scott	Muriel Burrows & Gordon McLennan	
1915 - 1919	W. W. 1 - NO COMPETITION HELD		
1920	Alden Godwin & Douglas Nelles	Beatrice McDougall & Allan Howard	
1921	Beatrice McDougall & Allan Howard	Dorothy Jenkins & C. J. Allan	
1922	Alden Godwin & A. G. McLennan	Jeanette Rathbun & Melville Rogers	D. F. Secord & Douglas Nelles
1923	Marjorie Anable & Duncan Hodgson	Dorothy Jenkins & A. G. McLennan	Cecil Smith & Melville Rogers
1924	Elizabeth Blair & John Machado	Margot Barclay & Norman Gregory	Evelyn Darling & Hugh Tarbox

Greg Fox

Year	Gold	Silver	Bronze
1925	Gladys Rogers & Melville Rogers	Elizabeth Machado & John Machado	
1926	Constance Wilson & Errol Morson	Marion McDougall & Chauncey Bangs	Isabel Blythe & Melville Rogers
1927	Marion McDougall & Chauncey Bangs	Constance Wilson & Montgomery Wilson	Elizabeth Machado & John Machado
1928	Marion McDougall & Chauncey Bangs	Gladys Rogers & Melville Rogers	Veronica Clarke & Stewart Reburn
1929	Constance Wilson & Montgomery Wilson	Maude Smith & Jack Eastwood	Gladys Rogers & Melville Rogers
1930	Constance Wilson Samuel & Montgomery Wilson	Margaret Winks & Lewis Elkin	
1931	Frances Claudet & Chauncey Bangs	Constance Wilson Samuel & Montgomery Wilson	Cecil Smith & Stewart Reburn
1932	Constance Wilson Samuel & Montgomery Wilson	Frances Claudet & Chauncey Bangs	Maude Smith & Jack Eastwood
1933	Constance Wilson Samuel & Montgomery Wilson	Maude Smith & Jack Eastwood	Kathleen Lopdell & Donald Cruikshank
1934	Constance Wilson Samuel & Montgomery Wilson	Louise Bertram & Stewart Reburn	Maude Smith & Jack Eastwood
1935	Louise Bertram & Stewart Reburn	Audrey Garland & Fraser Sweatman	Constance Wilson Samuel & Montgomery Wilson
1936	Veronica Clarke & Ralph McCreath	Aidrie Cruikshank & Donald Cruikshank	Mary Jane Halsted & Osborne Colson
1937	Veronica Clarke & Ralph McCreath	Aidrie Cruikshank & Donald Cruikshank	Mary Jane Halsted & Jack Eastwood

Year	Gold	Silver	Bronze
1938	Veronica Clarke & Ralph McCreath	Patricia Chown & Philip Lee	G. M. Black & Jack Kilgour
1939	Norah McCarthy & Ralph McCreath	Aidrie Cruikshank & Donald Cruikshank	Kathleen Lopdell & Peter Chance
1940	Norah McCarthy & Ralph McCreath	Christine Newson & Sandy McKechnie	Eleanor O'Meara & Donald Gilchrist
1941	Eleanor O'Meara & Ralph McCreath	Norah McCarthy & Sandy McKechnie	
1942	Eleanor O'Meara & Sandy McKechnie	Floraine Ducharme & Wallace Distelmeyer	
1943–1944	NO COMPETITION HELD – W.W. 2		
1945	Olga Bernyk & Alex Fulton	Sheila Smith & Ross Smith	
1946	Joyce Perkins & Wallace Distelmeyer	Suzanne Morrow & Norris Bowden	
1947	Suzanne Morrow & Wallace Distelmeyer	Margaret Roberts & Bruce Hyland	
1948	Suzanne Morrow & Wallace Distelmeyer	Sheila Smith & Ross Smith	
1949	Marlene Smith & Donald Gilchrist	Pearle Simmers & David Spalding	Joyce Perkins & Bruce Hyland
1950	Marlene Smith & Donald Gilchrist		
1951	Jane Kirby & Donald Tobin	Frances Dafoe & Norris Bowden	Gayle Wakely & David Spalding

Year	Gold	Silver	Bronze
1952	Frances Dafoe & Norris Bowden	Audrey Downie & Brian Power	
1953	Frances Dafoe & Norris Bowden	Dawn Steckley & David Lowery	
1954	Frances Dafoe & Norris Bowden	Audrey Downie & Brian Power	Dawn Steckley & David Lowery
1955	Frances Dafoe & Norris Bowden	Barbara Wagner & Robert Paul	Audrey Downie & Brian Power
1956	Barbara Wagner & Robert Paul	Maria Jelinek & Otto Jelinek	Dianne Neilson & Edwin Cossitt
1957	Barbara Wagner & Robert Paul	Maria Jelinek & Otto Jelinek	Barbara Bourne & Thomas Monypenny
1958	Barbara Wagner & Robert Paul	Maria Jelinek & Otto Jelinek	
1959	Barbara Wagner & Robert Paul	Jane Sinclair & Larry Rost	Lise Petit & Ian Knight
1960	Barbara Wagner & Robert Paul	Maria Jelinek & Otto Jelinek	Debbi Wilkes & Guy Revell
1961	Maria Jelinek & Otto Jelinek	Gertrude Desjardins & Maurice Lafrance	Debbi Wilkes & Guy Revell
1962	Maria Jelinek & Otto Jelinek	Gertrude Desjardins & Maurice Lafrance	Debbi Wilkes & Guy Revell
1963	Debbi Wilkes & Guy Revell	Gertrude Desjardins & Maurice Lafrance	Linda Ann Ward & Neil Carpenter
1964	Debbi Wilkes & Guy Revell	Linda Ann Ward & Neil Carpenter	Faye Strutt & Jim Watters
1965	Susan Huehnergard & Paul Huehnergard	Alexis Shields & Chris Shields	Faye Strutt & Jim Watters

Year	Gold	Silver	Bronze
1966	Susan Huehnergard & Paul Huehnergard	Alexis Shields & Chris Shields	Betty McKilligan & John McKilligan
1967	Betty McKilligan & John McKilligan	Alexis Shields & Chris Shields	Anna Forder & Richard Stephens
1968	Betty McKilligan & John McKilligan	Anna Forder & Richard Stephens	Alexis Shields & Chris Shields
1969	Anna Forder & Richard Stephens	Mary Petrie & Robert McAvoy	Sandra Bezic & Val Bezic
1970	Sandra Bezic & Val Bezic	Mary Petrie & Robert McAvoy	
1971	Sandra Bezic & Val Bezic	Mary Petrie & John Hubbell	Marian Murray & Glenn Moore
1972	Sandra Bezic & Val Bezic	Mary Petrie & John Hubbell	Marian Murray & Glenn Moore
1973	Sandra Bezic & Val Bezic	Marian Murray & Glenn Moore	Linda Tasker & Allen Carson
1974	Sandra Bezic & Val Bezic	Marian Murray & Glenn Moore	Kathy Hutchinson & Jamie McGrigor
1975	Candy Jones & Don Fraser	Kathy Hutchinson & Jamie McGrigor	Christine McBeth & Dennis Johnston
1976	Candy Jones & Don Fraser	Cheri Pinner & Dennis Pinner	Karen Newton & Glenn Laframboise
1977	Cheri Pinner & Dennis Pinner	Janet Hominuke & Mark Hominuke	
1978	Sherri Baier & Robin Cowan	Lea-Ann Jackson & Paul Mills	Susan Gowan & Eric Thomsen
1979	Barbara Underhill & Paul Martini	Susan Gowan & Eric Thomsen	Lea-Ann Jackson & Bernard Souche
1980	Barbara Underhill & Paul Martini	Lorrie Baier & Lloyd Eisler	Becky Gough & Mark Rowsom

Year	Gold	Silver	Bronze
1981	Barbara Underhill & Paul Martini	Lorrie Baier & Lloyd Eisler	Becky Gough & Mark Rowsom
1982	Barbara Underhill & Paul Martini	Lorrie Baier & Lloyd Eisler	Becky Gough & Mark Rowsom
1983	Barbara Underhill & Paul Martini	Cynthia Coull & Mark Rowsom	Katherina Matousek & Lloyd Eisler
1984	Katherina Matousek & Lloyd Eisler	Melinda Kunhegyi & Lyndon Johnston	Cynthia Coull & Mark Rowsom
1985	Cynthia Coull & Mark Rowsom	Melinda Kunhegyi & Lyndon Johnston	Christine Hough & Doug Ladret
1986	Cynthia Coull & Mark Rowsom	Denise Benning & Lyndon Johnston	Karen Westby & Lloyd Eisler
1987	Cynthia Coull & Mark Rowsom	Denise Benning & Lyndon Johnston	Christine Hough & Doug Ladret
1988	Christine Hough & Doug Ladret	Isabelle Brasseur & Lloyd Eisler	Denise Benning & Lyndon Johnston
1989	Isabelle Brasseur & Lloyd Eisler	Cindy Landry & Lyndon Johnston	Christine Hough & Doug Ladret
1990	Cindy Landry & Lyndon Johnston	Christine Hough & Doug Ladret	Isabelle Brasseur & Lloyd Eisler
1991	Isabelle Brasseur & Lloyd Eisler	Christine Hough & Doug Ladret	Stacey Ball & Jean-Michel Bombardier
1992	Isabelle Brasseur & Lloyd Eisler	Christine Hough & Doug Ladret	Sherry Ball & Kris Wirtz
1993	Isabelle Brasseur & Lloyd Eisler	Michelle Menzies & Jean-Michel Bombardier	Jodeyne Higgins & Sean Rice
1994	Isabelle Brasseur & Lloyd Eisler	Kristy Sargeant & Kris Wirtz	Jamie Salé & Jason Turner
1995	Michelle Menzies & Jean-Michel Bombardier	Allison Gaylor & David Pelletier	Jodeyne Higgins & Sean Rice

Year	Gold	Silver	Bronze
1996	Michelle Menzies & Jean-Michel Bombardier	Kristy Sargeant & Kris Wirtz	Marie-Claude Savard-Gagnon & Luc Bradet
1997	Marie-Claude Savard-Gagnon & Luc Bradet	Kristy Sargeant & Kris Wirtz	Michelle Menzies & Jean-Michel Bombardier
1998	Kristy Sargeant & Kris Wirtz	Marie-Claude Savard-Gagnon & Luc Bradet	Valerie Saurette & Jean-Sébastien Fecteau
1999	Kristy Sargeant & Kris Wirtz	Jamie Salé & David Pelletier	Valerie Saurette & Jean-Sébastien Fecteau
2000	Jamie Salé & David Pelletier	Kristy Sargeant & Kris Wirtz	Valerie Saurette & Jean-Sébastien Fecteau
2001	Jamie Salé & David Pelletier	Kristy Sargeant & Kris Wirtz	Anabelle Langlois & Patrice Archetto
2002	Jamie Salé & David Pelletier	Jacinthe Larivière & Lenny Faustino	Anabelle Langlois & Patrice Archetto
2003	Jacinthe Larivière & Lenny Faustino	Anabelle Langlois & Patrice Archetto	Elizabeth Putnam & Sean Wirtz
2004	Valérie Marcoux & Craig Buntin	Anabelle Langlois & Patrice Archetto	Elizabeth Putnam & Sean Wirtz
2005	Valérie Marcoux & Craig Buntin	Utako Wakamatsu & Jean-Sébastien Fecteau	Anabelle Langlois & Patrice Archetto
2006	Valérie Marcoux & Craig Buntin	Jessica Dubé & Bryce Davison	Utako Wakamatsu & Jean-Sébastien Fecteau
2007	Jessica Dubé & Bryce Davison	Valérie Marcoux & Craig Buntin	Anabelle Langlois & Cody Hay

Year	Gold	Silver	Bronze
2008	Anabelle Langlois & Cody Hay	Jessica Dubé & Bryce Davison	Meagan Duhamel & Craig Buntin
2009	Jessica Dubé & Bryce Davison	Meagan Duhamel & Craig Buntin	Mylène Brodeur & John Mattatall
2010	Jessica Dubé & Bryce Davison	Anabelle Langlois & Cody Hay	Meagan Duhamel & Craig Buntin
2011	Kirsten Moore-Towers & Dylan Moscovitch	Meagan Duhamel & Eric Radford	Paige Lawrence & Rudi Swiegers
2012	Meagan Duhamel & Eric Radford	Jessica Dubé & Sébastien Wolfe	Paige Lawrence & Rudi Swiegers
2013	Meagan Duhamel & Eric Radford	Kirsten Moore-Towers & Dylan Moscovitch	Paige Lawrence & Rudi Swiegers
2014	Meagan Duhamel & Eric Radford	Kirsten Moore-Towers & Dylan Moscovitch	Paige Lawrence & Rudi Swiegers
2015	Meagan Duhamel & Eric Radford	Lubov Iliushechkina & Dylan Moscovitch	Julianne Seguin & Charlie Bilodeau
2016	Meagan Duhamel & Eric Radford	Julianne Seguin & Charlie Bilodeau	Lubov Iliushechkina & Dylan Moscovitch
2017	Meagan Duhamel & Eric Radford	Lubov Iliushechkina & Dylan Moscovitch	Kirsten Moore-Towers & Michael Marinaro

Opposite Page: **Meagan Duhamel** and **Eric Radford**, Canadian pairs skaters who have won gold in the Canadian National Championships for 6 consecutive years, (2012-2017), and show no signs of stopping! They are also 2-time World Champions, 2-time Four Continents Champions, and Olympic silver medallists in the Team Event in 2014. They've also won numerous medals in various Grand Prix & ISU Challenger Series events. Off the ice, Eric Radford made news by coming out as gay in 2014, one of the few figure skaters ever to do so while at the peak of his competitive career.

Canadian Figure Skating Championships - WOMEN

Year	Gold	Silver	Bronze
1905	Anne Ewan		
1906	Aimee Haycock		
1907	NO COMPETITION HELD - Minto Club Rink destroyed by fire.		
1908	Aimee Haycock		
1909	NO COMPETITION HELD		
1910	Iris Mudge		
1911	Lady Evelyn Grey		
1912	Eleanor Kingsford		
1913	Eleanor Kingsford	Jeanne Chevalier	
1914	Muriel Maunsell	Jeanne Chevalier	
1915 – 1919	W. W. 1 - NO COMPETITION HELD		
1920	Jeanne Chevalier	Dorothy Jenkins	Alden Godwin
1921	Jeanne Chevalier	Dorothy Jenkins	Alden Godwin
1922	Dorothy Jenkins	Alden Godwin	Mrs. John Law
1923	Dorothy Jenkins	Cecil Smith	Constance Wilson
1924	Constance Wilson	Margot Barclay	Marjorie Annable
1925	Cecil Smith	Constance Wilson	
1926	Cecil Smith	Constance Wilson	Mrs. G. C. Secord
1927	Constance Wilson	Cecil Smith	Evelyn Darling
1928	Margot Barclay	Marion McDougall	Dorothy Benson
1929	Constance Wilson	Cecil Smith	Dorothy Benson
1930	Constance Wilson-Samuel	Elizabeth Fisher	Dorothy Benson
1931	Constance Wilson-Samuel	Cecil Smith	Elizabeth Fisher
1932	Constance Wilson-Samuel	Veronica Clarke	Elizabeth Fisher
1933	Constance Wilson-Samuel	Cecil Smith	Veronica Clarke
1934	Constance Wilson-Samuel	Veronica Clarke	Kathleen Lopdell
1935	Constance Wilson-Samuel	Veronica Clarke	Frances Claudet

Year	Gold	Silver	Bronze
1936	Eleanor O'Meara	Veronica Clarke	Margaret Leslie
1937	Dorothy Caley	Eleanor O'Meara	Veronica Clarke
1938	Eleanor O'Meara	Dorothy Caley	Eleanor Wilson
1939	Mary Rose Thacker	Norah McCarthy	Eleanor O'Meara
1940	Norah McCarthy	Mary Rose Thacker	Eleanor O'Meara
1941	Mary Rose Thacker	Barbara Ann Scott	Norah McCarthy
1942	Mary Rose Thacker	Barbara Ann Scott	Elizabeth McKellar
1943	W.W. 2 - NO COMPETITION HELD		
1944	Barbara Ann Scott	Marilyn Ruth Take	Nadine Phillips
1945	Barbara Ann Scott	Marilyn Ruth Take	Gloria Lillico
1946	Barbara Ann Scott	Marilyn Ruth Take	Nadine Phillips
1947	Marilyn Ruth Take	Nadine Phillips	Suzanne Morrow
1948	Barbara Ann Scott	Jeanne Matthews	Marlene Smith
1949	Suzanne Morrow	Patsy Earl	Jeanne Matthews
1950	Suzanne Morrow	Marlene Smith	Vevi Smith
1951	Suzanne Morrow	Vevi Smith	Jane Kirby
1952	Marlene Smith	Vevi Smith	Elizabeth Gratton
1953	Barbara Gratton	Dawn Steckley	Yarmila Pachl
1954	Barbara Gratton	Sonja Currie	Vevi Smith
1955	Carole Jane Pachl	Ann Johnston	Joan Shippam
1956	Carole Jane Pachl	Ann Johnston	Sonja Currie
1957	Carole Jane Pachl	Karen Dixon	Margaret Crosland
1958	Margaret Crosland	Doreen Lister	Sonia Snelling
1959	Margaret Crosland	Sonia Snelling	Sandra Tewkesbury
1960	Wendy Griner	Shirra Kenworthy	Sonia Snelling
1961	Wendy Griner	Shirra Kenworthy	Sonia Snelling
1962	Wendy Griner	Petra Burka	Shirra Kenworthy
1963	Wendy Griner	Petra Burka	Shirra Kenworthy
1964	Petra Burka	Wendy Griner	Shirra Kenworthy
1965	Petra Burka	Valerie Jones	Gloria Tatton
1966	Petra Burka	Valerie Jones	Roberta Laurent
1967	Valerie Jones	Karen Magnussen	Roberta Laurent
1968	Karen Magnussen	Linda Carbonetto	Lyndsai Cowan
1969	Linda Carbonetto	Karen Magnussen	Cathy Lee Irwin
1970	Karen Magnussen	Cathy Lee Irwin	Karen Grobba
1971	Karen Magnussen	Ruth Hutchinson	Diane Hall
1972	Karen Magnussen	Ruth Hutchinson	Cathy Lee Irwin

Year	Gold	Silver	Bronze
1973	Karen Magnussen	Cathy Lee Irwin	Lynn Nightingale
1974	Lynn Nightingale	Barbara Terpenning	Daria Prychun
1975	Lynn Nightingale	Kim Alletson	Barbara Terpenning
1976	Lynn Nightingale	Kim Alletson	Susan MacDonald
1977	Lynn Nightingale	Heather Kemkaran	Kim Alletson
1978	Heather Kemkaran	Cathie MacFarlane	Peggy McLean
1979	Janet Morrissey	Heather Kemkaran	Deborah Albright
1980	Heather Kemkaran	Janet Morrissey	Tracey Wainman
1981	Tracey Wainman	Kay Thomson	Elizabeth Manley
1982	Kay Thomson	Elizabeth Manley	Tracey Wainman
1983	Kay Thomson	Charlene Wong	Cynthia Coull
1984	Kay Thomson	Elizabeth Manley	Cynthia Coull
1985	Elizabeth Manley	Cynthia Coull	Charlene Wong
1986	Tracey Wainman	Elizabeth Manley	Patricia Schmidt
1987	Elizabeth Manley	Patricia Schmidt	Linda Florkevich
1988	Elizabeth Manley	Charlene Wong	Shannon Allison
1989	Karen Preston	Charlene Wong	Lisa Sargeant
1990	Lisa Sargeant	Charlene Wong	Josée Chouinard
1991	Josée Chouinard	Lisa Sargeant	Tanya Bingert
1992	Karen Preston	Josée Chouinard	Tanya Bingert
1993	Josée Chouinard	Karen Preston	Susan Humphreys
1994	Josée Chouinard	Susan Humphreys	Karen Preston
1995	Netty Kim	Jennifer Robinson	Susan Humphreys
1996	Jennifer Robinson	Josée Chouinard	Susan Humphreys
1997	Susan Humphreys	Angela Derochie	Jennifer Robinson
1998	Angela Derochie	Keyla Ohs	Jennifer Robinson
1999	Jennifer Robinson	Annie Bellemare	Angela Derochie
2000	Jennifer Robinson	Michelle Currie	Annie Bellemare
2001	Jennifer Robinson	Nicole Watt	Annie Bellemare
2002	Jennifer Robinson	Annie Bellemare	Joannie Rochette
2003	Jennifer Robinson	Joannie Rochette	Annie Bellemare
2004	Cynthia Phaneuf	Joannie Rochette	Jennifer Robinson
2005	Joannie Rochette	Cynthia Phaneuf	Mira Leung
2006	Joannie Rochette	Mira Leung	Lesley Hawker
2007	Joannie Rochette	Mira Leung	Lesley Hawker
2008	Joannie Rochette	Mira Leung	Cynthia Phaneuf
2009	Joannie Rochette	Cynthia Phaneuf	Amélie Lacoste

Year	Gold	Silver	Bronze
2010	Joannie Rochette	Cynthia Phaneuf	Myriane Samson
2011	Cynthia Phaneuf	Myriane Samson	Amélie Lacoste
2012	Amélie Lacoste	Cynthia Phaneuf	Kaetlyn Osmond
2013	Kaetlyn Osmond	Gabrielle Daleman	Alaine Chartrand
2014	Kaetlyn Osmond	Gabrielle Daleman	Amélie Lacoste
2015	Gabrielle Daleman	Alaine Chartrand	Veronik Mallet
2016	Alaine Chartrand	Gabrielle Daleman	Kaetlyn Osmond
2017	Kaetlyn Osmond	Gabrielle Daleman	Alaine Chartrand

Canadian Figure Skating Championships - ICE DANCING

Year	Gold	Silver	Bronze
1947	Margaret Roberts & Bruce Hyland	Joyce Perkins & William de Nance, Jr.	Marnie Brereton & Richard McLaughlin
1948	Suzanne Morrow & Wallace Diestelmeyer	Joy Forsyth & Donald Taylor	
1949	Joyce Perkins & Bruce Hyland	Pierrette Paquin & Donald Tobin	Joy Forsyth & Ronald Vincent
1950	Pierrette Paquin & Donald Tobin	Joy Forsyth & William de Nance	Frances Dafoe & Norris Bowden
1951	Pierrette Paquin & Donald Tobin	Mary Diane Trimble & David Ross	Frances Dafoe & Norris Bowden
1952	Frances Dafoe & Norris Bowden	Joyce Kornacher & William de Nance, Jr.	Pierrette Paquin & Malcolm Wickson
1953	Frances Abbott & David Ross	Patty Lou Montgomery & George Montgomery	Marion Wattie & Harry Ball
1954	Doreen Leech & Norman Walker	Geraldine Fenton & William McLachlan	Claudette Lacaille & Jeffrey Johnston
1955	Lindis Johnston & Jeffrey Johnston	Geraldine Fenton & Gordon Crossland	Beverley de Nance & William de Nance
1956	Lindis Johnston & Jeffrey Johnston	Geraldine Fenton & William McLachlan	Beverley Orr & Hugh Smith

Year	Gold	Silver	Bronze
1957	Geraldine Fenton & William McLachlan	Beverley Orr & Hugh Smith	Elaine Protheroe & William Trimble
1958	Geraldine Fenton & William McLachlan	Ann Martin & Edward Collins	Svata Staroba & Mirek Staroba
1959	Geraldine Fenton & William McLachlan	Ann Martin & Edward Collins	Svata Staroba & Mirek Staroba
1960	Virginia Thompson & William McLachlan	Ann Martin & Gilles Vanasse	Svata Staroba & Mirek Staroba
1961	Virginia Thompson & William McLachlan	Donna Lee Mitchell & John Mitchell	Paulette Doan & Kenneth Ormsby
1962	Virginia Thompson & William McLachlan	Donna Lee Mitchell & John Mitchell	Paulette Doan & Kenneth Ormsby
1963	Paulette Doan & Kenneth Ormsby	Donna Lee Mitchell & John Mitchell	Carole Forrest & Kevin Lethbridge
1964	Paulette Doan & Kenneth Ormsby	Carole Forrest & Kevin Lethbridge	Marilyn Crawford & Blair Armitage
1965	Carole Forrest & Kevin Lethbridge	Lynn Matthews & Bryon Topping	Judy Henderson & John Bailey
1966	Carole Forrest & Kevin Lethbridge	Gail Snyder & Wayne Palmer	Judy Henderson & John Bailey
1967	Joni Graham & Don Phillips	Judy Henderson & John Bailey	Maureen Peever & Wayne Palmer
1968	Joni Graham & Don Phillips	Donna Taylor & Bruce Lennie	Mary Church & Tom Falls
1969	Donna Taylor & Bruce Lennie	Mary Church & Tom Falls	Hazel Pike & Phillip Boskill
1970	Mary Church & David Sutton	Hazel Pike & Phillip Boskill	Louise Lind & Barry Soper
1971	Louise Lind & Barry Soper	Mary Church & David Sutton	Brenda Sandys & James Holden
1972	Louise Lind & Barry Soper	Barbara Berezowski & David Porter	Linda Roe & Michael Bradley

Year	Gold	Silver	Bronze
1973	Louise Soper & Barry Soper	Barbara Berezowski & David Porter	Linda Roe & Michael Bradley
1974	Louise Soper & Barry Soper	Barbara Berezowski & David Porter	Linda Roe & Michael Bradley
1975	Barbara Berezowski & David Porter	Susan Carscallen & Eric Gillies	Shelley MacLeod & Bob Knapp
1976	Barbara Berezowski & David Porter	Susan Carscallen & Eric Gillies	Lorna Wighton & John Dowding
1977	Susan Carscallen & Eric Gillies	Lorna Wighton & John Dowding	Debbie Young & Greg Young
1978	Lorna Wighton & John Dowding	Patricia Fletcher & Michael de la Penotiere	Marie McNeil & Rob McCall
1979	Lorna Wighton & John Dowding	Patricia Fletcher & Michael de la Penotiere	Marie McNeil & Rob McCall
1980	Lorna Wighton & John Dowding	Marie McNeil & Rob McCall	Gina Aucoin & Hans Peter Ponikau
1981	Marie McNeil & Rob McCall	Kelly Johnson & Kris Barber	Joanne French & John Thomas
1982	Tracy Wilson & Rob McCall	Kelly Johnson & Kris Barber	Joanne French & John Thomas
1983	Tracy Wilson & Rob McCall	Kelly Johnson & John Thomas	Karyn Garossino & Rod Garossino
1984	Tracy Wilson & Rob McCall	Kelly Johnson & John Thomas	Karyn Garossino & Rod Garossino
1985	Tracy Wilson & Rob McCall	Karyn Garossino & Rod Garossino	Isabelle Duchesnay & Paul Duchesnay
1986	Tracy Wilson & Rob McCall	Karyn Garossino & Rod Garossino	Jo-Anne Borlase & Scott Chalmers
1987	Tracy Wilson & Rob McCall	Karyn Garossino & Rod Garossino	Jo-Anne Borlase & Scott Chalmers
1988	Tracy Wilson & Rob McCall	Karyn Garossino & Rod Garossino	Melanie Cole & Michael Farrington

Greg Fox

Year	Gold	Silver	Bronze
1989	Karyn Garossino & Rod Garossino	Michelle McDonald & Mark Mitchell	Jo-Anne Borlase & Martin Smith
1990	Jo-Anne Borlase & Martin Smith	Michelle McDonald & Mark Mitchell	Jacqueline Petr & Mark Janoschak
1991	Michelle McDonald & Martin Smith	Jacqueline Petr & Mark Janoschak	Penny Mann & Juan-Carlos Noria
1992	Jacqueline Petr & Mark Janoschak	Penny Mann & Juan-Carlos Noria	Michelle McDonald & Martin Smith
1993	Shae-Lynn Bourne & Victor Kraatz	Penny Mann & Juan-Carlos Noria	Jacqueline Petr & Mark Janoschak
1994	Shae-Lynn Bourne & Victor Kraatz	Jennifer Boyce & Michel Brunet	Martine Patenaude & Eric Masse
1995	Shae-Lynn Bourne & Victor Kraatz	Jennifer Boyce & Michel Brunet	Janet Emerson & Steve Kavanagh
1996	Shae-Lynn Bourne & Victor Kraatz	Chantal Lefebvre & Michel Brunet	Janet Emerson & Steve Kavanagh
1997	Shae-Lynn Bourne & Victor Kraatz	Chantal Lefebvre & Michel Brunet	Megan Wing & Aaron Lowe
1998	Shae-Lynn Bourne & Victor Kraatz	Chantal Lefebvre & Michel Brunet	Megan Wing & Aaron Lowe
1999	Shae-Lynn Bourne & Victor Kraatz	Chantal Lefebvre & Michel Brunet	Marie-France Dubreuil & Patrice Lauzon
2000	Marie-France Dubreuil & Patrice Lauzon	Megan Wing & Aaron Lowe	Josée Piché & Pascal Denis
2001	Shae-Lynn Bourne & Victor Kraatz	Marie-France Dubreuil & Patrice Lauzon	Megan Wing & Aaron Lowe
2002	Shae-Lynn Bourne & Victor Kraatz	Marie-France Dubreuil & Patrice Lauzon	Megan Wing & Aaron Lowe
2003	Shae-Lynn Bourne & Victor Kraatz	Marie-France Dubreuil & Patrice Lauzon	Megan Wing & Aaron Lowe

Year	Gold	Silver	Bronze
2004	Marie-France Dubreuil & Patrice Lauzon	Megan Wing & Aaron Lowe	Chantal Lefebvre & Arseniy Markov
2005	Marie-France Dubreuil & Patrice Lauzon	Megan Wing & Aaron Lowe	Chantal Lefebvre & Arseni Markov
2006	Marie-France Dubreuil & Patrice Lauzon	Megan Wing & Aaron Lowe	Tessa Virtue & Scott Moir
2007	Marie-France Dubreuil & Patrice Lauzon	Tessa Virtue & Scott Moir	Kaitlyn Weaver & Andrew Poje
2008	Tessa Virtue & Scott Moir	Kaitlyn Weaver & Andrew Poje	Allie Hann-McCurdy & Michael Coreno
2009	Tessa Virtue & Scott Moir	Vanessa Crone & Paul Poirier	Kaitlyn Weaver & Andrew Poje
2010	Tessa Virtue & Scott Moir	Vanessa Crone & Paul Poirier	Kaitlyn Weaver & Andrew Poje
2011	Vanessa Crone & Paul Poirier	Kaitlyn Weaver & Andrew Poje	Alexandra Paul & Mitchell Islam
2012	Tessa Virtue & Scott Moir	Kaitlyn Weaver & Andrew Poje	Piper Gilles & Paul Poirier
2013	Tessa Virtue & Scott Moir	Piper Gilles & Paul Poirier	Nicole Orford & Thomas Williams
2014	Tessa Virtue & Scott Moir	Kaitlyn Weaver & Andrew Poje	Alexandra Paul & Mitchell Islam
2015	Kaitlyn Weaver & Andrew Poje	Piper Gilles & Paul Poirier	Alexandra Paul & Mitchell Islam
2016	Kaitlyn Weaver & Andrew Poje	Piper Gilles & Paul Poirier	Elisabeth Paradis & Francois-Xavier Ouellette
2017	Tessa Virtue & Scott Moir	Kaitlyn Weaver & Andrew Poje	Piper Gilles & Paul Poirier

British Figure Skating Championships

Above: **Ethel Muckelt**, British figure skater who had a rather astounding career. Like Madge Syers and some other British female skaters, she entered competition against male skaters in the British National Championships before there ever was a separate ladies event. And, in fact, won silver in 1922 and 1923. Once the ladies event was established, she also won silver, in 1927. She would fare better in pairs skating. Starting in 1914, paired with Sydney Wallwork, she won silver. And then, paired with John Ferguson Page, she won the gold medal in pairs a whopping 9 times, from 1923-1931, and then the silver medal from 1933-1934. Outside of Britain, she also had success, winning the bronze medal at the 1924 Olympics, (at the age of 38!), in the ladies single event, and silver in pairs with John Ferguson Page at the World Championships in 1924. By the time she won her last British Nationals medal, she was competing at the age of 48.

The British National Championships are normally held in November or December of each year, (hence, as an example, the 2017 championship took place in December, 2016). The competition is open to all countries in the British commonwealth, and thus have sometimes attracted competitors from Canada and Australia. Prior to 1927, when the ladies competition was first held, female competitors occasionally competed, (and won medals), in the men's competition. Madge Syers, Dorothy Greenhough-Smith, Phyllis Johnson, Ethel Muckelt, and Kathleen Shaw were female competitors who won gold or silver in the men's competition. In some years, due to lack of entrants to compete, certain disciplines were not included in that year's event.

My deepest gratitude to Elaine Hooper, Historian and Archivist for the National Ice Skating Association of Great Britain, for providing access to their historical database, which uncovered many medal winners names which might have been lost to history. For some of the early years shown here, there are still some gaps; for many of these, there simply weren't any other competitors to fill all of the positions in that year's event. Other years, it is possible some names may not have been recorded at the time. But I am, again, very grateful to Elaine Hooper for opening the British database to help make this, possibly, the most comprehensive list of British Championship medal winners ever published.

British Championships - MEN

Year	Gold	Silver	Bronze
1903	Madge Syers	Hoatio Torrome	
1904	Madge Syers	Edgar Syers	
1905	Hoatio Torrome	H R Yglesias	
1906	Hoatio Torrome	J Keiller Grieg	H R Yglesias
1907	J Keiller Grieg	Hoatio Torrome	
1908	Dorothy Greenhough Smith	A March	
1909	J Keiller Grieg	A March	
1910	J Keiller Grieg	Arthur Cumming	
1911	Dorothy Greenhough Smith	A March	
1912	Arthur Cumming	Basil Williams	A March
1913	Basil Williams	Phyllis Johnson	
1914	Arthur Cumming	Phyllis Johnson	
1915 - 1920	NOT HELD DUE TO W.W. 1		

Year	Gold	Silver	Bronze
1921	Phyllis Johnson	Kenneth Beaumont	
1922	John Ferguson Page	Ethel Muckelt	
1923	John Ferguson Page	Ethel Muckelt	
1924	John Ferguson Page	Ian Bowhill	
1925	John Ferguson Page	Kathleen Shaw	
1926	John Ferguson Page	Kathleen Shaw	
1927	John Ferguson Page	Ian Bowhill	Dr H O J White
1928	John Ferguson Page	M S Wilson	
1929	John Ferguson Page	Ian Bowhill	
1930	John Ferguson Page	A Proctor Burman	*No other competitors*
1931	John Ferguson Page	W M Clunie	H White
1932	Ian Bowhill	L G Cox	H Constantine
1933	John Ferguson Page	H Graham Sharp	
1934	H Graham Sharp	Jackie Dunn	
1935	H Graham Sharp	Jackie Dunn	
1936	H Graham Sharp	Freddie Tomlins	
1937	H Graham Sharp	Freddie Tomlins	Geoff Yates
1938	H Graham Sharp	Freddie Tomlins	Geoff Yates
1939	H Graham Sharp	Freddie Tomlins	Tony Austin
1940 - 1945	**NOT HELD DUE**	**TO W.W. 2**	
1946	H Graham Sharp	Arthur Apfel	Adrian Pryce-Jones
1947	Arthur Apfel	*No other competitors*	
1948	H Graham Sharp	Dennis Silverthorne	Adrian Pryce-Jones
1949	*Senior Men's*	*competition*	*not held*
1950	Michael Carrington	Reg Park	John Elliot
1951	Michael Carrington	Ian Small	*No other competitors*
1952	Adrian Swan	*No other competitors*	
1953	Michael Booker	Geoffrey Duncan	*No other competitors*
1954	Michael Booker	*No other competitors*	
1955	Michael Booker	Brian Tuck	
1956	Michael Booker	Brian Tuck	Keith Kelley
1957	Michael Booker	Brian Tuck	Keith Kelley
1958	Michael Booker	Keith Kelley	Rodney Ward
1959	David Clements	Peter Burrows	Keith Kelley
1960	C. Robin Jones	David Clements	*No other competitors*
1961	*Title not awarded*		
1962	C. Robin Jones	Malcolm Cannon	Hywel Evans
1963	Malcolm Cannon	Hywel Evans	*No other competitors*
1964	Hywel Evans	Malcolm Cannon	Harold Williams
1965	Hywel Evans	Malcolm Cannon	Michael Williams
1966	Malcolm Cannon	Michael Williams	Harold Williams
1967	Michael Williams	Haig Oundjian	Harold Williams
1968	Michael Williams	Haig Oundjian	Harold Williams
1969	Haig Oundjian	John Curry	Michael Edmonds
1970	Haig Oundjian	John Curry	Michael Fish
1971	John Curry	Haig Oundjian	Michael Fish

Year	Gold	Silver	Bronze
1972	Haig Oundjian	John Curry	Gordon Andison
1973	John Curry	Michael Fish	Robin Cousins
1974	John Curry	Robin Cousins	Glyn Jones
1975	John Curry	Robin Cousins	Stefan Wertans
1976	John Curry	Robin Cousins	Glyn Jones
1977	Robin Cousins	Glyn Jones	Andrew Bestwick
1978	Robin Cousins	Andrew Bestwick	Christopher Howarth
1979	Robin Cousins	Christopher Howarth	Mark Pepperday
1980	Robin Cousins	Christopher Howarth	Andrew Bestwick
1981	Christopher Howarth	Andrew Bestwick	Mark Pepperday
1982	Mark Pepperday	Christopher Howarth	Paul Robinson
1983	Mark Pepperday	Paul Robinson	Neil Cushley
1984	Mark Pepperday	Paul Robinson	Stephen Pickavance
1985	Stephen Pickavance	Paul Robinson	Spencer Durrant
1986	Stephen Pickavance	Paul Robinson	David Reynolds
1987	Paul Robinson	Spencer Durrant	Ashley Moore
1988	Paul Robinson	Ashley Moore	David Reynolds
1989	Christian Newberry	John Martin	David Reynolds
1990	Steven Cousins	Christian Newberry	Leigh Yip
1991	Steven Cousins	Leigh Yip	Simon Briggs
1992	Steven Cousins	John Martin	Gary Ballantine
1993	Steven Cousins	John Martin	David Ings
1994	Steven Cousins	John Martin	David Ings
1995	Steven Cousins	Clive Shorten	Stuart Bell
1996	Steven Cousins	Neil Wilson	David Ings
1997	Neil Wilson	Steven Cousins	Clive Shorten
1998	Steven Cousins	Neil Wilson	Clive Shorten
1999	Clive Shorten	Matthew Davies	Stuart Bell
2000	Neil Wilson	Alan Street	Matthew Davies
2001	Alan Street	Neil Wilson	James Black
2002	Matthew Davies	James Black	David Hartley
2003	Neil Wilson	James Black	Matthew Wilkinson
2004	Matthew Davies	Neil Wilson	Stuart Bell
2005	John Hamer	James Black	David Hartley
2006	John Hamer	Thomas Paulson	David Hartley
2007	John Hamer	Thomas Paulson	David Richardson
2008	Elliot Hilton	Thomas Paulson	Tristan Cousins
2009	Matthew Parr	David Richardson	Robert Murray
2010	Matthew Parr	Thomas Paulson	David Richardson
2011	David Richardson	Matthew Parr	Phillip Harris
2012	Jason Thompson	Luke Chilcott	Phillip Harris
2013	Matthew Parr	Harry Mattick	David Richardson
2014	Matthew Parr	Lewis Gibson	David Richardson
2015	Phillip Harris	Peter James Hallam	Harry Mattick
2016	Phillip Harris	Peter James Hallam	Jamie Wright
2017	Graham Newberry	Peter James Hallam	Phillip Harris

British Championships - PAIRS

Year	Gold	Silver	Bronze
1914	James Johnson & Phyllis Johnson	Sydney Wallwork & Ethel Muckelt	
1915 - 1920	NOT HELD	DUE TO W.W. 1	
1921	Mjr. Kenneth Beaumont & Mrs Kenneth Beaumont	C. Cormack & Kathleen Lovett	
1922	Mjr. Kenneth Beaumont & Mrs Kenneth Beaumont	W.E. Kay & Miss Barnes	
1923	John Ferguson Page & Ethel Muckelt	Captain TD Richardson & Mildred Richardson	
1924	John Ferguson Page & Ethel Muckelt	A. Proctor Burman & Kathleen Lovett	
1925	John Ferguson Page & Ethel Muckelt	A. Proctor Burman & Kathleen Lovett	
1926	John Ferguson Page & Ethel Muckelt	A. Proctor Burman & Kathleen Lovett	
1927	John Ferguson Page & Ethel Muckelt	A. Proctor Burman & Kathleen Lovett	
1928	John Ferguson Page & Ethel Muckelt	A. Proctor Burman & Kathleen Lovett	
1929	John Ferguson Page & Ethel Muckelt	*NO OTHER COMPETITORS*	
1930	John Ferguson Page & Ethel Muckelt	Mr. K Ord Mackenzie & Mrs. K Ord Mackenzie	H Constantine & E J McCleary
1931	John Ferguson Page & Ethel Muckelt	Mr. K Ord Mackenzie & Mrs. K Ord Mackenzie	Mr. W. Anderson & Mrs. W. Anderson
1932	Mr. K Ord Mackenzie & Mrs. K Ord Mackenzie	Rodney Murdoch & Mollie Philliips	Mr. Proctor Burman & Mrs. Proctor Burman
1933	Rodney Murdoch & Mollie Philliips	John Ferguson Page & Ethel Muckelt	Leslie Cliff & Violet Supple

Year	Gold	Silver	Bronze
1934	Leslie Cliff & Violet Supple	John Ferguson Page & Ethel Muckelt	H. Constantine & M. Thorpe
1935	Leslie Cliff & Violet Cliff	Ernest Yates & Rosemarie Stewart	H. Constantine & M. Thorpe
1936	Leslie Cliff & Violet Cliff	Ernest Yates & Rosemarie Stewart	*No Other Competitors*
1937	Leslie Cliff & Violet Cliff	Reginald Wilkie & Daphne Wallis	Harry Levy & Cissy Krieger
1938	Leslie Cliff & Violet Cliff	Reginald Wilkie & Daphne Wallis	H. Constantine & Iris Howles
1939	Leslie Cliff & Violet Cliff	Reginald Wilkie & Daphne Wallis	H. Constantine & Iris Howles
1940 - 1945	**NOT HELD**	**DUE TO W.W. 2**	
1946	Dennis Silverthorn & Winifred Silverthorn	Leslie Cliff & Violet Cliff	Mr. R. Griffiths & Mrs. R. Griffiths
1947	Dennis Silverthorn & Winifred Silverthorn	Captain Ernest Yates & Pamela Davis	John Nicks & Jennifer Nicks
1948	Jennifer Nicks & John Nicks	Jean Thompson & Robert Ogilvie	Mrs. R. Griffiths & Mr. R. Griffiths
1949	Jennifer Nicks & John Nicks	Pamela Davis & Peter Scholes	Doris Clayden & Ron Clayden
1948	Jennifer Nicks & John Nicks	Jean Thompson & Robert Ogilvie	Mrs. R. Griffiths & Mr. R. Griffiths
1949	Jennifer Nicks & John Nicks	Pamela Davis & Peter Scholes	Doris Clayden & Ron Clayden
1950	Jennifer Nicks & John Nicks	Sybil Cooke & Robert Hudson	Doris Clayden & Ron Clayden
1951	Jennifer Nicks & John Nicks	E. Williams & J. McCann	
1952	Jennifer Nicks & John Nicks	Peri Horne & Ray Lockwood	Jacqueline Mason & Mervyn Bower

Year	Gold	Silver	Bronze
1953	Jennifer Nicks & John Nicks	Peri Horne & Ray Lockwood	Jean Higson & Robert Hudson
1954	Jean Higson & Robert Hudson	A. Smith & J. Dixon	
1955	Vivien Higson & Robert Hudson	Joyce Coates & Anthony Holles	
1956	Joyce Coates & Anthony Holles	Carolyn Krau & Rodney Ward	Jacqueline Mason & Mervyn Bower
1957	Joyce Coates & Anthony Holles	Lesley Norfolk & John Pearse	*No Other Competitors*
1958	Joyce Coates & Anthony Holles	Carolyn Krau & Rodney Ward	June Markham & Courtney Jones
1959	Joyce Coates & Anthony Holles	Jaqueline Pintp & John Anderson	Carolyn Hayward & Richard Edwards
1960	*Senior Pairs*	*competition not held*	
1961	Valerie Holman Hunt & Peter Burrows	Vera Jeffery & Peter Webb	Jean Harby & Malcolm Balchin
1962	Valerie Holman Hunt & Peter Burrows	Vera Jeffery & Peter Webb	*No other competitors*
1963	Vera Jeffery & Peter Webb	Diane Ward & Raymond Wilson	Fiona Hunt & John Bayman
1964	Vera Jeffery & Peter Webb	Diane Ward & Raymond Wilson	Verona Tosh & Ken Babbington
1965	Glennis Parry & John Bayman	Diane Ward & Raymond Wilson	Verona Tosh & Ken Babbington
1966	Linda Connolly & Colin Taylforth	Verona Tosh & Ken Babbington	Valerie Taylor & Raymond Wilson
1967	Linda Bernard & Ray Wilson	Verona Tosh & Ken Babbington	*No other competitors*
1968	Linda Bernard & Ray Wilson	Linda Connolly & Colin Taylforth	*No other competitors*

Year	Gold	Silver	Bronze
1969	Linda Bernard & Raymond Wilson	Verona Tosh & Ken Babbington	*No other competitors*
1970	Linda Connolly & Colin Taylforth	Elizabeth Todd & Alan Merchant	*No other competitors*
1971	Linda Connolly & Colin Taylforth	Jayne Torvill & Michael Hutchison	Ann Angus & Hamish Angus
1972	Jayne Torvill & Michael Hutchinson	Ann Angus & Hamish Angus	Carol Merchant & Alan Merchant
1973	Linda McCafferty & Colin Taylforth	Jayne Torvill & Michael Hutchison	Sara Smith & Roland Hailston
1974	Wendy Sessions & Christopher Harrison		*No other competitors*
1975	Linda McCafferty & Colin Taylforth	Penny Booth & Roland Hailston	Ruth Lindsey & Alan Beckwith
1976	Erika Taylforth & Colin Taylforth	Ruth Lindsey & Alan Beckwith	Elizabeth Cain & Peter Cain
1977	Ruth Lindsey & Alan Beckwith	Karen Wood & Stephen Baker	*No other competitors*
1978	Ruth Lindsey & Alan Beckwith	Susan Garland & Robert Daw	Beverley Stewart & Mark Stewart
1979	Susan Garland & Robert Daw	*No other competitors*	
1980	Susan Garland & Robert Daw	Karen Gingell & Ian Jenkins	*No other competitors*
1981	Susan Garland & Robert Daw	Dawn Packe & Ian Jenkins	Carol Nelson & Carl Nelson
1982	Susan Garland & Ian Jenkins	Carol Nelson & Carl Nelson	Maxine Hague & Andrew Naylor
1983	Susan Garland & Ian Jenkins	Lisa Cushley & Neil Cushley	Maxine Hague & Andrew Naylor
1984	Susan Garland & Ian Jenkins	Lisa Cushley & Neil Cushley	Maxine Hague & Andrew Naylor

Year	Gold	Silver	Bronze
1985	Lisa Cushley & Neil Cushley	Cheryl Peake & Andrew Naylor	Colette Kay & Carl Nelson
1986	Cheryl Peake & Andrew Naylor	Lisa Cushley & Neil Cushley	Colette Kay & Carl Nelson
1987	Cheryl Peake & Andrew Naylor	Lisa Cushley & Neil Cushley	
1988	Cheryl Peake & Andrew Naylor	Lisa Cushley & Neil Cushley	*No other competitors*
1989	Cheryl Peake & Andrew Naylor		
1990	Cheryl Peake & Andrew Naylor		Hayley Williams & John Herring
1991	Cheryl Peake & Andrew Naylor	Catherine Barker & Michael Aldred	Kathryn Pritchard & Jason Briggs
1992	Kathryn Pritchard & Jason Briggs	Cheryl Peake & Andrew Naylor	Vicky Pearce & Clive Shorten
1993	Vicky Pearce & Clive Shorten	Jackie Soames & John Jenkins	Dana Mednick & Jason Briggs
1994	Dana Mednick & Jason Briggs	Jackie Soames & John Jenkins	Lesley Rogers & Michael Aldred
1995	Lesley Rogers & Michael Aldred	Jackie Soames & John Jenkins	Nicola Thomas & Daniel Thomas
1996	Lesley Rogers & Michael Aldred		
1997	Lesley Rogers & Michael Aldred		
1998	Marsha Poluliaschenko & Andrew Seabrook	*No other competitors*	
1999	Marsha Poluliaschenko & Andrew Seabrook	Katie Wenger & Daniel Thomas	Sarah Kemp & Michael Aldred
2000	Sarah Kemp & Daniel Thomas	Rebecca Corne & Richard Rowland	*No other competitors*

Year	Gold	Silver	Bronze
2001	Tiffany Sfikas & Andrew Seabrook	Sarah Kemp & Daniel Thomas	*No other competitors*
2002	Tiffany Sfikas & Andrew Seabrook	*No other competitors*	
2003	*Senior Pairs*	*competition not held*	
2004	*Senior Pairs*	*competition not held*	
2005	*Senior Pairs*	*competition not held*	
2006	*Senior Pairs*	*competition not held*	
2007	Stacey Kemp & David King	*No other competitors*	
2008	Stacey Kemp & David King	*No other competitors*	
2009	Stacey Kemp & David King	Erica Risseeuw & Robert Paxton	*No other competitors*
2010	Stacey Kemp & David King	Erica Risseeuw & Robert Paxton	*No other competitors*
2011	Stacey Kemp & David King	Sally Riding & Jakub Safranek	*No other competitors*
2012	Stacey Kemp & David King	*No other competitors*	
2013	Stacey Kemp & David King	*No other competitors*	
2014	Amani Fancy & Christopher Boyadji	Stacey Kemp & David King	Caitlin Yankowskas & Hamish Gaman
2015	Caitlin Yankowskas & Hamish Gaman	*No other competitors*	
2016	Amani Fancy & Christopher Boyadji	*No other competitors*	
2017	Zoe Wilkinson & Christopher Boyadji	*No other competitors*	

British Championships - LADIES

Year	Gold	Silver	Bronze
1927	G. Kathleen Shaw	Ethel Muckelt	
1928	Constance Wilson	C. Smith	
1929	G. Kathleen Shaw	Kathleen Lovett	
1930	G. Kathleen Shaw	Joyce Macbeth	Kathleen Lovett
1931	Marion Field (Lay)	Joyce Macbeth	Cecilia Colledge
1932	Megan Taylor	Cecilia Colledge	Jean Dix
1933	Megan Taylor	Cecilia Colledge	
1934	Megan Taylor	Cecilia Colledge	Mollie Phillips
1935	Cecilia Colledge	Gweneth Butler	Mollie Phillips
1936	Cecilia Colledge	Mollie Phillips	
1937	Cecilia Colledge	Megan Taylor	Gladys Jagger
1938	Cecilia Colledge	Megan Taylor	Daphne Walker
1939	Cecilia Colledge	Megan Taylor	Daphne Walker
1940 - 1945	NOT HELD DUE TO W.W. 2		
1946	Cecilia Colledge	Daphne Walker	Marion Davies
1947	Daphne Walker	Marion Davies	Jeannette Altwegg
1948	Jeannette Altwegg	Marion Davies	Jill Hood-Linzee
1949	Jeannette Altwegg	Barbara Wyatt	Bridgett Shirley Adams
1950	Jeannette Altwegg	Barbara Wyatt	Beryl Bailey
1951	Jeannette Altwegg	Barbara Wyatt	
1952	Valda Osborn	Barbara Wyatt	
1953	Valda Osborn	Yvonne Sugden	Erica Batchelor
1954	Yvonne Sugden	Erica Batchelor	
1955	Yvonne Sugden	Erica Batchelor	Dawn Hunter
1956	Yvonne Sugden	Erica Batchelor	Diana Clifton-Peach
1957	Erica Batchelor	Diana Clifton-Peach	Patricia Pauley
1958	Diana Clifton-Peach	Patricia Pauley	
1959	Patricia Pauley	Diana Clifton-Peach	Carolyn Krau
1960	Patricia Pauley	Carolyn Krau	Anne Reynolds
1961	Diana Clifton-Peach	Anne Reynolds	Carolyn Krau
1962	Jacqueline Harbord	Diana Clifton-Peach	Barbara Conniff
1963	Diana Clifton-Peach	Jacqueline Harbord	Sally-Anne Stapleford
1964	Sally-Anne Stapleford	Diana Clifton-Peach	Carol Ann Warner
1965	Sally-Anne Stapleford	Diana Clifton-Peach	Janet Sawbridge
1966	Sally-Anne Stapleford	Diana Clifton-Peach Stevens	Sylvia Oundjian
1967	Sally-Anne Stapleford	Patricia Dodd	Linda Davis
1968	Sally-Anne Stapleford	Patricia Dodd	Frances Waghorn
1969	Patricia Dodd	Frances Waghorn	Rita Pokorski
1970	Patricia Dodd	Frances Waghorn	Jean Scott
1971	Patricia Dodd	Jean Scott	Rita Pokorski

Year	Gold	Silver	Bronze
1972	Jean Scott	Maria McLean	Gail Keddie
1973	Maria McLean	Jean Scott	Gail Keddie
1974	Jean Scott	Maria McLean	Gail Keddie
1975	Gail Keddie	Yvonne Kavanagh	Karena Richardson
1976	Karena Richardson	Gail Keddie	Deborah Cottrill
1977	Karena Richardson	Deborah Cottrill	Phyllida Beck
1978	Karena Richardson	Deborah Cottrill	Teresa Foy
1979	Deborah Cottrill	Karena Richardson	Teresa Foy
1980	Karena Richardson	Deborah Cottrill	Alison Southwood
1981	Karen Wood	Deborah Cottrill	Beverley Dempsey
1982	Deborah Cottrill	Karen Wood	Diana Rankin
1983	Karen Wood	Alison Southwood	Susan Jackson
1984	Susan Jackson	Diana Rankin	Karen Wood
1985	Susan Jackson	Karen Wood	Fiona Hamilton
1986	Joanne Conway	Susan Jackson	Fiona Ritchie
1987	Joanne Conway	Susan Jackson	Gina Fulton
1988	Joanne Conway	Gina Fulton	Fiona Ritchie
1989	Joanne Conway	Jacqueline Soames	Louisa Danskin
1990	Emma Murdoch	Joanne Conway	Gina Fulton
1991	Joanne Conway	Jacqueline Soames	Andrea Law
1992	Joanne Conway	Charlene Von Saher	Susanne Otterson
1993	Charlene Von Saher	Emma Warmington	Helen Preece
1994	Stephanie Main	Natalia Gorbenko-Risk	Emma Warmington
1995	Jenna Arrowsmith	Zoe Jones	Stephanie Main
1996	Stephanie Main	Zoe Jones	Kelly McDermott
1997	Jenna Arrowsmith	Zoe Jones	
1998	Jenna Arrowsmith	Nancy Manning	Tammy Sear
1999	Stephanie Main	Tammy Sear	Zoe Jones
2000	Tammy Sear	Zoe Jones	Jennifer Holmes
2001	Zoe Jones	Jennifer Holmes	Tammy Sear
2002	Zoe Jones	Vicki Hodges	Dannielle Guppy
2003	Jenna McCorkell	Vicki Hodges	Kathryn Hedley
2004	Jenna McCorkell	Dannielle Guppy	Kathryn Hedley
2005	Jenna McCorkell	Sarah Daniel	Kathryn Hedley
2006	Vanessa James	Joanna Webber	Sarah Daniel
2007	Jenna McCorkell	Vanessa James	Joanna Webber
2008	Jenna McCorkell	Karly Robertson	Phillipa Pickard
2009	Jenna McCorkell	Karly Robertson	Karla Quinn
2010	Jenna McCorkell	Karly Robertson	Laura Kean
2011	Jenna McCorkell	Karly Robertson	Laura Kean
2012	Jenna McCorkell	Karly Robertson	Toni Murray
2013	Jenna McCorkell	Karly Robertson	Katie Powell
2014	Jenna McCorkell	Karly Robertson	Katie Powell
2015	Karly Robertson	Michelle Callison	Natasha McKay
2016	Danielle Harrison	Zoe Wilkinson	Nina Povey
2017	Natasha McKay	Karly Robertson	Danielle Harrison

British Championships - ICE DANCING

Year	Gold	Silver	Bronze
1937	Daphne Wallis & Reginald Wilkie	E. Thompson & D. Veitch	M. Longster & H. MacKeown
1938	Daphne Wallis & Reginald Wilkie	Pauline Borrajo & E. Appleby	G. Grover & R. T. James
1939	Daphne Wallis & Reginald Wilkie	Pauline Borrajo & Harry Levy	Isobel Clive-Smith & G. Edmonds
1940 - 1946	NOT HELD DUE TO W.W. 2		
1947	Pauline Borrajo & Albert Edmonds	Mrs. W. R. Barrett & Mr. W. R. Barrett	
1948	Pauline Borrajo & Albert Edmonds	Mrs. W. R. Barrett & Mr. W. R. Barrett	
1949	Sybil Cooke & Robert Hudson	Mrs. W. R. Barrett & Mr. W. R. Barrett	Barbara Radford & Alec Gordon
1950	Sybil Cooke & Robert Hudson	J. Chessman & Gordon Bellchambers	Mrs. W. R. Barrett & Mr. W. R. Barrett
1951	Joan Dewhurst & John Slater	Jean Westwood & Lawrence Demmy	Kay Morrison & Michael Robinson
1952	Joan Dewhurst & John Slater	Jean Westwood & Lawrence Demmy	Nesta Davies & Paul Thomas
1953	Joan Dewhurst & John Slater	Nesta Davies & Paul Thomas	
1954	Jean Westwood & Lawrence Demmy	Nesta Davies & Paul Thomas	Barbara Radford & Raymond Lockwood
1955	Jean Westwood & Lawrence Demmy	Pamela Weight & Paul Thomas	Barbara Radford & Raymond Lockwood
1956	Pamela Weight & Paul Thomas	June Markham & Courtney Jones	Barbara Thompson & Gerald Rigby

Year	Gold	Silver	Bronze
1957	June Markham & Courtney Jones	Barbara Thompson & Gerald Rigby	Kay Morris & Michael Robinson
1958	June Markham & Courtney Jones	Kay Morris & Michael Robinson	Barbara Thompson & Gerald Rigby
1959	Doreen Denny & Courtney Jones	Barbara Thompson & Gerald Rigby	Kay Morris & Michael Robinson
1960	Doreen Denny & Courtney Jones	Mary Parry & Roy Mason	Anne Cross & Francis Leonard Williams
1961	Doreen Denny & Courtney Jones	Mary Parry & Roy Mason	Linda Shearman & Michael Phillips
1962	Linda Shearman & Michael Phillips	Mary Parry & Roy Mason	Virginia Thompson & William MacLachlan
1963	Linda Shearman & Michael Phillips	Janet Sawbridge & David Hickinbottom	Mary Parry & Roy Mason
1964	Janet Sawbridge & David Hickinbottom	Yvonne Suddick & Roger Kennerson	Marjorie McCoy & Ian Phillips
1965	Janet Sawbridge & David Hickinbottom	Yvonne Suddick & Roger Kennerson	Diane Towler & Bernard Ford
1966	Diane Towler & Bernard Ford	Yvonne Suddick & Roger Kennerson	Janet Sawbridge & Jon Lane
1967	Diane Towler & Bernard Ford	Yvonne Suddick & Malcolm Cannon	Janet Sawbridge & Jon Lane
1968	Diane Towler & Bernard Ford	Yvonne Suddick & Malcolm Cannon	Janet Sawbridge & Jon Lane
1969	Diane Towler & Bernard Ford	Janet Sawbridge & Jon Lane	Susan Getty & Roy Bradshaw

Year	Gold	Silver	Bronze
1970	Susan Getty & Roy Bradshaw	Janet Sawbridge & Peter Dalby	Hilary Green & Glyn Watts
1971	Susan Getty & Roy Bradshaw	Hilary Green & Glyn Watts	Kay Webster & Malcolm Taylor
1972	Janet Sawbridge & Peter Dalby	Hilary Green & Glyn Watts	Rosalind Druce & David Barker
1973	Susan Getty & Roy Bradshaw	Janet Sawbridge & Peter Dalby	Hilary Green & Glyn Watts
1974	Susan Getty & Roy Bradshaw	Hilary Green & Glyn Watts	Kay Webster & Malcolm Taylor
1975	Janet Sawbridge & Peter Dalby	Hilary Green & Glyn Watts	Rosalind Druce & David Barker
1976	Hilary Green & Glyn Watts	Kay Barsdell & Ken Foster	Janet Thompson & Warren Maxwell
1977	Janet Thompson & Warren Maxwell	Kay Barsdell & Ken Foster	Kathryn Winter & Nicky Slater
1978	Janet Thompson & Warren Maxwell	Kay Barsdell & Ken Foster	Jayne Torvill & Christopher Dean
1979	Jayne Torvill & Christopher Dean	Karen Barber & Nicky Slater	Kathryn Winter & Kim Speyer
1980	Jayne Torvill & Christopher Dean	Karen Barber & Nicky Slater	Carol Long & John Philpott
1981	Jayne Torvill & Christopher Dean	Karen Barber & Nicky Slater	Wendy Sessions & Stephen Williams
1982	Jayne Torvill & Christopher Dean	Karen Barber & Nicky Slater	Wendy Sessions & Stephen Williams
1983	Jayne Torvill & Christopher Dean	Karen Barber & Nicky Slater	Wendy Sessions & Stephen Williams
1984	Jayne Torvill & Christopher Dean	Wendy Sessions & Stephen Williams	Sharon Jones & Paul Askham
1985	Karen Barber & Nicky Slater	Sharon Jones & Paul Askham	Sharon Wilkinson & Panos Pierre Panayi

Year	Gold	Silver	Bronze
1986	Sharon Jones & Paul Askham	Elizabeth Coates & Alan Abretti	Danielle Biss & David Crofts
1987	Sharon Jones & Paul Askham	Elizabeth Coates & Alan Abretti	Danielle Biss & David Crofts
1988	Sharon Jones & Paul Askham	Annalisa Meyers & Justin Green	Julie Linney & Graham Linney
1989	Sharon Jones & Paul Askham	Karen Quinn & Alan Abretti	Lynn Burton & Andrew Place
1990	Lynn Burton & Andrew Place	Anne Hall & Jason Blomfield	Karen Quinn & Alan Abretti
1991	Anne Hall & Jason Blomfield	Lisa Bradby & Alan Towers	Melanie Bruce & Andrew Place
1992	Melanie Bruce & Andrew Place	Anne Hall & Jason Blomfield	Cheryl Rushton & Colin Sturgess
1993	Marika Humphreys & Justin Lanning	Michelle Fitzgerald & Vincent Kyle	Anne Hall & Jason Blomfield
1994	Jayne Torvill & Christopher Dean	Marika Humphreys & Justin Lanning	Michelle Fitzgerald & Vincent Kyle
1995	Michelle Fitzgerald & Vincent Kyle	Clair Wileman & Andrew Place	Lynn Burton & Duncan Lenard
1996	Marika Humphreys & Philip Askew	Clair Wileman & Andrew Place	Lisa Dunn & John Dunn
1997	Marika Humphreys & Philip Askew	Marie James & Daniel Gray	Lisa Dunn & John Dunn
1998	Charlotte Clements & Gary Shortland	Radmila Chrobokova & Justin Lanning	Sinead Kerr & Jamie Ferguson
1999	Charlotte Clements & Gary Shortland	Sinead Kerr & Jamie Ferguson	Marika Humphreys & Vitaliy Baranov
2000	Julie Keeble & Lukasz Zalewski	Charlotte Clements & Gary Shortland	Sinead Kerr & Jamie Ferguson
2001	Marika Humphreys & Vitaliy Baranov	Sinead Kerr & John Kerr	Pam O'Connor & Jonathon O'Dougherty

Year	Gold	Silver	Bronze
2002	Marika Humphreys & Vitaliy Baranov	Pam O'Connor & Jonathon O'Dougherty	Sinead Kerr & John Kerr
2003	Pam O'Connor & Jonathon O'Dougherty	Sinead Kerr & John Kerr	Charlotte Clements & Phillip Poole
2004	Sinead Kerr & John Kerr	Pam O'Connor & Jonathon O'Dougherty	Marika Humphreys & Vitaliy Baranov
2005	Sinead Kerr & John Kerr	Pam O'Connor & Jonathon O'Dougherty	Phillipa Towler-Green & Phillip Poole
2006	Sinead Kerr & John Kerr	Phillipa Towler-Green & Phillip Poole	Kira Geil & Andrew Smykowski
2007	Sinead Kerr & John Kerr	Phillipa Towler-Green & Phillip Poole	Nicola Trippick & Jamie Burns
2008	Sinead Kerr & John Kerr	Phillipa Towler-Green & Phillip Poole	Christina Chitwood & Mark Hanretty
2009	Sinead Kerr & John Kerr	Phillipa Towler-Green & Phillip Poole	Louise Walden & Owen Edwards
2010	Sinead Kerr & John Kerr	Penny Coomes & Nicholas Buckland	Christina Chitwood & Mark Hanretty
2011	Louise Walden & Owen Edwards	*No other competitors*	
2012	Penny Coomes & Nicholas Buckland	Louise Walden & Owen Edwards	*No other competitors*
2013	Penny Coomes & Nicholas Buckland	Charlotte Aiken & Josh Whidborne	Louise Walden & Owen Edwards
2014	Penny Coomes & Nicholas Buckland	Carter Marie Jones & Richard Sharpe	Sophie Jones & Jordan Brown
2015	Olivia Smart & Joseph Buckland	Carter Marie Jones & Richard Sharpe	*No other competitors*
2016	Penny Coomes & Nicholas Buckland	Carter Marie Jones & Richard Sharpe	Eleanor Hirst & Jordan Barrett
2017	Lilah Fear & Lewis Gibson	Robynne Tweedale & Joseph Buckland	Ekaterina Fedyushchenko & Lucas Kitteridge

European Figure Skating Championships

The European Figure Skating Championships, founded in 1891 in Hamburg, Germany, is the oldest figure skating competition in existence, actually predating the formation of the International Skating Union (ISU).

Up until 1948, the European Championships were open to competitors from any nation that was part of the ISU. But at that point, after Dick Button (US), and Barbara Ann Scott (Canada), won gold in the men's and ladies competitions respectively, the decision was made to only allow skaters who represented European countries. (This ultimately led to the establishment of the Four Continents Championships, an ISU-sanctioned competition of equal weight for non-European skaters).

Right: **Per Thorén**, Swedish men's figure skater, won the gold medal at the 1911 European Championships, as well as bronze at the 1906, 1909, and 1910 events. He also won the bronze medal at the 1908 Olympics, silver, (1909) and bronze, (1905) at the World Championships, and in his home country of Sweden, won gold twice and silver three times in the national championships. In Europe, the half loop jump came to be know as the Thorén Jump.

European Figure Skating Championships - MEN

Year	Location	Gold	Silver	Bronze
1891	GER Hamburg	GER Oskar Uhlig	GER Anon Schmitson	GER Franz Zilly
1892	AUT Vienna	AUT Eduard Engelmann	HUN Tibor von Földváry	AUT Georg Zachariades
1893	GER Berlin	AUT Eduard Engelmann	SWE Henning Grenander	AUT Georg Zachariades
1894	AUT Vienna	AUT Eduard Engelmann	AUT Gustav Hügel	HUN Tibor von Földváry
1895	HUN Budapest	HUN Tibor von Földváry	AUT Gustav Hügel	GER Gilbert Fuchs
1898	NOR Trondheim	SWE Ulrich Salchow	NOR Johan Lefstad	NOR Oscar Holthe
1899	SWI Davos	SWE Ulrich Salchow	AUT Gustav Hügel	AUT Ernst Fellner
1900	GER Berlin	SWE Ulrich Salchow	AUT Gustav Hügel	NOR Oscar Holthe
1901	AUT Vienna	AUT Gustav Hügel	GER Gilbert Fuchs	SWE Ulrich Salchow
1904	SWI Davos	SWE Ulrich Salchow	AUT Max Bohatsch	RUS Nikolai Panin
1905	GER Bonn	AUT Max Bohatsch	GER Heinrich Burger	GER Karl Zenger
1906	SWI Davos	SWE Ulrich Salchow	AUT Ernst Herz	SWE Per Thorén
1907	GER Berlin	SWE Ulrich Salchow	GER Gilbert Fuchs	AUT Ernst Herz
1908	RUS Warsaw	AUT Ernst Herz	RUS Nikolai Panin	AUT Henryk Juliusz Krukowicz-Przedrzymirski
1909	HUN Budapest	SWE Ulrich Salchow	GER Gilbert Fuchs	SWE Per Thorén
1910	GER Berlin	SWE Ulrich Salchow	GER Werner Rittberger	SWE Per Thorén
1911	RUS St Petersburg	SWE Per Thorén	RUS Karl Ollo	GER Werner Rittberger
1912	SWE Stockholm	SWE Gösta Sandahl	RUS Ivan Malinin	NOR Martin Stixrud
1913	NOR Oslo	SWE Ulrich Salchow	HUN Andor Szende	AUT Willy Böckl

Year	Location	Gold	Silver	Bronze
1914	AUT Vienna	AUT Fritz Kachler	NOR Alexander Krogh	AUT Willy Böckl
1915-1921	**NOT HELD DUE TO W.W. 1**			
1922	SWI Davos	AUT Willy Böckl	AUT Fritz Kachler	AUT Ernst Oppacher
1923	NOR Oslo	AUT Willy Böckl	NOR Martin Stixrud	FIN Gunnar Jakobsson
1924	SWI Davos	AUT Fritz Kachler	AUT Ludwig Wrede	GER Werner Rittberger
1925	GER Triberg	AUT Willy Böckl	GER Werner Rittberger	AUT Otto Preißecker
1926	SWI Davos	AUT Willy Böckl	AUT Otto Preißecker	SWI Georges Gautschi
1927	AUT Vienna	AUT Willy Böckl	AUT Hugo Distler	AUT Karl Schäfer
1928	CZE Troppau	AUT Willy Böckl	AUT Karl Schäfer	AUT Otto Preißecker
1929	SWI Davos	AUT Karl Schäfer	SWI Georges Gautschi	AUT Ludwig Wrede
1930	AUT Vienna	AUT Karl Schäfer	CZE Otto Gold	FIN Markus Nikkanen
1931	SWI St. Moritz	AUT Karl Schäfer	GER Ernst Baier	AUT Hugo Distler
1932	FRA Paris	AUT Karl Schäfer	GER Ernst Baier	AUT Erich Erdös
1933	GBR London	AUT Karl Schäfer	GER Ernst Baier	AUT Erich Erdös
1934	CZE Prague	AUT Karl Schäfer	HUN Dénes Pataky	HUN Elemér Terták
1935	SWI St. Moritz	AUT Karl Schäfer	AUT Felix Kaspar	GER Ernst Baier
1936	GER Berlin	AUT Karl Schäfer	GBR Graham Sharp	GER Ernst Baier
1937	CZE Prague	AUT Felix Kaspar	GBR Graham Sharp	HUN Elemér Terták
1938	SWI St. Moritz	AUT Felix Kaspar	GBR Graham Sharp	AUT Herbert Alward
1939	GBR London	GBR Graham Sharp	GBR Freddie Tomlins	GER Horst Faber
1940-1946	**NOT HELD DUE TO W.W. 2**			
1947	SWI Davos	SWI Hans Gerschwiler	CZE Vladislav Čáp	BEL Fernand Leemans
1948	CZE Prague	USA Dick Button	SWI Hans Gerschwiler	AUT Edi Rada
1949	ITA Milan	AUT Edi Rada	HUN Ede Király	AUT Helmut Seibt

Greg Fox

Year	Location	Gold	Silver	Bronze
1950	NOR Oslo	HUN Ede Király	AUT Helmut Seibt	ITA Carlo Fassi
1951	SWI Zürich	AUT Helmut Seibt	GDR Horst Faber	ITA Carlo Fassi
1952	AUT Vienna	AUT Helmut Seibt	ITA Carlo Fassi	GBR Michael Carrington
1953	GDR Dortmund	ITA Carlo Fassi	FRA Alain Giletti	GDR Freimut Stein
1954	ITA Bolzano	ITA Carlo Fassi	FRA Alain Giletti	CZE Karol Divín
1955	HUN Budapest	FRA Alain Giletti	GBR Michael Booker	CZE Karol Divín
1956	FRA Paris	FRA Alain Giletti	GBR Michael Booker	CZE Karol Divín
1957	AUT Vienna	FRA Alain Giletti	CZE Karol Divín	GBR Michael Booker
1958	CZE Bratislava	CZE Karol Divín	FRA Alain Giletti	FRA Alain Calmat
1959	SWI Davos	CZE Karol Divín	FRA Alain Giletti	AUT Norbert Felsinger
1960	GDR Garmisch-Partenkirchen	FRA Alain Giletti	AUT Norbert Felsinger	GDR Manfred Schnelldorfer
1961	West Berlin West Berlin	FRA Alain Giletti	FRA Alain Calmat	GDR Manfred Schnelldorfer
1962	SWI Geneva	FRA Alain Calmat	CZE Karol Divín	GDR Manfred Schnelldorfer
1963	HUN Budapest	FRA Alain Calmat	GDR Manfred Schnelldorfer	AUT Emmerich Danzer
1964	FRA Grenoble	FRA Alain Calmat	GDR Manfred Schnelldorfer	CZE Karol Divín
1965	SOV Moscow	AUT Emmerich Danzer	FRA Alain Calmat	AUT Peter Jonas
1966	CZE Bratislava	AUT Emmerich Danzer	AUT Wolfgang Schwarz	CZE Ondrej Nepela
1967	YUG Ljubljana	AUT Emmerich Danzer	AUT Wolfgang Schwarz	CZE Ondrej Nepela
1968	SWE Västerås	AUT Emmerich Danzer	AUT Wolfgang Schwarz	CZE Ondrej Nepela

Year	Location	Gold	Silver	Bronze
1969	GDR Garmisch-Partenkirchen	CZE Ondrej Nepela	FRA Patrick Péra	SOV Sergei Chetverukhin
1970	SOV Leningrad	CZE Ondrej Nepela	FRA Patrick Péra	GDR Günter Zöller
1971	SWI Zürich	CZE Ondrej Nepela	SOV Sergei Chetverukhin	GBR Haig Oundjian
1972	SWE Gothenburg	CZE Ondrej Nepela	SOV Sergei Chetverukhin	FRA Patrick Péra
1973	GDR Cologne	CZE Ondrej Nepela	SOV Sergei Chetverukhin	GDR Jan Hoffmann
1974	YUG Zagreb	GDR Jan Hoffmann	SOV Sergei Volkov	GBR John Curry
1975	DEN Copenhagen	SOV Vladimir Kovalev	GBR John Curry	SOV Yuri Ovchinnikov
1976	SWI Geneva	GBR John Curry	SOV Vladimir Kovalev	GDR Jan Hoffmann
1977	FIN Helsinki	GDR Jan Hoffmann	SOV Vladimir Kovalev	GBR Robin Cousins
1978	FRA Strasbourg	GDR Jan Hoffmann	SOV Vladimir Kovalev	GBR Robin Cousins
1979	YUG Zagreb	GDR Jan Hoffmann	SOV Vladimir Kovalev	GBR Robin Cousins
1980	SWE Gothenburg	GBR Robin Cousins	GDR Jan Hoffmann	SOV Vladimir Kovalev
1981	AUT Innsbruck	SOV Igor Bobrin	FRA Jean-Christophe Simond	GDR Norbert Schramm
1982	FRA Lyon	GDR Norbert Schramm	FRA Jean-Christophe Simond	SOV Igor Bobrin
1983	GDR Dortmund	GDR Norbert Schramm	CZE Jozef Sabovčík	SOV Alexander Fadeev
1984	HUN Budapest	SOV Alexander Fadeev	GDR Rudi Cerne	GDR Norbert Schramm
1985	SWE Gothenburg	CZE Jozef Sabovčík	SOV Vladimir Kotin	POL Grzegorz Filipowski
1986	DEN Copenhagen	CZE Jozef Sabovčík	SOV Vladimir Kotin	SOV Alexander Fadeev
1987	YUG Sarajevo	SOV Alexander Fadeev	SOV Vladimir Kotin	SOV Viktor Petrenko
1988	CZE Prague	SOV Alexander Fadeev	SOV Vladimir Kotin	SOV Viktor Petrenko
1989	GBR Birmingham	SOV Alexander Fadeev	POL Grzegorz Filipowski	CZE Petr Barna

Year	Location	Gold	Silver	Bronze
1990	SOV Leningrad	SOV Viktor Petrenko	CZE Petr Barna	SOV Viacheslav Zagorodniuk
1991	BUL Sofia	SOV Viktor Petrenko	CZE Petr Barna	SOV Viacheslav Zagorodniuk
1992	SWI Lausanne	CZE Petr Barna	UKR Viktor Petrenko	RUS Alexei Urmanov
1993	FIN Helsinki	UKR Dmitri Dmitrenko	FRA Philippe Candeloro	FRA Éric Millot
1994	DEN Copenhagen	UKR Viktor Petrenko	UKR Viacheslav Zagorodniuk	RUS Alexei Urmanov
1995	GER Dortmund	RUS Ilia Kulik	RUS Alexei Urmanov	UKR Viacheslav Zagorodniuk
1996	BUL Sofia	UKR Viacheslav Zagorodniuk	RUS Igor Pashkevich	RUS Ilia Kulik
1997	FRA Paris	RUS Alexei Urmanov	FRA Philippe Candeloro	UKR Viacheslav Zagorodniuk
1998	ITA Milan	RUS Alexei Yagudin	RUS Evgeni Plushenko	RUS Alexander Abt
1999	CZE Prague	RUS Alexei Yagudin	RUS Evgeni Plushenko	RUS Alexei Urmanov
2000	AUT Vienna	RUS Evgeni Plushenko	RUS Alexei Yagudin	UKR Dmitri Dmitrenko
2001	SVK Bratislava	RUS Evgeni Plushenko	RUS Alexei Yagudin	FRA Stanick Jeannette
2002	SWI Lausanne	RUS Alexei Yagudin	RUS Alexander Abt	FRA Brian Joubert
2003	SWE Malmö	RUS Evgeni Plushenko	FRA Brian Joubert	FRA Stanick Jeannette
2004	HUN Budapest	FRA Brian Joubert	RUS Evgeni Plushenko	RUS Ilia Klimkin
2005	ITA Turin	RUS Evgeni Plushenko	FRA Brian Joubert	GER Stefan Lindemann
2006	FRA Lyon	RUS Evgeni Plushenko	SWI Stéphane Lambiel	FRA Brian Joubert
2007	POL Warsaw	FRA Brian Joubert	CZE Tomáš Verner	BEL Kevin van der Perren

Year	Location	Gold	Silver	Bronze
2008	CRO Zagreb	CZE Tomáš Verner	SWI Stéphane Lambiel	FRA Brian Joubert
2009	FIN Helsinki	FRA Brian Joubert	ITA Samuel Contesti	BEL Kevin van der Perren
2010	EST Tallinn	RUS Evgeni Plushenko	SWI Stéphane Lambiel	FRA Brian Joubert
2011	SWI Bern	FRA Florent Amodio	FRA Brian Joubert	CZE Tomáš Verner
2012	GBR Sheffield	RUS Evgeni Plushenko	RUS Artur Gachinski	FRA Florent Amodio
2013	CRO Zagreb	SPA Javier Fernández	FRA Florent Amodio	CZE Michal Březina
2014	HUN Budapest	SPA Javier Fernández	RUS Sergei Voronov	RUS Konstantin Menshov
2015	SWE Stockholm	SPA Javier Fernández	RUS Maxim Kovtun	RUS Sergei Voronov
2016	SVK Bratislava	SPA Javier Fernández	ISR Oleksii Bychenko	RUS Maxim Kovtun
2017	CZE Ostrova	SPA Javier Fernández	RUS Maxim Kovtun	RUS Mikhail Kolyada

European Figure Skating Championships - PAIRS

Year	Location	Gold	Silver	Bronze
1930	AUT Vienna	HUN Olga Orgonista & Sándor Szalay	HUN Emília Rotter & László Szollás	AUT Gisela Hochaltinger & Otto Preißecker
1931	SWI St. Moritz	HUN Olga Orgonista & Sándor Szalay	HUN Emília Rotter & László Szollás	AUT Lilly Gaillard & Willy Petter
1932	FRA Paris	FRA Andrée Brunet & Pierre Brunet	AUT Lilly Gaillard & Willy Petter	AUT Idi Papez & Karl Zwack
1933	GBR London	AUT Idi Papez & Karl Zwack	AUT Lilly Gaillard & Willy Petter	GBR Mollie Phillips & Rodney Murdoch
1934	CZE Prague	HUN Emília Rotter & László Szollás	AUT Idi Papez & Karl Zwack	POL Zofia Bilorówna & Tadeusz Kowalski

Year	Location	Gold	Silver	Bronze
1935	SWI St. Moritz	GER Maxi Herber & Ernst Baier	AUT Idi Papez & Karl Zwack	HUN Lucy Gallo & Rezső Dillinger
1936	GER Berlin	GER Maxi Herber & Ernst Baier	GBR Violet Cliff & Leslie Cliff	HUN Piroska Szekrényessy & Attila Szekrényessy
1937	CZE Prague	GER Maxi Herber & Ernst Baier	AUT Ilse Pausin & Erich Pausin	HUN Piroska Szekrényessy & Attila Szekrényessy
1938	SWI St. Moritz	GER Maxi Herber & Ernst Baier	AUT Ilse Pausin & Erich Pausin	GER Inge Koch & Gunther Noack
1939	GBR London	GER Maxi Herber & Ernst Baier	GER Ilse Pausin & Erich Pausin	GER Inge Koch & Gunther Noack
1940-1946		NOT HELD DUE TO W.W. 2		
1947	SWI Davos	BEL Micheline Lannoy & Pierre Baugniet	GBR Winifred Silverthorne & Dennis Silverthorne	BEL Suzanne Diskeuve & Edmond Verbustel
1948	CZE Prague	HUN Andrea Kékesy & Ede Király	CZE Blažena Knittlová & Karel Vosátka	AUT Herta Ratzenhofer & Emil Ratzenhofer
1949	ITA Milan	HUN Andrea Kékesy & Ede Király	HUN Marianne Nagy & Lászlo Nagy	AUT Herta Ratzenhofer & Emil Ratzenhofer
1950	NOR Oslo	HUN Marianne Nagy & Lászlo Nagy	SWI Eliane Steinemann & Andre Calame	GBR Jennifer Nicks & John Nicks
1951	SWI Zürich	GDR Ria Baran & Paul Falk	SWI Eliane Steinemann & Andre Calame	GBR Jennifer Nicks & John Nicks
1952	AUT Vienna	GDR Ria Baran & Paul Falk	GBR Jennifer Nicks & John Nicks	HUN Marianne Nagy & Lászlo Nagy

Year	Location	Gold	Silver	Bronze
1953	GDR Dortmund	GBR Jennifer Nicks & John Nicks	HUN Marianne Nagy & Lászlo Nagy	AUT Sissy Schwarz & Kurt Oppelt
1954	ITA Bolzano	SWI Silvia Grandjean & Michel Grandjean	AUT Sissy Schwarz & Kurt Oppelt	CZE Soňa Balůnova & Miroslav Balůn
1955	HUN Budapest	HUN Marianne Nagy & Lászlo Nagy	CZE Věra Suchánková & Zdeněk Doležal	GDR Marika Kilius & Franz Ningel
1956	FRA Paris	AUT Sissy Schwarz & Kurt Oppelt	HUN Marianne Nagy & Lászlo Nagy	GDR Marika Kilius & Franz Ningel
1957	AUT Vienna	CZE Věra Suchánková & Zdeněk Doležal	HUN Marianne Nagy & Lászlo Nagy	GDR Marika Kilius & Franz Ningel
1958	CZE Bratislava	CZE Věra Suchánková & Zdeněk Doležal	SOV Nina Zhuk & Stanislav Zhuk	GBR Joyce Coates & Anthony Holles
1959	SWI Davos	GDR Marika Kilius & Hans-Jürgen Bäumler	SOV Nina Zhuk & Stanislav Zhuk	GBR Joyce Coates & Anthony Holles
1960	GDR Garmisch-Partenkirchen	GDR Marika Kilius & Hans-Jürgen Bäumler	SOV Nina Zhuk & Stanislav Zhuk	GDR Margret Göbl & Franz Ningel
1961	West Berlin West Berlin	GDR Marika Kilius & Hans-Jürgen Bäumler	GDR Margret Göbl & Franz Ningel	GDR Margit Senf & Peter Göbel
1962	SWI Geneva	GDR Marika Kilius & Hans-Jürgen Bäumler	SOV Liudmila Belousova & Oleg Protopopov	GDR Margret Göbl & Franz Ningel
1963	HUN Budapest	GDR Marika Kilius & Hans-Jürgen Bäumler	SOV Liudmila Belousova & Oleg Protopopov	SOV Tatiana Zhuk & Alexander Gavrilov

Year	Location	Gold	Silver	Bronze
1964	FRA Grenoble	GDR Marika Kilius & Hans-Jürgen Bäumler	SOV Liudmila Belousova & Oleg Protopopov	SOV Tatiana Zhuk & Alexander Gavrilov
1965	SOV Moscow	SOV Liudmila Belousova & Oleg Protopopov	SWI Gerda Johner & Rüdi Johner	SOV Tatiana Zhuk & Alexander Gorelik
1966	CZE Bratislava	SOV Liudmila Belousova & Oleg Protopopov	SOV Tatiana Zhuk & Alexander Gorelik	GDR Margot Glockshuber & Wolfgang Danne
1967	YUG Ljubljana	SOV Liudmila Belousova & Oleg Protopopov	GDR Margot Glockshuber & Wolfgang Danne	GDR Heidemarie Steiner & Heinz-Ulrich Walther
1968	SWE Västerås	SOV Liudmila Belousova & Oleg Protopopov	SOV Tamara Moskvina & Alexei Mishin	GDR Heidemarie Steiner & Heinz-Ulrich Walther
1969	GDR Garmisch-Partenkirchen	SOV Irina Rodnina & Alexei Ulanov	SOV Liudmila Belousova & Oleg Protopopov	SOV Tamara Moskvina & Alexei Mishin
1970	SOV Leningrad	SOV Irina Rodnina & Alexei Ulanov	SOV Liudmila Smirnova & Andrei Suraikin	GDR Heidemarie Steiner & Heinz-Ulrich Walther
1971	SWI Zürich	SOV Irina Rodnina & Alexei Ulanov	SOV Liudmila Smirnova & Andrei Suraikin	SOV Galina Karelina & Georgi Proskurin
1972	SWE Gothenburg	SOV Irina Rodnina & Alexei Ulanov	SOV Liudmila Smirnova & Andrei Suraikin	GDR Manuela Groß & Uwe Kagelmann
1973	GDR Cologne	SOV Irina Rodnina & Alexander Zaitsev	SOV Liudmila Smirnova & Alexei Ulanov	GDR Almut Lehmann & Herbert Wiesinger
1974	YUG Zagreb	SOV Irina Rodnina & Alexander Zaitsev	GDR Romy Kermer & Rolf Österreich	SOV Liudmila Smirnova & Alexei Ulanov

Year	Location	Gold	Silver	Bronze
1975	DEN Copenhagen	SOV Irina Rodnina & Alexander Zaitsev	GDR Romy Kermer & Rolf Österreich	GDR Manuela Groß & Uwe Kagelmann
1976	SWI Geneva	SOV Irina Rodnina & Alexander Zaitsev	GDR Romy Kermer & Rolf Österreich	SOV Irina Vorobieva & Alexander Vlasov
1977	FIN Helsinki	SOV Irina Rodnina & Alexander Zaitsev	SOV Irina Vorobieva & Alexander Vlasov	SOV Marina Cherkasova & Sergei Shakhrai
1978	FRA Strasbourg	SOV Irina Rodnina & Alexander Zaitsev	SOV Marina Cherkasova & Sergei Shakhrai	GDR Manuela Mager & Uwe Bewersdorf
1979	YUG Zagreb	SOV Marina Cherkasova & Sergei Shakhrai	SOV Irina Vorobieva & Igor Lisovski	GDR Sabine Baeß & Tassilo Thierbach
1980	SWE Gothenburg	SOV Irina Rodnina & Alexander Zaitsev	SOV Marina Cherkasova & Sergei Shakhrai	SOV Marina Pestova & Stanislav Leonovich
1981	AUT Innsbruck	SOV Irina Vorobieva & Igor Lisovski	GDR Christina Riegel & Andreas Nischwitz	SOV Marina Cherkasova & Sergei Shakhrai
1982	FRA Lyon	GDR Sabine Baeß & Tassilo Thierbach	SOV Marina Pestova & Stanislav Leonovich	SOV Irina Vorobieva & Igor Lisovski
1983	GDR Dortmund	GDR Sabine Baeß & Tassilo Thierbach	SOV Elena Valova & Oleg Vasiliev	GDR Birgit Lorenz & Knut Schubert
1984	HUN Budapest	SOV Elena Valova & Oleg Vasiliev	GDR Sabine Baeß & Tassilo Thierbach	GDR Birgit Lorenz & Knut Schubert
1985	SWE Gothenburg	SOV Elena Valova & Oleg Vasiliev	SOV Larisa Selezneva & Oleg Makarov	SOV Veronika Pershina & Marat Akbarov

Year	Location	Gold	Silver	Bronze
1986	DEN Copenhagen	SOV Elena Valova & Oleg Vasiliev	SOV Ekaterina Gordeeva & Sergei Grinkov	SOV Elena Bechke & Valeri Kornienko
1987	YUG Sarajevo	SOV Larisa Selezneva & Oleg Makarov	SOV Elena Valova & Oleg Vasiliev	GDR Katrin Kanitz & Tobias Schröter
1988	CZE Prague	SOV Ekaterina Gordeeva & Sergei Grinkov	SOV Larisa Selezneva & Oleg Makarov	GDR Peggy Schwarz & Alexander König
1989	GBR Birmingham	SOV Larisa Selezneva & Oleg Makarov	GDR Mandy Wötzel & Axel Rauschenbach	SOV Natalia Mishkutenok & Artur Dmitriev
1990	SOV Leningrad	SOV Ekaterina Gordeeva & Sergei Grinkov	SOV Larisa Selezneva & Oleg Makarov	SOV Natalia Mishkutenok & Artur Dmitriev
1991	BUL Sofia	SOV Natalia Mishkutenok & Artur Dmitriev	SOV Elena Bechke & Denis Petrov	SOV Evgenia Shishkova & Vadim Naumov
1992	SWI Lausanne	RUS Natalia Mishkutenok & Artur Dmitriev	RUS Elena Bechke & Denis Petrov	RUS Evgenia Shishkova & Vadim Naumov
1993	FIN Helsinki	RUS Marina Eltsova & Andrei Bushkov	GER Mandy Wötzel & Ingo Steuer	RUS Evgenia Shishkova & Vadim Naumov
1994	DEN Copenhagen	RUS Ekaterina Gordeeva & Sergei Grinkov	RUS Evgenia Shishkova & Vadim Naumov	RUS Natalia Mishkutenok & Artur Dmitriev
1995	GER Dortmund	GER Mandy Wötzel & Ingo Steuer	CZE Radka Kovaříková & René Novotný	RUS Evgenia Shishkova & Vadim Naumov
1996	BUL Sofia	RUS Oksana Kazakova & Artur Dmitriev	GER Mandy Wötzel & Ingo Steuer	FRA Sarah Abitbol & Stéphane Bernadis

Year	Location	Gold	Silver	Bronze
1997	FRA Paris	RUS Marina Eltsova & Andrei Bushkov	GER Mandy Wötzel & Ingo Steuer	RUS Elena Berezhnaya & Anton Sikharulidze
1998	ITA Milan	RUS Elena Berezhnaya & Anton Sikharulidze	RUS Oksana Kazakova & Artur Dmitriev	FRA Sarah Abitbol & Stéphane Bernadis
1999	CZE Prague	RUS Maria Petrova & Alexei Tikhonov	POL Dorota Zagórska & Mariusz Siudek	FRA Sarah Abitbol & Stéphane Bernadis
2000	AUT Vienna	RUS Maria Petrova & Alexei Tikhonov	POL Dorota Zagórska & Mariusz Siudek	FRA Sarah Abitbol & Stéphane Bernadis
2001	SVK Bratislava	RUS Elena Berezhnaya & Anton Sikharulidze	RUS Tatiana Totmianina & Maxim Marinin	FRA Sarah Abitbol & Stéphane Bernadis
2002	SWI Lausanne	RUS Tatiana Totmianina & Maxim Marinin	FRA Sarah Abitbol & Stéphane Bernadis	RUS Maria Petrova & Alexei Tikhonov
2003	SWE Malmö	RUS Tatiana Totmianina & Maxim Marinin	FRA Sarah Abitbol & Stéphane Bernadis	RUS Maria Petrova & Alexei Tikhonov
2004	HUN Budapest	RUS Tatiana Totmianina & Maxim Marinin	RUS Maria Petrova & Alexei Tikhonov	POL Dorota Zagórska & Mariusz Siudek
2005	ITA Turin	RUS Tatiana Totmianina & Maxim Marinin	RUS Julia Obertas & Sergei Slavnov	RUS Maria Petrova & Alexei Tikhonov
2006	FRA Lyon	RUS Tatiana Totmianina & Maxim Marinin	GER Aliona Savchenko & Robin Szolkowy	RUS Maria Petrova & Alexei Tikhonov
2007	POL Warsaw	GER Aliona Savchenko & Robin Szolkowy	RUS Maria Petrova & Alexei Tikhonov	POL Dorota Siudek & Mariusz Siudek

Year	Location	Gold	Silver	Bronze
2008	CRO Zagreb	GER Aliona Savchenko & Robin Szolkowy	RUS Maria Mukhortova & Maxim Trankov	RUS Yuko Kawaguchi & Alexander Smirnov
2009	FIN Helsinki	GER Aliona Savchenko & Robin Szolkowy	RUS Yuko Kawaguchi & Alexander Smirnov	RUS Maria Mukhortova & Maxim Trankov
2010	EST Tallinn	RUS Yuko Kavaguti & Alexander Smirnov	GER Aliona Savchenko & Robin Szolkowy	RUS Maria Mukhortova & Maxim Trankov
2011	SWI Bern	GER Aliona Savchenko & Robin Szolkowy	RUS Yuko Kavaguti & Alexander Smirnov	RUS Vera Bazarova & Yuri Larionov
2012	GBR Sheffield	RUS Tatiana Volosozhar & Maxim Trankov	RUS Vera Bazarova & Yuri Larionov	RUS Ksenia Stolbova & Fedor Klimov
2013	CRO Zagreb	RUS Tatiana Volosozhar & Maxim Trankov	GER Aliona Savchenko & Robin Szolkowy	ITA Stefania Berton & Ondřej Hotárek
2014	HUN Budapest	RUS Tatiana Volosozhar & Maxim Trankov	RUS Ksenia Stolbova & Fedor Klimov	RUS Vera Bazarova & Yuri Larionov
2015	SWE Stockholm	RUS Yuko Kavaguti & Alexander Smirnov	RUS Ksenia Stolbova & Fedor Klimov	RUS Evgenia Tarasova & Vladimir Morozov
2016	SVK Bratislava	RUS Tatiana Volosozhar & Maxim Trankov	GER Aliona Savchenko & Bruno Massot	RUS Evgenia Tarasova & Vladimir Morozov
2017	CZE Ostrova	RUS Evgenia Tarasova & Vladimir Morozov	GER Aliona Savchenko & Bruno Massot	FRA Vanessa James & Morgan Ciprès

European Figure Skating Championships - LADIES

Year	Location	Gold	Silver	Bronze
1930	AUT Vienna	AUT Fritzi Burger	AUT Ilse Hornung	SWE Vivi-Anne Hultén
1931	SWI St. Moritz	NOR Sonja Henie	AUT Fritzi Burger	AUT Hilde Holovsky
1932	FRA Paris	NOR Sonja Henie	AUT Fritzi Burger	SWE Vivi-Anne Hultén
1933	GBR London	NOR Sonja Henie	GBR Cecilia Colledge	AUT Fritzi Burger
1934	CZE Prague	NOR Sonja Henie	AUT Liselotte Landbeck	USA Maribel Vinson
1935	SWI St. Moritz	NOR Sonja Henie	AUT Liselotte Landbeck	GBR Cecilia Colledge
1936	GER Berlin	NOR Sonja Henie	GBR Cecilia Colledge	GBR Megan Taylor
1937	CZE Prague	GBR Cecilia Colledge	GBR Megan Taylor	AUT Emmy Putzinger
1938	SWI St. Moritz	GBR Cecilia Colledge	GBR Megan Taylor	AUT Emmy Putzinger
1939	GBR London	GBR Cecilia Colledge	GBR Megan Taylor	GBR Daphne Walker
1940 - 1946	NOT HELD DUE	TO W.W. 2		
1947	SWI Davos	CAN Barbara Ann Scott	USA Gretchen Merrill	GBR Daphne Walker
1948	CZE Prague	CAN Barbara Ann Scott	AUT Eva Pawlik	CZE Alena Vrzáňová
1949	ITA Milan	AUT Eva Pawlik	CZE Alena Vrzáňová	GBR Jeannette Altwegg
1950	NOR Oslo	CZE Alena Vrzáňová	GBR Jeannette Altwegg	FRA Jacqueline du Bief
1951	SWI Zürich	GBR Jeannette Altwegg	FRA Jacqueline du Bief	GBR Barbara Wyatt
1952	AUT Vienna	GBR Jeannette Altwegg	FRA Jacqueline du Bief	GBR Barbara Wyatt
1953	GDR Dortmund	GBR Valda Osborn	GDR Gundi Busch	GBR Erica Batchelor
1954	ITA Bolzano	GDR Gundi Busch	GBR Erica Batchelor	GBR Yvonne Sugden
1955	HUN Budapest	AUT Hanna Eigel	GBR Yvonne Sugden	GBR Erica Batchelor
1956	FRA Paris	AUT Ingrid Wendl	GBR Yvonne Sugden	GBR Erica Batchelor

Greg Fox

Year	Location	Gold	Silver	Bronze
1958	CZE Bratislava	AUT Ingrid Wendl	AUT Hanna Walter	NED Joan Haanappel
1959	SWI Davos	AUT Hanna Walter	NED Sjoukje Dijkstra	NED Joan Haanappel
1960	GDR Garmisch-Partenkirchen	NED Sjoukje Dijkstra	AUT Regine Heitzer	NED Joan Haanappel
1961	West Berlin West Berlin	NED Sjoukje Dijkstra	AUT Regine Heitzer	CZE Jana Mrázková
1962	SWI Geneva	NED Sjoukje Dijkstra	AUT Regine Heitzer	AUT Karin Frohner
1963	HUN Budapest	NED Sjoukje Dijkstra	FRA Nicole Hassler	AUT Regine Heitzer
1964	FRA Grenoble	NED Sjoukje Dijkstra	AUT Regine Heitzer	FRA Nicole Hassler
1965	SOV Moscow	AUT Regine Heitzer	GBR Sally-Anne Stapleford	FRA Nicole Hassler
1966	CZE Bratislava	AUT Regine Heitzer	GDR Gabriele Seyfert	FRA Nicole Hassler
1967	YUG Ljubljana	GDR Gabriele Seyfert	CZE Hana Mašková	HUN Zsuzsa Almássy
1968	SWE Västerås	CZE Hana Mašková	GDR Gabriele Seyfert	AUT Beatrix Schuba
1969	GDR Garmisch-Partenkirchen	GDR Gabriele Seyfert	CZE Hana Mašková	AUT Beatrix Schuba
1970	SOV Leningrad	GDR Gabriele Seyfert	AUT Beatrix Schuba	HUN Zsuzsa Almássy
1971	SWI Zürich	AUT Beatrix Schuba	HUN Zsuzsa Almássy	ITA Rita Trapanese
1972	SWE Gothenburg	AUT Beatrix Schuba	ITA Rita Trapanese	GDR Sonja Morgenstern
1973	GDR Cologne	GDR Christine Errath	GBR Jean Scott	SWI Karin Iten
1974	YUG Zagreb	GDR Christine Errath	NED Dianne de Leeuw	CZE Liana Drahová
1975	DEN Copenhagen	GDR Christine Errath	NED Dianne de Leeuw	GDR Anett Pötzsch
1976	SWI Geneva	NED Dianne de Leeuw	GDR Anett Pötzsch	GDR Christine Errath
1977	FIN Helsinki	GDR Anett Pötzsch	GDR Dagmar Lurz	ITA Susanna Driano

Year	Location	Gold	Silver	Bronze
1978	FRA Strasbourg	GDR Anett Pötzsch	GDR Dagmar Lurz	SOV Elena Vodorezova
1979	YUG Zagreb	GDR Anett Pötzsch	GDR Dagmar Lurz	SWI Denise Biellmann
1980	SWE Gothenburg	GDR Anett Pötzsch	GDR Dagmar Lurz	ITA Susanna Driano
1981	AUT Innsbruck	SWI Denise Biellmann	YUG Sanda Dubravčić	AUT Claudia Kristofics-Binder
1982	FRA Lyon	AUT Claudia Kristofics-Binder	GDR Katarina Witt	SOV Elena Vodorezova
1983	GDR Dortmund	GDR Katarina Witt	SOV Elena Vodorezova	GDR Claudia Leistner
1984	HUN Budapest	GDR Katarina Witt	GDR Manuela Ruben	SOV Anna Kondrashova
1985	SWE Gothenburg	GDR Katarina Witt	SOV Kira Ivanova	GDR Claudia Leistner
1986	DEN Copenhagen	GDR Katarina Witt	SOV Kira Ivanova	SOV Anna Kondrashova
1987	YUG Sarajevo	GDR Katarina Witt	SOV Kira Ivanova	SOV Anna Kondrashova
1988	CZE Prague	GDR Katarina Witt	SOV Kira Ivanova	SOV Anna Kondrashova
1989	GBR Birmingham	GDR Claudia Leistner	SOV Natalia Lebedeva	GDR Patricia Neske
1990	SOV Leningrad	GDR Evelyn Großmann	SOV Natalia Lebedeva	GDR Marina Kielmann
1991	BUL Sofia	FRA Surya Bonaly	GER Evelyn Großmann	GER Marina Kielmann
1992	SWI Lausanne	FRA Surya Bonaly	GER Marina Kielmann	GER Patricia Neske
1993	FIN Helsinki	FRA Surya Bonaly	UKR Oksana Baiul	GER Marina Kielmann
1994	DEN Copenhagen	FRA Surya Bonaly	UKR Oksana Baiul	RUS Olga Markova
1995	GER Dortmund	FRA Surya Bonaly	RUS Olga Markova	UKR Elena Liashenko
1996	BUL Sofia	RUS Irina Slutskaya	FRA Surya Bonaly	RUS Maria Butyrskaya
1997	FRA Paris	RUS Irina Slutskaya	HUN Krisztina Czakó	UKR Yulia Lavrenchuk
1998	ITA Milan	RUS Maria Butyrskaya	RUS Irina Slutskaya	GER Tanja Szewczenko

Year	Location	Gold	Silver	Bronze
1999	CZE Prague	RUS Maria Butyrskaya	RUS Julia Soldatova	RUS Viktoria Volchkova
2000	AUT Vienna	RUS Irina Slutskaya	RUS Maria Butyrskaya	RUS Viktoria Volchkova
2001	SVK Bratislava	RUS Irina Slutskaya	RUS Maria Butyrskaya	RUS Viktoria Volchkova
2002	SWI Lausanne	RUS Maria Butyrskaya	RUS Irina Slutskaya	RUS Viktoria Volchkova
2003	SWE Malmö	RUS Irina Slutskaya	RUS Elena Sokolova	HUN Júlia Sebestyén
2004	HUN Budapest	HUN Júlia Sebestyén	UKR Elena Liashenko	RUS Elena Sokolova
2005	ITA Turin	RUS Irina Slutskaya	FIN Susanna Pöykiö	UKR Elena Liashenko
2006	FRA Lyon	RUS Irina Slutskaya	RUS Elena Sokolova	ITA Carolina Kostner
2007	POL Warsaw	ITA Carolina Kostner	SWI Sarah Meier	FIN Kiira Korpi
2008	CRO Zagreb	ITA Carolina Kostner	SWI Sarah Meier	FIN Laura Lepistö
2009	FIN Helsinki	FIN Laura Lepistö	ITA Carolina Kostner	FIN Susanna Pöykiö
2010	EST Tallinn	ITA Carolina Kostner	FIN Laura Lepistö	Georgia (country) Elene Gedevanishvili
2011	SWI Bern	SWI Sarah Meier	ITA Carolina Kostner	FIN Kiira Korpi
2012	GBR Sheffield	ITA Carolina Kostner	FIN Kiira Korpi	Georgia (country) Elene Gedevanishvili
2013	CRO Zagreb	ITA Carolina Kostner	RUS Adelina Sotnikova	RUS Elizaveta Tuktamysheva
2014	HUN Budapest	RUS Yulia Lipnitskaya	RUS Adelina Sotnikova	ITA Carolina Kostner
2015	SWE Stockholm	RUS Elizaveta Tuktamysheva	RUS Elena Radionova	RUS Anna Pogorilaya
2016	SVK Bratislava	RUS Evgenia Medvedeva	RUS Elena Radionova	RUS Anna Pogorilaya
2017	CZE Ostrova	RUS Evgenia Medvedeva	RUS Anna Pogorilaya	ITA Carolina Kostner

Opposite Page: **Katarina Witt**, 2-time Olympic gold medallist, (in 1984 & 1988), and 4-time World Champion. One of the most successful figure skaters in history, she has also won gold at the European Championships six years in a row, (1983-1988).

European Figure Skating Championships - ICE DANCING

Year	Location	Gold	Silver	Bronze
1954	ITA Bolzano	GBR Jean Westwood & Lawrence Demmy	GBR Nesta Davies & Paul Thomas	GBR Barbara Radford & Raymond Lockwood
1955	HUN Budapest	GBR Jean Westwood & Lawrence Demmy	GBR Pamela Weight & Paul Thomas	GBR Barbara Radford & Raymond Lockwood
1956	FRA Paris	GBR Pamela Weight & Paul Thomas	GBR June Markham & Courtney Jones	GBR Barbara Thompson & Gerard Rigby
1957	AUT Vienna	GBR June Markham & Courtney Jones	GBR Barbara Thompson & Gerard Rigby	GBR Catherine Morris & Michael Robinson
1958	CZE Bratislava	GBR June Markham & Courtney Jones	GBR Catherine Morris & Michael Robinson	GBR Barbara Thompson & Gerard Rigby
1959	SWI Davos	GBR Doreen Denny & Courtney Jones	GBR Catherine Morris & Michael Robinson	FRA Christiane Guhel & Jean Paul Guhel
1960	GDR Garmisch-Partenkirchen	GBR Doreen Denny & Courtney Jones	FRA Christiane Guhel & Jean Paul Guhel	GBR Mary Parry & Roy Mason
1961	West Berlin West Berlin	GBR Doreen Denny & Courtney Jones	FRA Christiane Guhel & Jean Paul Guhel	GBR Linda Shearman & Michael Phillips
1962	SWI Geneva	FRA Christiane Guhel & Jean Paul Guhel	GBR Linda Shearman & Michael Phillips	CZE Eva Romanová & Pavel Roman
1963	HUN Budapest	GBR Linda Shearman & Michael Phillips	CZE Eva Romanová & Pavel Roman	GBR Janet Sawbridge & David Hickinbottom

Year	Location	Gold	Silver	Bronze
1964	FRA Grenoble	CZE Eva Romanová & Pavel Roman	GBR Janet Sawbridge & David Hickinbottom	GBR Yvonne Suddick & Roger Kennerson
1965	SOV Moscow	CZE Eva Romanová & Pavel Roman	GBR Janet Sawbridge & David Hickinbottom	GBR Yvonne Suddick & Roger Kennerson
1966	CZE Bratislava	GBR Diane Towler & Bernard Ford	GBR Yvonne Suddick & Roger Kennerson	CZE Jitka Babická & Jaromír Holan
1967	YUG Ljubljana	GBR Diane Towler & Bernard Ford	GBR Yvonne Suddick & Malcolm Cannon	FRA Brigitte Martin & Francis Gamichon
1968	SWE Vasteras	GBR Diane Towler & Bernard Ford	GBR Yvonne Suddick & Malcolm Cannon	GBR Janet Sawbridge & Jon Lane
1969	GDR Garmisch-Partenkirchen	GBR Diane Towler & Bernard Ford	GBR Janet Sawbridge & Jon Lane	SOV Liudmila Pakhomova & Alexander Gorshkov
1970	SOV Leningrad	SOV Liudmila Pakhomova & Alexander Gorshkov	GDR Angelika Buck & Erich Buck	SOV Tatiana Voitiuk & Viacheslav Zhigalin
1971	SWI Zurich	SOV Liudmila Pakhomova & Alexander Gorshkov	GDR Angelika Buck & Erich Buck	GBR Susan Getty & Roy Bradshaw
1972	SWE Gothenburg	GDR Angelika Buck & Erich Buck	SOV Liudmila Pakhomova & Alexander Gorshkov	GBR Janet Sawbridge & Peter Dalby
1973	GDR Cologne	SOV Liudmila Pakhomova & Alexander Gorshkov	GDR Angelika Buck & Erich Buck	GBR Hilary Green & Glyn Watts
1974	YUG Zagreb	SOV Liudmila Pakhomova & Alexander Gorshkov	GBR Hilary Green & Glyn Watts	SOV Natalia Linichuk & Gennadi Karponosov

Year	Location	Gold	Silver	Bronze
1975	DEN Copenhagen	SOV Liudmila Pakhomova & Alexander Gorshkov	GBR Hilary Green & Glyn Watts	SOV Natalia Linichuk & Gennadi Karponosov
1976	SWI Geneva	SOV Liudmila Pakhomova & Alexander Gorshkov	SOV Irina Moiseeva & Andrei Minenkov	SOV Natalia Linichuk & Gennadi Karponosov
1977	FIN Helsinki	SOV Irina Moiseeva Andrei Minenkov	HUN Krisztina Regőczy András Sallay	SOV Natalia Linichuk Gennadi Karponosov
1978	FRA Strasbourg	SOV Irina Moiseeva & Andrei Minenkov	SOV Natalia Linichuk & Gennadi Karponosov	HUN Krisztina Regőczy & András Sallay
1979	YUG Zagreb	SOV Natalia Linichuk & Gennadi Karponosov	SOV Irina Moiseeva & Andrei Minenkov	HUN Krisztina Regőczy & András Sallay
1980	SWE Gothenburg	SOV Natalia Linichuk & Gennadi Karponosov	HUN Krisztina Regőczy & András Sallay	SOV Irina Moiseeva & Andrei Minenkov
1981	AUT Innsbruck	GBR Jayne Torvill & Christopher Dean	SOV Irina Moiseeva & Andrei Minenkov	SOV Natalia Linichuk & Gennadi Karponosov
1982	FRA Lyon	GBR Jayne Torvill & Christopher Dean	SOV Natalia Bestemianova & Andrei Bukin	SOV Irina Moiseeva & Andrei Minenkov
1983	GDR Dortmund	SOV Natalia Bestemianova & Andrei Bukin	SOV Olga Volozhinskaya & Alexander Svinin	GBR Karen Barber & Nicholas Slater

Year	Location	Gold	Silver	Bronze
1984	HUN Budapest	GBR Jayne Torvill & Christopher Dean	SOV Natalia Bestemianova & Andrei Bukin	SOV Marina Klimova & Sergei Ponomarenko
1985	SWE Gothenburg	SOV Natalia Bestemianova & Andrei Bukin	SOV Marina Klimova & Sergei Ponomarenko	GDR Petra Born & Rainer Schönborn
1986	DEN Copenhagen	SOV Natalia Bestemianova & Andrei Bukin	SOV Marina Klimova & Sergei Ponomarenko	SOV Natalia Annenko & Genrikh Sretenski
1987	YUG Sarajevo	SOV Natalia Bestemianova & Andrei Bukin	SOV Marina Klimova & Sergei Ponomarenko	SOV Natalia Annenko & Genrikh Sretenski
1988	CZE Prague	SOV Natalia Bestemianova & Andrei Bukin	SOV Natalia Annenko & Genrikh Sretenski	FRA Isabelle Duchesnay & Paul Duchesnay
1989	GBR Birmingham	SOV Marina Klimova & Sergei Ponomarenko	SOV Maya Usova & Alexander Zhulin	SOV Natalia Annenko & Genrikh Sretenski
1990	SOV Leningrad	SOV Marina Klimova & Sergei Ponomarenko	SOV Maya Usova & Alexander Zhulin	FRA Isabelle Duchesnay & Paul Duchesnay
1991	BUL Sofia	SOV Marina Klimova & Sergei Ponomarenko	FRA Isabelle Duchesnay & Paul Duchesnay	SOV Maya Usova & Alexander Zhulin

Year	Location	Gold	Silver	Bronze
1992	SWI Lausanne	RUS Marina Klimova & Sergei Ponomarenko	RUS Maya Usova & Alexander Zhulin	RUS Pasha Grishuk & Evgeni Platov
1993	FIN Helsinki	RUS Maya Usova & Alexander Zhulin	RUS Pasha Grishuk & Evgeni Platov	FIN Susanna Rahkamo & Petri Kokko
1994	DEN Copenhagen	GBR Jayne Torvill & Christopher Dean	RUS Pasha Grishuk & Evgeni Platov	RUS Maya Usova & Alexander Zhulin
1995	GER Dortmund	FIN Susanna Rahkamo & Petri Kokko	FRA Sophie Moniotte & Pascal Lavanchy	RUS Anjelika Krylova & Oleg Ovsyannikov
1996	BUL Sofia	RUS Pasha Grishuk & Evgeni Platov	RUS Anjelika Krylova & Oleg Ovsyannikov	UKR Irina Romanova & Igor Yaroshenko
1997	FRA Paris	RUS Pasha Grishuk & Evgeni Platov	RUS Anjelika Krylova & Oleg Ovsyannikov	FRA Sophie Moniotte & Pascal Lavanchy
1998	ITA Milan	RUS Pasha Grishuk & Evgeni Platov	RUS Anjelika Krylova & Oleg Ovsyannikov	FRA Marina Anissina & Gwendal Peizerat
1999	CZE Prague	RUS Anjelika Krylova & Oleg Ovsyannikov	FRA Marina Anissina & Gwendal Peizerat	RUS Irina Lobacheva & Ilia Averbukh
2000	AUT Vienna	FRA Marina Anissina & Gwendal Peizerat	ITA Barbara Fusar-Poli & Maurizio Margaglio	LIT Margarita Drobiazko & Povilas Vanagas
2001	SVK Bratislava	ITA Barbara Fusar-Poli & Maurizio Margaglio	FRA Marina Anissina & Gwendal Peizerat	RUS Irina Lobacheva & Ilia Averbukh
2002	SWI Lausanne	FRA Marina Anissina & Gwendal Peizerat	ITA Barbara Fusar-Poli & Maurizio Margaglio	RUS Irina Lobacheva & Ilia Averbukh

Year	Location	Gold	Silver	Bronze
2003	SWE Malmö	RUS Irina Lobacheva & Ilia Averbukh	BUL Albena Denkova & Maxim Staviski	RUS Tatiana Navka & Roman Kostomarov
2004	HUN Budapest	RUS Tatiana Navka & Roman Kostomarov	BUL Albena Denkova & Maxim Staviski	UKR Elena Grushina & Ruslan Goncharov
2005	ITA Turin	RUS Tatiana Navka & Roman Kostomarov	UKR Elena Grushina & Ruslan Goncharov	FRA Isabelle Delobel & Olivier Schoenfelder
2006	FRA Lyon	RUS Tatiana Navka & Roman Kostomarov	UKR Elena Grushina & Ruslan Goncharov	LIT Margarita Drobiazko & Povilas Vanagas
2007	POL Warsaw	FRA Isabelle Delobel & Olivier Schoenfelder	RUS Oksana Domnina & Maxim Shabalin	BUL Albena Denkova & Maxim Staviski
2008	CRO Zagreb	RUS Oksana Domnina & Maxim Shabalin	FRA Isabelle Delobel & Olivier Schoenfelder	RUS Jana Khokhlova & Sergei Novitski
2009	FIN Helsinki	RUS Jana Khokhlova & Sergei Novitski	ITA Federica Faiella & Massimo Scali	GBR Sinead Kerr & John Kerr
2010	EST Tallinn	RUS Oksana Domnina & Maxim Shabalin	ITA Federica Faiella & Massimo Scali	RUS Jana Khokhlova & Sergei Novitski
2011	SWI Bern	FRA Nathalie Péchalat & Fabian Bourzat	RUS Ekaterina Bobrova & Dmitri Soloviev	GBR Sinead Kerr & John Kerr
2012	GBR Sheffield	FRA Nathalie Péchalat & Fabian Bourzat	RUS Ekaterina Bobrova & Dmitri Soloviev	RUS Elena Ilinykh & Nikita Katsalapov
2013	CRO Zagreb	RUS Ekaterina Bobrova & Dmitri Soloviev	RUS Elena Ilinykh & Nikita Katsalapov	ITA Anna Cappellini & Luca Lanotte

Year	Location	Gold	Silver	Bronze
2014	HUN Budapest	ITA Anna Cappellini & Luca Lanotte	RUS Elena Ilinykh & Nikita Katsalapov	GBR Penny Coomes & Nicholas Buckland
2015	SWE Stockholm	FRA Gabriella Papadakis & Guillaume Cizeron	ITA Anna Cappellini & Luca Lanotte	RUS Alexandra Stepanova & Ivan Bukin
2016	SVK Bratislava	FRA Gabriella Papadakis & Guillaume Cizeron	ITA Anna Cappellini & Luca Lanotte	RUS Ekaterina Bobrova & Dmitri Soloviev
2017	CZE Ostrova	FRA Gabriella Papadakis & Guillaume Cizeron	ITA Anna Cappellini & Luca Lanotte	RUS Ekaterina Bobrova & Dmitri Soloviev

Grand Prix Competitions

Above: **Mirai Nagasu**, American figure skater, has won multiple medals at a variety of Grand Prix competitions. (She's also medalled at Four Continents & at the US National Championships, where she won gold in 2008 and silver, bronze and pewter in other years). She kicked off the 2017/2018 season in powerful form, landing two triple axels, one in each program at one competition, the first female skater to do so since Tonya Harding in 1991. She looks to be a strong contender for the 2018 Winter Olympics.

Grand Prix Competitions

The ISU Grand Prix of Figure Skating is a series of international figure skating competitions, sanctioned by the International Skating Union (ISU), starting in the Fall season each year. Although the Grand Prix series was first initiated in the mid-1990s, many of the events that comprise it had existed for years before. The events are Skate America, Skate Canada, NHK Trophy (Japan), Cup of China, Trophée de France, Cup of Russia-Rostelecom Cup, Bofrost Cup On Ice (Germany, discontinued after 2004), and the Grand Prix of Figure Skating Finals.

Skate America

Skate America was initiated in 1979 in Lake Placid, New York, and was considered a "test event" for the 1980 Winter Olympic Games. In 1995 it was incorporated into the Grand Prix Series.

Skate Canada International

Skate Canada was first held in 1973 in Calgary, Alberta. The 1987 competition, (also held in Calgary). was considered a "test event" for the 1988 Winter Olympic Games. In 1995 it was incorporated into the Grand Prix Series.

NHK Trophy

NHK Trophy, organized by the Japanese Skating Federation, was initiated in 1979 in Tokyo. In 1995 it was incorporated into the Grand Prix Series.

Cup of China

Cup of China, organized by the Chinese Skating Association, was initiated in 2003 in Beijing, replacing the discontinued German event Bofrost Cup on Ice in the Grand Prix Series.

Trophée de France / Internationaux de France

First held in 1987 in Paris, the competition was initially known as the Grand Prix International de Paris. The title changed in 1994 to Trophée de France. Incorporated into the Grand Prix series in 1995, the competition changed names again in 1996 to the Trophée Lalique, (to reflect the name of its sponsor, the Lalique glassware company). The title was changed yet again in 2004, when another corporate sponsor, the Éric Bompard company, had it renamed as the Trophée Éric Bompard. The 2015 competition was cut short after one day because of the November, 2015 Paris attacks. (The short program results were ultimately considered as final results). In 2016, the competition returned to its original title of Trophée de France, and then in 2017, was retitled once again as Internationaux de France.

Cup of Russia / Rostelecom Cup

The Cup of Russia has been held since 1996, put together by the Figure Skating Federation of Russia. It is, essentially, a replacement for the Prize of Moscow News, an international competition held in Russia from 1966 to 1990 (except for 1989). The competition changed its name to Rostelecom Cup in 2009, (after its sponsor).

Bofrost Cup On Ice

The Bofrost Cup on Ice (also known as the Fujifilm Trophy from 1986 to 1987, the Nations Cup from 1989 to 1997, and the Sparkassen Cup on Ice from 1998 to 2001), became part of the Grand Prix series in 1995, but was ultimately dropped and replaced by the Cup of China in 2003. The event was held twice more after being dropped from the Grand Prix series, but was discontinued after the 2004 competition.

Grand Prix of Figure Skating Finals

Begun in 1995, (and originally known as the Champions Series Final for its first three years), the Grand Prix Finals is the finishing event in the ISU Grand Prix Figure Skating series. Although it doesn't technically qualify as an ISU Championship, the Grand Prix Finals are generally considered to be the second most important competition (after the World Championships) of the season.

Skate America - MEN

Year	Location	Gold	Silver	Bronze
1979	Lake Placid	USA Scott Hamilton	USA Scott Cramer	GDR Jan Hoffmann
1980		*Competition not held*		
1981	Lake Placid	USA Scott Hamilton	USA Robert Wagenhoffer	USA Brian Boitano
1982	Lake Placid	USA Scott Hamilton	FRG Heiko Fischer	CZE Jozef Sabovčík
1983	Rochester	USA Brian Boitano	FRG Rudi Cerne	USA Bobby Beauchamp
1984		*Competition not held*		
1985	St. Paul	CZE Jozef Sabovčík	USA Brian Boitano	URS Viktor Petrenko
1986	Portland	USA Brian Boitano	URS Viktor Petrenko	USA Daniel Doran
1987		*Competition not held*		
1988	Portland	USA Christopher Bowman	USA Daniel Doran	USA Todd Eldredge
1989	Indianapolis	USA Christopher Bowman	URS Viktor Petrenko	CAN Kurt Browning
1990	Buffalo	URS Viktor Petrenko	USA Christopher Bowman	USA Todd Eldredge
1991	Oakland	USA Christopher Bowman	CZE Petr Barna	USA Todd Eldredge
1992	Atlanta	USA Todd Eldredge	USA Scott Davis	USA Mark Mitchell
1993	Dallas	UKR Viktor Petrenko	USA Brian Boitano	RUS Alexei Urmanov
1994	Pittsburgh	USA Todd Eldredge	FRA Philippe Candeloro	FRA Éric Millot
1995	Detroit	USA Todd Eldredge	USA Michael Weiss	RUS Alexander Abt
1996	Springfield	USA Todd Eldredge	RUS Alexei Urmanov	RUS Alexei Yagudin
1997	Detroit	USA Todd Eldredge	RUS Evgeni Plushenko	RUS Alexander Abt
1998	Detroit	RUS Alexei Yagudin	USA Michael Weiss	RUS Alexei Urmanov
1999	Colorado Springs	RUS Alexei Yagudin	USA Timothy Goebel	CAN Elvis Stojko
1995	HUN Budapest	RUS Ilia Kulik	FRA Thierry Cerez	JPN Seiichi Suzuki
1996	AUS Brisbane	RUS Alexei Yagudin	JPN Takeshi Honda	CHN Guo Zhengxin

Greg Fox

Year	Location	Gold	Silver	Bronze
1997	Detroit	USA Todd Eldredge	RUS Evgeni Plushenko	RUS Alexander Abt
1998	Detroit	RUS Alexei Yagudin	USA Michael Weiss	RUS Alexei Urmanov
1999	Colorado Springs	RUS Alexei Yagudin	USA Timothy Goebel	CAN Elvis Stojko
2000	Colorado Springs	USA Timothy Goebel	RUS Alexei Yagudin	USA Todd Eldredge
2001	Colorado Springs	USA Timothy Goebel	JPN Takeshi Honda	RUS Alexander Abt
2002	Spokane	FRA Brian Joubert	RUS Alexander Abt	USA Matthew Savoie
2003	Reading	USA Michael Weiss	JPN Takeshi Honda	CHN Zhang Min
2004	Pittsburgh	FRA Brian Joubert	USA Ryan Jahnke	USA Michael Weiss
2005	Atlantic City	JPN Daisuke Takahashi	USA Evan Lysacek	FRA Brian Joubert
2006	Hartford	JPN Nobunari Oda	USA Evan Lysacek	FRA Alban Préaubert
2007	Reading	JPN Daisuke Takahashi	USA Evan Lysacek	CAN Patrick Chan
2008	Everett	JPN Takahiko Kozuka	USA Johnny Weir	USA Evan Lysacek
2009	Lake Placid	USA Evan Lysacek	CAN Shawn Sawyer	USA Ryan Bradley
2010	Portland	JPN Daisuke Takahashi	JPN Nobunari Oda	USA Armin Mahbanoozadeh
2011	Ontario	CZE Michal Březina	BEL Kevin van der Perren	JPN Takahiko Kozuka
2012	Kent	JPN Takahiko Kozuka	JPN Yuzuru Hanyu	JPN Tatsuki Machida
2013	Detroit	JPN Tatsuki Machida	USA Adam Rippon	USA Max Aaron
2014	Chicago	JPN Tatsuki Machida	USA Jason Brown	CAN Nam Nguyen
2015	Milwaukee	USA Max Aaron	JPN Shoma Uno	USA Jason Brown
2016	Chicago	JPN Shoma Uno	USA Jason Brown	USA Adam Rippon

Opposite page: **Brian Joubert**, French men's figure skater, has racked up a number of medals at various Grand Prix competitions, including gold at Skate America in 2002 & 2004. He won gold in his native France's National Championships 8 times, and 3 times in the European Championships. And, oh yes, he was World Champion in 2007!

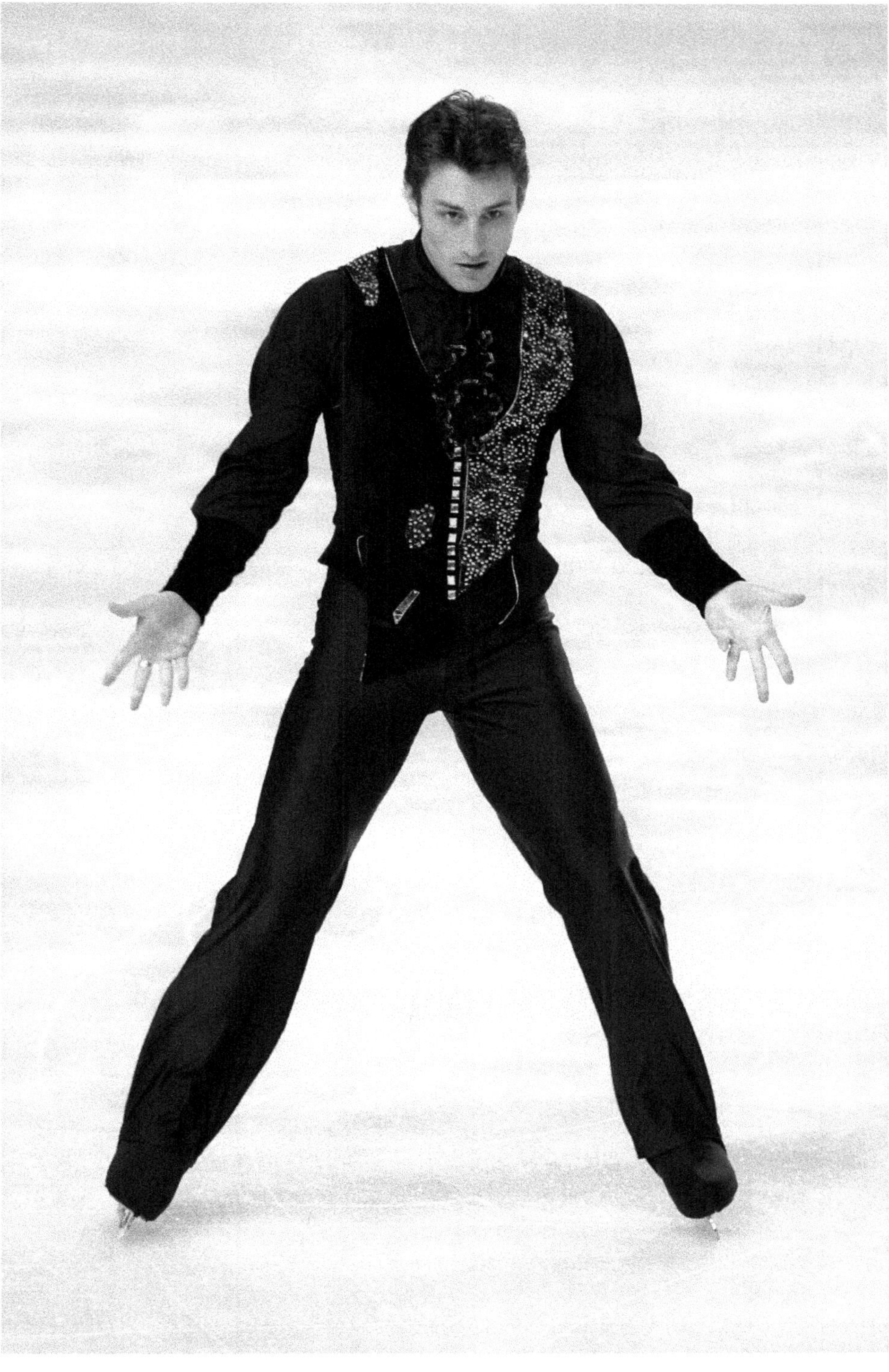

Olga Besnard/Shutterstock.com

Skate America - PAIRS

Year	Location	Gold	Silver	Bronze
1979	Lake Placid	GDR Sabine Baeß & Tassilo Thierbach	USA Caitlin Carruthers & Peter Carruthers	USA Vickie Heasley & Robert Wagenhoffer
1980		*Competition not held*		
1981	Lake Placid	CAN Barbara Underhill & Paul Martini	USA Caitlin Carruthers & Peter Carruthers	URS Elena Valova & Oleg Vasiliev
1982	Lake Placid	URS Elena Valova & Oleg Vasiliev	USA Lea Ann Miller & William Fauver	URS Nellie Chervotkina & Viktor Teslya
1983	Rochester	USA Caitlin Carruthers & Peter Carruthers	USA Jill Watson & Burt Lancon	CAN Melinda Kunhegyi & Lyndon Johnston
1984		*Competition not held*		
1985	St. Paul	USA Jill Watson & Peter Oppegard	URS Elena Bechke & Valeri Kornienko	USA Gillian Wachsman & Todd Waggoner
1986	Portland	USA Katy Keeley & Joseph Mero	CAN Denise Benning & Lyndon Johnston	URS Liudmila Koblova & Andrei Kalitin
1987		*Competition not held*		
1988	Portland	URS Natalia Mishkutenok & Artur Dmitriev	URS Marina Eltsova & Sergei Zaitsev	USA Natalie Seybold & Wayne Seybold
1989	Indianapolis	URS Natalia Mishkutenok & Artur Dmitriev	USA Kristi Yamaguchi & Rudy Galindo	GDR Peggy Schwarz & Alexander König
1990	Buffalo	URS Marina Eltsova & Andrei Bushkov	CZE Radka Kovaříková & René Novotný	GER Mandy Wötzel & Axel Rauschenbach

Year	Location	Gold	Silver	Bronze
1991	Oakland	USA Calla Urbanski & Rocky Marval	URS Elena Nikonova & Nikolai Apter	GER Peggy Schwarz & Alexander König
1992	Atlanta	RUS Marina Eltsova & Andrei Bushkov	CZE Radka Kovaříková & René Novotný	RUS Evgenia Shishkova & Vadim Naumov
1993	Dallas	RUS Evgenia Shishkova & Vadim Naumov	USA Kyoko Ina & Jason Dungjen	USA Karen Courtland & Todd Reynolds
1994	Pittsburgh	RUS Marina Eltsova & Andrei Bushkov	RUS Evgenia Shishkova & Vadim Naumov	CZE Radka Kovaříková & René Novotný
1995	Detroit	RUS Marina Eltsova & Andrei Bushkov	USA Jenni Meno & Todd Sand	LAT Elena Berezhnaya & Oleg Shliakhov
1996	Springfield	RUS Oksana Kazakova & Artur Dmitriev	USA Shelby Lyons & Brian Wells	USA Stephanie Stiegler & John Zimmerman
1997	Detroit	RUS Marina Eltsova & Andrei Bushkov	USA Kyoko Ina & Jason Dungjen	RUS Evgenia Shishkova & Vadim Naumov
1998	Detroit	RUS Elena Berezhnaya & Anton Sikharulidze	CAN Kristy Wirtz & Kris Wirtz	RUS Viktoria Maxiuta & Vladislav Zhovnirski
1999	Colorado Springs	CAN Jamie Salé & David Pelletier	FRA Sarah Abitbol & Stéphane Bernadis	RUS Elena Berezhnaya & Anton Sikharulidze
2000	Colorado Springs	CAN Jamie Salé & David Pelletier	CHN Shen Xue & Zhao Hongbo	RUS Tatiana Totmianina & Maxim Marinin
2001	Colorado Springs	CAN Jamie Salé & David Pelletier	USA Kyoko Ina & John Zimmerman	RUS Tatiana Totmianina & Maxim Marinin

Year	Location	Gold	Silver	Bronze
2002	Spokane	RUS Tatiana Totmianina & Maxim Marinin	CAN Anabelle Langlois & Patrice Archetto	CHN Pang Qing & Tong Jian
2003	Reading	CHN Pang Qing & Tong Jian	RUS Maria Petrova & Alexei Tikhonov	CHN Zhang Dan & Zhang Hao
2004	Pittsburgh	CHN Zhang Dan & Zhang Hao	RUS Julia Obertas & Sergei Slavnov	USA Rena Inoue & John Baldwin
2005	Atlantic City	CHN Zhang Dan & Zhang Hao	USA Rena Inoue & John Baldwin	RUS Julia Obertas & Sergei Slavnov
2006	Hartford	USA Rena Inoue & John Baldwin	POL Dorota Siudek & Mariusz Siudek	USA Naomi Nari Nam & Themistocles Leftheris
2007	Reading	CAN Jessica Dubé & Bryce Davison	CHN Pang Qing & Tong Jian	RUS Vera Bazarova & Yuri Larionov
2008	Everett	GER Aliona Savchenko & Robin Szolkowy	USA Keauna McLaughlin & Rockne Brubaker	RUS Maria Mukhortova & Maxim Trankov
2009	Lake Placid	CHN Shen Xue & Zhao Hongbo	UKR Tatiana Volosozhar & Stanislav Morozov	CHN Zhang Dan & Zhang Hao
2010	Portland	GER Aliona Savchenko & Robin Szolkowy	CAN Kirsten Moore-Towers & Dylan Moscovitch	CHN Sui Wenjing & Han Cong
2011	Ontario	GER Aliona Savchenko & Robin Szolkowy	CHN Zhang Dan & Zhang Hao	CAN Kirsten Moore-Towers & Dylan Moscovitch
2012	Kent	RUS Tatiana Volosozhar & Maxim Trankov	CHN Pang Qing & Tong Jian	USA Caydee Denney & John Coughlin

Year	Location	Gold	Silver	Bronze
2013	Detroit	RUS Tatiana Volosozhar & Maxim Trankov	CAN Kirsten MooreTowers & Dylan Moscovitch	RUS Ksenia Stolbova & Fedor Klimov
2014	Hoffman Estates	RUS Yuko Kavaguti & Alexander Smirnov	USA Haven Denney & Brandon Frazier	CHN Peng Cheng & Zhang Hao
2015	Milwaukee	CHN Sui Wenjing & Han Cong	USA Alexa Scimeca & Chris Knierim	CAN Julianne Séguin & Charlie Bilodeau
2016	Chicago	CAN Julianne Séguin & Charlie Bilodeau	USA Haven Denney & Brandon Frazier	RUS Evgenia Tarasova & Vladimir Morozov

Skate America - LADIES

Year	Location	Gold	Silver	Bronze
1979	Lake Placid	USA Lisa-Marie Allen	ITA Susanna Driano	USA Sandy Lenz
1980		*Competition*	*not held*	
1981	Lake Placid	USA Vikki de Vries	USA Elaine Zayak	AUT Claudia Kristofics-Binder
1982	Lake Placid	USA Rosalynn Sumners	FRG Claudia Leistner	FIN Kristiina Wegelius
1983	Rochester	USA Tiffany Chin	USA Jill Frost	USA Kelly Webster
1984		*Competition*	*not held*	
1985	St. Paul	USA Debi Thomas	CAN Tracey Wainman	BEL Katrien Pauwels
1986	Portland	USA Tiffany Chin	USA Tonya Harding	FRA Agnès Gosselin
1987		*Competition*	*not held*	
1988	Portland	FRG Claudia Leistner	JPN Midori Ito	USA Kristi Yamaguchi
1989	Indianapolis	USA Tonya Harding	USA Jill Trenary	GDR Simone Lang
1990	Buffalo	USA Kristi Yamaguchi	JPN Midori Ito	USA Tonia Kwiatkowski
1991	Oakland	USA Tonya Harding	USA Kristi Yamaguchi	FRA Surya Bonaly
1992	Atlanta	JPN Yuka Sato	USA Nancy Kerrigan	CHN Chen Lu

Greg Fox

Year	Location	Gold	Silver	Bronze
1993	Dallas	UKR Oksana Baiul	FRA Surya Bonaly	USA Tonya Harding
1994	Pittsburgh	FRA Surya Bonaly	USA Michelle Kwan	RUS Irina Slutskaya
1995	Detroit	USA Michelle Kwan	CHN Chen Lu	RUS Irina Slutskaya
1996	Springfield	USA Michelle Kwan	USA Tonia Kwiatkowski	USA Sydne Vogel
1997	Detroit	USA Michelle Kwan	USA Tara Lipinski	RUS Elena Sokolova
1998	Detroit	RUS Maria Butyrskaya	RUS Elena Sokolova	USA Angela Nikodinov
1999	Colorado Springs	USA Michelle Kwan	RUS Julia Soldatova	RUS Elena Sokolova
2000	Colorado Springs	USA Michelle Kwan	USA Sarah Hughes	RUS Elena Sokolova
2001	Colorado Springs	USA Michelle Kwan	USA Sarah Hughes	RUS Viktoria Volchkova
2002	Spokane	USA Michelle Kwan	USA Ann Patrice McDonough	UKR Elena Liashenko
2003	Reading	USA Sasha Cohen	USA Jennifer Kirk	JPN Shizuka Arakawa
2004	Pittsburgh	USA Angela Nikodinov	CAN Cynthia Phaneuf	JPN Miki Ando
2005	Atlantic City	RUS Elena Sokolova	USA Alissa Czisny	JPN Yoshie Onda
2006	Hartford	JPN Miki Ando	USA Kimmie Meissner	JPN Mao Asada
2007	Reading	USA Kimmie Meissner	JPN Miki Ando	USA Caroline Zhang
2008	Everett	KOR Kim Yuna	JPN Yukari Nakano	JPN Miki Ando
2009	Lake Placid	KOR Kim Yuna	USA Rachael Flatt	HUN Júlia Sebestyén
2010	Portland	JPN Kanako Murakami	USA Rachael Flatt	ITA Carolina Kostner
2011	Ontario	USA Alissa Czisny	ITA Carolina Kostner	SWE Viktoria Helgesson
2012	Kent	USA Ashley Wagner	USA Christina Gao	RUS Adelina Sotnikova
2013	Detroit	JPN Mao Asada	USA Ashley Wagner	RUS Elena Radionova
2014	Chicago	RUS Elena Radionova	RUS Elizaveta Tuktamysheva	USA Gracie Gold
2015	Milwaukee	RUS Evgenia Medvedeva	USA Gracie Gold	JPN Satoko Miyahara
2016	Chicago	USA Ashley Wagner	USA Mariah Bell	JPN Mai Mihara

Skate America - ICE DANCING

Year	Location	Gold	Silver	Bronze
1979	Lake Placid	HUN Krisztina Regőczy & András Sallay	URS Natalia Bestemianova & Andrei Bukin	CAN Lorna Wighton & John Dowding
1980		*Competition not held*		
1981	Lake Placid	USA Judy Blumberg & Michael Seibert	URS Elena Garanina & Igor Zavozin	GBR Karen Barber & Nicky Slater
1982	Lake Placid	USA Elisa Spitz & Scott Gregory	URS Elena Garanina & Igor Zavozin	CAN Karyn Garossino & Rod Garossino
1983	Rochester	USA Elisa Spitz & Scott Gregory	CAN Kelly Johnson & John Thomas	GBR Wendy Sessions & Stephen Williams
1984		*Competition not held*		
1985	St. Paul	USA Renée Roca & Donald Adair	URS Irina Zhuk & Oleg Petrov	FRG Antonia Becherer & Ferdinand Becherer
1986	Portland	FRA Isabelle Duchesnay & Paul Duchesnay	USA Suzanne Semanick & Scott Gregory	CAN Jo-Anne Borlase & Scott Chalmers
1987		*Competition not held*		
1988	Portland	USA Susan Wynne & Joseph Druar	URS Svetlana Liapina & Gorsha Sur	USA Renée Roca & James Yorke
1989	Indianapolis	URS Maya Usova & Alexander Zhulin	USA April Sargent & Russ Witherby	CAN Jo-Anne Borlase & Martin Smith
1990	Buffalo	ITA Stefania Calegari & Pasquale Camerlengo	FRA Isabelle Sarech & Xavier Debernis	URS Ilona Melnichenko & Gennadi Kaskov
1991	Oakland	URS Tatiana Navka & Samuel Gezalian	FIN Susanna Rahkamo & Petri Kokko	FRA Dominique Yvon & Frédéric Palluel

Year	Location	Gold	Silver	Bronze
1992	Atlanta	RUS Maya Usova & Alexander Zhulin	FRA Sophie Moniotte & Pascal Lavanchy	USA Elizabeth Punsalan & Jerod Swallow
1993	Dallas	FRA Sophie Moniotte & Pascal Lavanchy	CZE Kateřina Mrázová & Martin Šimeček	USA Renée Roca & Gorsha Sur
1994	Pittsburgh	USA Elizabeth Punsalan & Jerod Swallow	FRA Marina Anissina & Gwendal Peizerat	KAZ Elizaveta Stekolnikova & Dmitri Kazarliga
1995	Detroit	RUS Oksana Grishuk & Evgeni Platov	RUS Anjelika Krylova & Oleg Ovsyannikov	USA Renée Roca & Gorsha Sur
1996	Springfield	RUS Anjelika Krylova & Oleg Ovsyannikov	RUS Irina Lobacheva & Ilia Averbukh	FRA Sophie Moniotte & Pascal Lavanchy
1997	Detroit	USA Elizabeth Punsalan & Jerod Swallow	ITA Barbara Fusar-Poli & Maurizio Margaglio	RUS Anna Semenovich & Vladimir Fedorov
1998	Detroit	FRA Marina Anissina & Gwendal Peizerat	RUS Irina Lobacheva & Ilia Averbukh	ITA Barbara Fusar-Poli & Maurizio Margaglio
1999	Colorado Springs	ITA Barbara Fusar-Poli & Maurizio Margaglio	RUS Irina Lobacheva & Ilia Averbukh	USA Naomi Lang & Peter Tchernyshev
2000	Colorado Springs	ITA Barbara Fusar-Poli & Maurizio Margaglio	LTU Margarita Drobiazko & Povilas Vanagas	CAN Shae-Lynn Bourne & Viktor Kraatz
2001	Colorado Springs	CAN Shae-Lynn Bourne & Victor Kraatz	ISR Galit Chait & Sergei Sakhnovski	LTU Margarita Drobiazko & Povilas Vanagas
2002	Spokane	UKR Elena Grushina & Ruslan Goncharov	RUS Tatiana Navka & Roman Kostomarov	USA Tanith Belbin & Benjamin Agosto
2003	Reading	USA Tanith Belbin & Benjamin Agosto	UKR Elena Grushina & Ruslan Goncharov	FRA Isabelle Delobel & Olivier Schoenfelder

Year	Location	Gold	Silver	Bronze
2004	Pittsburgh	USA Tanith Belbin & Benjamin Agosto	ISR Galit Chait & Sergei Sakhnovski	CAN Megan Wing & Aaron Lowe
2005	Atlantic City	USA Tanith Belbin & Benjamin Agosto	FRA Isabelle Delobel & Olivier Schoenfelder	RUS Oksana Domnina & Maxim Shabalin
2006	Hartford	BUL Albena Denkova & Maxim Staviski	USA Melissa Gregory & Denis Petukhov	FRA Nathalie Péchalat & Fabian Bourzat
2007	Reading	USA Tanith Belbin & Benjamin Agosto	FRA Nathalie Péchalat & Fabian Bourzat	ITA Federica Faiella & Massimo Scali
2008	Everett	FRA Isabelle Delobel & Olivier Schoenfelder	USA Tanith Belbin & Benjamin Agosto	GBR Sinead Kerr & John Kerr
2009	Lake Placid	USA Tanith Belbin & Benjamin Agosto	ITA Anna Cappellini & Luca Lanotte	ISR Alexandra Zaretsky & Roman Zaretsky
2010	Portland	USA Meryl Davis & Charlie White	CAN Vanessa Crone & Paul Poirier	USA Maia Shibutani & Alex Shibutani
2011	Ontario	USA Meryl Davis & Charlie White	FRA Nathalie Péchalat & Fabian Bourzat	LTU Isabella Tobias & Deividas Stagniūnas
2012	Kent	USA Meryl Davis & Charlie White	RUS Ekaterina Bobrova & Dmitri Soloviev	CAN Kaitlyn Weaver & Andrew Poje
2013	Detroit	USA Meryl Davis & Charlie White	ITA Anna Cappellini & Luca Lanotte	USA Maia Shibutani & Alex Shibutani
2014	Chicago	USA Madison Chock & Evan Bates	USA Maia Shibutani & Alex Shibutani	RUS Alexandra Stepanova & Ivan Bukin
2015	Milwaukee	USA Madison Chock & Evan Bates	RUS Victoria Sinitsina & Nikita Katsalapov	CAN Piper Gilles & Paul Poirier
2016	Chicago	USA Maia Shibutani & Alex Shibutani	USA Madison Hubbell & Zachary Donohue	RUS Ekaterina Bobrova & Dmitri Soloviev

Skate Canada International - MEN

Year	Location	Gold	Silver	Bronze
1973	Calgary	CAN Toller Cranston	CAN Ron Shaver	JPN Minoru Sano
1974	Kitchener	CAN Ron Shaver	JPN Minoru Sano	USA Charles Tickner
1975	Edmonton	CAN Toller Cranston	CAN Ron Shaver	USA Terry Kubicka
1976	Ottawa	CAN Ron Shaver	GBR Robin Cousins	USA David Santee
1977	Moncton	GBR Robin Cousins	USA Charles Tickner	USA Scott Cramer
1978	Vancouver	JPN Fumio Igarashi	USA Charles Tickner	CAN Brian Pockar
1979		*Competition not held*		
1980	Calgary	USA Scott Hamilton	CAN Brian Pockar	USA David Santee
1981	Ottawa	FRG Norbert Schramm	CAN Brian Orser	CZE Jozef Sabovčík
1982	Kitchener	USA Brian Boitano	CAN Brian Orser	FRG Heiko Fischer
1983	Halifax	CAN Brian Orser	POL Grzegorz Filipowski	JPN Masaru Ogawa
1984	Victoria	CAN Brian Orser	POL Grzegorz Filipowski	JPN Masaru Ogawa
1985	London	CZE Jozef Sabovčík	USA Scott Williams	POL Grzegorz Filipowski
1986	Regina	URS Vitali Egorov	USA Christopher Bowman	POL Grzegorz Filipowski
1987	Calgary	CAN Brian Orser	USA Brian Boitano	URS Viktor Petrenko
1988	Thunder Bay	CAN Kurt Browning	URS Viktor Petrenko	USA Angelo D'Agostino
1989	Cornwall	CZE Petr Barna	USA Paul Wylie	FRG Daniel Weiss
1990	Lethbridge	CAN Kurt Browning	POL Grzegorz Filipowski	USA Mark Mitchell
1991	London	CAN Elvis Stojko	URS Vasili Eremenko	USA Paul Wylie
1992	Victoria	CAN Elvis Stojko	USA Scott Davis	FRA Éric Millot
1993	Ottawa	CAN Kurt Browning	USA Mark Mitchell	GBR Steven Cousins

Year	Location	Gold	Silver	Bronze
1994	Red Deer	CAN Elvis Stojko	ISR Michael Shmerkin	CAN Sébastien Britten
1995	Saint John	RUS Alexei Urmanov	ISR Michael Shmerkin	FRA Éric Millot
1996	Kitchener	CAN Elvis Stojko	RUS Ilia Kulik	USA Scott Davis
1997	Halifax	CAN Elvis Stojko	RUS Ilia Kulik	DEN Michael Tyllesen
1998	Kamloops	RUS Evgeni Plushenko	CAN Elvis Stojko	HUN Szabolcs Vidrai
1999	Saint John	RUS Alexei Yagudin	CAN Elvis Stojko	JPN Takeshi Honda
2000	Mississauga	RUS Alexei Yagudin	USA Todd Eldredge	USA Matthew Savoie
2001	Saskatoon	RUS Alexei Yagudin	CAN Elvis Stojko	USA Todd Eldredge
2002	Quebec City	JPN Takeshi Honda	CAN Emanuel Sandhu	RUS Stanislav Timchenko
2003	Mississauga	RUS Evgeni Plushenko	CAN Jeffrey Buttle	JPN Takeshi Honda
2004	Halifax	CAN Emanuel Sandhu	CAN Ben Ferreira	CAN Jeffrey Buttle
2005	St. John's	CAN Emanuel Sandhu	CAN Jeffrey Buttle	JPN Nobunari Oda
2006	Victoria	SUI Stéphane Lambiel	JPN Daisuke Takahashi	USA Johnny Weir
2007	Quebec City	FRA Brian Joubert	BEL Kevin van der Perren	CAN Jeffrey Buttle
2008	Ottawa	CAN Patrick Chan	USA Ryan Bradley	USA Evan Lysacek
2009	Kitchener	USA Jeremy Abbott	JPN Daisuke Takahashi	FRA Alban Préaubert
2010	Kingston	CAN Patrick Chan	JPN Nobunari Oda	USA Adam Rippon
2011	Mississauga	CAN Patrick Chan	ESP Javier Fernández	JPN Daisuke Takahashi
2012	Windsor	ESP Javier Fernández	CAN Patrick Chan	JPN Nobunari Oda
2013	Saint John	CAN Patrick Chan	JPN Yuzuru Hanyu	JPN Nobunari Oda
2014	Kelowna	JPN Takahito Mura	ESP Javier Fernández	USA Max Aaron
2015	Lethbridge	CAN Patrick Chan	JPN Yuzuru Hanyu	JPN Daisuke Murakami
2016	Mississauga	CAN Patrick Chan	JPN Yuzuru Hanyu	CAN Kevin Reynolds

Skate Canada International - PAIRS

Year	Location	Gold	Silver	Bronze
1973-1983		NO PAIRS	COMPETITION	HELD
1984	Victoria	URS Elena Bechke & Valeri Kornienko	CAN Cynthia Coull & Mark Rowsom	CAN Katherina Matousek & Lloyd Eisler
1985	London	URS Ekaterina Gordeeva & Sergei Grinkov	URS Veronika Pershina & Marat Akbarov	CAN Denise Benning & Lyndon Johnston
1986	Regina	CAN Cynthia Coull & Mark Rowsom	URS Ekaterina Gordeeva & Sergei Grinkov	USA Natalie Seybold & Wayne Seybold
1987	Calgary	CAN Christine Hough & Doug Ladret	URS Elena Kvitchenko & Rashid Kadyrkaev	USA Katy Keely & Joseph Mero
1988	Thunder Bay	CAN Isabelle Brasseur & Lloyd Eisler	GDR Peggy Schwarz & Alexander König	URS Ekaterina Murugova & Artem Torgashev
1989	Cornwall	URS Elena Leonova & Gennadi Krasnitski	CAN Cindy Landry & Lyndon Johnston	CAN Michelle Menzies & Kevin Wheeler
1990	Lethbridge	CAN Isabelle Brasseur & Lloyd Eisler	URS Evgenia Shishkova & Vadim Naumov	CAN Michelle Menzies & Kevin Wheeler
1991	London	CAN Stacey Ball & Jean-Michel Bombardier	CAN Michelle Menzies & Kevin Wheeler	URS Marina Eltsova & Andrei Bushkov
1992	Victoria	GER Mandy Wötzel & Ingo Steuer	CAN Michelle Menzies & Jean-Michel Bombardier	AUS Danielle Carr & Stephen Carr

Year	Location	Gold	Silver	Bronze
1993	Ottawa	RUS Ekaterina Gordeeva & Sergei Grinkov	CZE Radka Kovaříková & René Novotný	CAN Michelle Menzies & Jean-Michel Bombardier
1994	Red Deer	CAN Kristy Sargeant & Kris Wirtz	LAT Elena Berezhnaya & Oleg Shliakhov	FRA Sarah Abitbol & Stéphane Bernadis
1995	Saint John	RUS Evgenia Shishkova & Vadim Naumov	RUS Maria Petrova & Anton Sikharulidze	CAN Jodeyne Higgins & Sean Rice
1996	Kitchener	GER Mandy Wötzel & Ingo Steuer	RUS Marina Eltsova & Andrei Bushkov	USA Kyoko Ina & Jason Dungjen
1997	Halifax	RUS Oksana Kazakova & Artur Dmitriev	KAZ Marina Khalturina & Andrei Kroukov	FRA Sarah Abitbol & Stéphane Bernadis
1998	Kamloops	CHN Shen Xue & Zhao Hongbo	RUS Maria Petrova & Alexei Tikhonov	CAN Jamie Salé & David Pelletier
1999	Saint John	RUS Elena Berezhnaya & Anton Sikharulidze	USA Kyoko Ina & John Zimmerman	CAN Kristy Wirtz & Kris Wirtz
2000	Mississauga	CAN Jamie Salé & David Pelletier	RUS Elena Berezhnaya & Anton Sikharulidze	RUS Maria Petrova & Alexei Tikhonov
2001	Saskatoon	CAN Jamie Salé & David Pelletier	RUS Tatiana Totmianina & Maxim Marinin	CAN Anabelle Langlois & Patrice Archetto
2002	Quebec City	RUS Tatiana Totmianina & Maxim Marinin	CHN Pang Qing & Tong Jian	CAN Anabelle Langlois & Patrice Archetto
2003	Mississauga	RUS Tatiana Totmianina & Maxim Marinin	CHN Shen Xue & Zhao Hongbo	POL Dorota Zagórska & Mariusz Siudek

Year	Location	Gold	Silver	Bronze
2004	Halifax	CHN Shen Xue & Zhao Hongbo	CHN Pang Qing & Tong Jian	POL Dorota Zagórska & Mariusz Siudek
2005	St. John's	GER Aliona Savchenko & Robin Szolkowy	RUS Maria Petrova & Alexei Tikhonov	CAN Valérie Marcoux & Craig Buntin
2006	Victoria	CHN Zhang Dan & Zhang Hao	USA Rena Inoue & John Baldwin	CAN Valérie Marcoux & Craig Buntin
2007	Quebec City	GER Aliona Savchenko & Robin Szolkowy	CAN Jessica Dubé & Bryce Davison	RUS Yuko Kawaguchi & Alexander Smirnov
2008	Ottawa	RUS Yuko Kawaguchi & Alexander Smirnov	CAN Jessica Dubé & Bryce Davison	USA Keauna McLaughlin & Rockne Brubaker
2009	Kitchener	GER Aliona Savchenko & Robin Szolkowy	RUS Maria Mukhortova & Maxim Trankov	CAN Jessica Dubé & Bryce Davison
2010	Kingston	RUS Lubov Iliushechkina & Nodari Maisuradze	CAN Kirsten Moore-Towers & Dylan Moscovitch	CAN Paige Lawrence & Rudi Swiegers
2011	Mississauga	RUS Tatiana Volosozhar & Maxim Trankov	CHN Sui Wenjing & Han Cong	CAN Meagan Duhamel & Eric Radford
2012	Windsor	GER Aliona Savchenko & Robin Szolkowy	CAN Meagan Duhamel & Eric Radford	ITA Stefania Berton & Ondřej Hotárek
2013	Saint John	ITA Stefania Berton & Ondřej Hotárek	CHN Sui Wenjing & Han Cong	CAN Meagan Duhamel & Eric Radford
2014	Kelowna	CAN Meagan Duhamel & Eric Radford	CHN Sui Wenjing & Han Cong	RUS Evgenia Tarasova & Vladimir Morozov
2015	Lethbridge	CAN Meagan Duhamel & Eric Radford	RUS Evgenia Tarasova & Vladimir Morozov	CAN Kirsten Moore-Towers & Michael Marinaro
2016	Mississauga	CAN Meagan Duhamel & Eric Radford	CHN Yu Xiaoyu & Zhang Hao	CAN Lubov Ilyushechkina & Dylan Moscovitch

Skate Canada International - LADIES

Year	Location	Gold	Silver	Bronze
1973	Calgary	CAN Lynn Nightingale	CAN Barbara Terpenning	GBR Jean Scott
1974	Kitchener	CAN Lynn Nightingale	GDR Anett Pötzsch	USA Wendy Burge
1975	Edmonton	ITA Susanna Driano	USA Kath Malmberg	JPN Emi Watanabe
1976	Ottawa	CAN Kim Alletson	GBR Karena Richardson	GDR Garnet Ostermeier
1977	Moncton	USA Linda Fratianne	USA Lisa-Marie Allen	CAN Heather Kemkaran
1978	Vancouver	USA Lisa-Marie Allen	AUT Claudia Kristofics-Binder	FIN Kristiina Wegelius
1979		*Competition not held*		
1980	Calgary	USA Elaine Zayak	CAN Tracey Wainman	AUT Claudia Kristofics-Binder
1981	Ottawa	CAN Tracey Wainman	USA Rosalynn Sumners	URS Kira Ivanova
1982	Kitchener	USA Vikki De Vries	FIN Kristiina Wegelius	USA Rosalynn Sumners
1983	Halifax	GDR Katarina Witt	CAN Kay Thomson	USA Tiffany Chin
1984	Victoria	JPN Midori Ito	USA Tiffany Chin	URS Natalia Lebedeva
1985	London	USA Caryn Kadavy	CAN Elizabeth Manley	FRG Patricia Neske
1986	Regina	CAN Elizabeth Manley	FRG Claudia Leistner	GBR Joanne Conway
1987	Calgary	USA Debi Thomas	CAN Elizabeth Manley	GBR Joanne Conway
1988	Thunder Bay	URS Natalia Lebedeva	USA Jill Trenary	FRG Patricia Neske
1989	Cornwall	USA Kristi Yamaguchi	GDR Simone Lang	URS Natalia Lebedeva
1990	Lethbridge	CAN Josée Chouinard	CAN Lisa Sargeant	USA Holly Cook
1991	London	FRA Surya Bonaly	GER Marina Kielmann	CAN Karen Preston
1992	Victoria	RUS Maria Butyrskaya	BEL Alice Sue Claeys	CAN Josée Chouinard

Greg Fox

Year	Location	Gold	Silver	Bronze
1993	Ottawa	CHN Chen Lu	RUS Olga Markova	CAN Karen Preston
1994	Red Deer	HUN Krisztina Czakó	FRA Laetitia Hubert	USA Jessica Mills
1995	Saint John	USA Michelle Kwan	JPN Hanae Yokoya	CAN Josée Chouinard
1996	Kitchener	RUS Irina Slutskaya	USA Tara Lipinski	SUI Lucinda Ruh
1997	Halifax	USA Michelle Kwan	RUS Maria Butyrskaya	FRA Surya Bonaly
1998	Kamloops	UKR Elena Liashenko	JPN Fumie Suguri	RUS Irina Slutskaya
1999	Saint John	USA Michelle Kwan	RUS Julia Soldatova	CAN Jennifer Robinson
2000	Mississauga	RUS Irina Slutskaya	USA Michelle Kwan	JPN Fumie Suguri
2001	Saskatoon	USA Sarah Hughes	RUS Irina Slutskaya	USA Michelle Kwan
2002	Quebec City	USA Sasha Cohen	JPN Fumie Suguri	RUS Viktoria Volchkova
2003	Mississauga	USA Sasha Cohen	JPN Shizuka Arakawa	HUN Júlia Sebestyén
2004	Halifax	CAN Cynthia Phaneuf	JPN Yoshie Onda	FIN Susanna Pöykiö
2005	St. John's	USA Alissa Czisny	CAN Joannie Rochette	JPN Yukari Nakano
2006	Victoria	CAN Joannie Rochette	JPN Fumie Suguri	KOR Kim Yuna
2007	Quebec City	JPN Mao Asada	JPN Yukari Nakano	CAN Joannie Rochette
2008	Ottawa	CAN Joannie Rochette	JPN Fumie Suguri	USA Alissa Czisny
2009	Kitchener	CAN Joannie Rochette	USA Alissa Czisny	FIN Laura Lepistö
2010	Kingston	USA Alissa Czisny	RUS Ksenia Makarova	CAN Amélie Lacoste
2011	Mississauga	RUS Elizaveta Tuktamysheva	JPN Akiko Suzuki	USA Ashley Wagner
2012	Windsor	CAN Kaetlyn Osmond	JPN Akiko Suzuki	JPN Kanako Murakami
2013	Saint John	RUS Yulia Lipnitskaya	JPN Akiko Suzuki	USA Gracie Gold
2014	Kelowna	RUS Anna Pogorilaya	USA Ashley Wagner	JPN Satoko Miyahara
2015	Lethbridge	USA Ashley Wagner	RUS Elizaveta Tuktamysheva	JPN Yuka Nagai
2016	Mississauga	RUS Evgenia Medvedeva	CAN Kaetlyn Osmond	JPN Satoko Miyahara

Skate Canada International - ICE DANCING

Year	Location	Gold	Silver	Bronze
1973	Calgary	CAN Louise Soper & Barry Soper		URS Irina Moiseeva & Andrei Minenkov
1974	Kitchener	URS Irina Moiseeva & Andrei Minenkov	USA Colleen O'Connor & Jim Millns	GBR Janet Thompson & Warren Maxwell
1975	Edmonton	URS Natalia Linichuk & Gennadi Karponosov	CAN Barbara Berezowski & David Porter	ITA Matilde Ciccia & Lamberto Ceserani
1976	Ottawa	URS Natalia Linichuk & Gennadi Karponosov	GBR Janet Thompson & Warren Maxwell	CAN Susan Carscallen & Eric Gillies
1977	Moncton	GBR Janet Thompson & Warren Maxwell	URS Marina Zueva & Andrei Vitman	CAN Lorna Wighton & John Dowding
1978	Vancouver	HUN Krisztina Regőczy & András Sallay	CAN Lorna Wighton & John Dowding	URS Marina Zueva & Andrei Vitman
1979		*Competition not held*		
1980	Calgary	USA Judy Blumberg & Michael Seibert	GBR Karen Barber & Nicky Slater	CAN Marie McNeill & Rob McCall
1981	Ottawa	USA Carol Fox & Richard Dalley	GBR Karen Barber & Nicky Slater	URS Natalia Karamy-sheva & Rostislav Sinitsyn
1982	Kitchener	USA Elisa Spitz & Scott Gregory	CAN Tracy Wilson & Rob McCall	URS Natalia Annenko & Genrikh Sretenski

Year	Location	Gold	Silver	Bronze
1983	Halifax	CAN Tracy Wilson & Rob McCall	GBR Wendy Sessions & Stephen Williams	URS Natalia Annenko & Genrikh Sretenski
1984	Victoria	URS Olga Volozhinskaya & Alexander Svinin	FRG Petra Born & Rainer Schönborn	CAN Kelly Johnson & John Thomas
1985	London	USA Renée Roca & Donald Adair	URS Olga Volozhinskaya & Alexander Svinin	AUT Kathrin Beck & Christoff Beck
1986	Regina	URS Natalia Annenko & Genrikh Sretenski	USA Suzanne Semanick & Scott Gregory	CAN Karyn Garossino & Rod Garossino
1987	Calgary	CAN Tracy Wilson & Rob McCall	AUT Kathrin Beck & Christoff Beck	ITA Lia Trovati & Roberto Pelizzola
1988	Thunder Bay	URS Natalia Annenko & Genrikh Sretenski	USA April Sargent & Russ Witherby	CAN Melanie Cole & Michael Farrington
1989	Cornwall	USA Suzanne Semanick & Ron Kravette	CAN Michelle McDonald & Mark Mitchell	CAN Jacqueline Petr & Mark Janoschak
1990	Lethbridge	CAN Jacqueline Petr & Mark Janoschak	URS Irina Romanova & Igor Yaroshenko	POL Małgorzata Grajcar & Andrzej Dostatni
1991	London	ITA Stefania Calegari & Pasquale Camerlengo	FRA Sophie Moniotte & Pascal Lavanchy	CZE Kateřina Mrázová & Martin Šimeček
1992	Victoria	FIN Susanna Rahkamo & Petri Kokko	RUS Yaroslava Nechaeva & Yuri Chesnichenko	CZE Kateřina Mrázová & Martin Šimeček
1993	Ottawa	FRA Sophie Moniotte & Pascal Lavanchy	BLR Tatiana Navka & Samuel Gezolian	CAN Shae-Lynn Bourne & Victor Kraatz

Year	Location	Gold	Silver	Bronze
1994	Red Deer	CAN Shae-Lynn Bourne & Victor Kraatz	LTU Margarita Drobiazko & Povilas Vanagas	USA Renée Roca & Gorsha Sur
1995	Saint John	CAN Shae-Lynn Bourne & Viktor Kraatz	FRA Marina Anissina & Gwendal Peizerat	UKR Irina Romanova & Igor Yaroshenko
1996	Kitchener	CAN Shae-Lynn Bourne & Viktor Kraatz	FRA Marina Anissina & Gwendal Peizerat	ITA Barbara Fusar-Poli & Maurizio Margaglio
1997	Halifax	CAN Shae-Lynn Bourne & Viktor Kraatz	USA Elizabeth Punsalan & Jerod Swallow	RUS Irina Lobacheva & Ilia Averbukh
1998	Kamloops	CAN Shae-Lynn Bourne & Viktor Kraatz	LTU Margarita Drobiazko & Povilas Vanagas	POL Sylwia Nowak & Sebastian Kolasiński
1999	Saint John	LTU Margarita Drobiazko & Povilas Vanagas	UKR Elena Grushina & Ruslan Goncharov	FRA Isabelle Delobel & Olivier Schoenfelder
2000	Mississauga	FRA Marina Anissina & Gwendal Peizerat	ISR Galit Chait & Sergei Sakhnovski	CAN Marie-France Dubreuil & Patrice Lauzon
2001	Saskatoon	CAN Shae-Lynn Bourne & Victor Kraatz	ISR Galit Chait & Sergei Sakhnovski	FRA Isabelle Delobel & Olivier Schoenfelder
2002	Quebec City	UKR Elena Grushina & Ruslan Goncharov	CAN Marie-France Dubreuil & Patrice Lauzon	RUS Svetlana Kulikova & Arseni Markov
2003	Mississauga	RUS Tatiana Navka & Roman Kostomarov	BUL Albena Denkova & Maxim Staviyski	CAN Marie-France Dubreuil & Patrice Lauzon

Year	Location	Gold	Silver	Bronze
2004	Halifax	BUL Albena Denkova & Maxim Staviyski	CAN Marie-France Dubreuil & Patrice Lauzon	ISR Galit Chait & Sergei Sakhnovski
2005	St. John's	CAN Marie-France Dubreuil & Patrice Lauzon	UKR Elena Grushina & Ruslan Goncharov	USA Melissa Gregory & Denis Petukhov
2006	Victoria	CAN Marie-France Dubreuil & Patrice Lauzon	CAN Tessa Virtue & Scott Moir	ITA Federica Faiella & Massimo Scali
2007	Quebec City	CAN Tessa Virtue & Scott Moir	ITA Anna Cappellini & Luca Lanotte	FRA Pernelle Carron & Mathieu Jost
2008	Ottawa	USA Meryl Davis & Charlie White	CAN Vanessa Crone & Paul Poirier	FRA Nathalie Péchalat & Fabian Bourzat
2009	Kitchener	CAN Tessa Virtue & Scott Moir	FRA Nathalie Péchalat & Fabian Bourzat	CAN Kaitlyn Weaver & Andrew Poje
2010	Kingston	CAN Vanessa Crone & Paul Poirier	GBR Sinead Kerr & John Kerr	USA Madison Chock & Greg Zuerlein
2011	Mississauga	CAN Tessa Virtue & Scott Moir	CAN Kaitlyn Weaver & Andrew Poje	ITA Anna Cappellini & Luca Lanotte
2012	Windsor	CAN Tessa Virtue & Scott Moir	ITA Anna Cappellini & Luca Lanotte	RUS Ekaterina Riazanova & Ilia Tkachenko
2013	Saint John	CAN Tessa Virtue & Scott Moir	CAN Kaitlyn Weaver & Andrew Poje	USA Madison Hubbell & Zachary Donohue
2014	Kelowna	CAN Kaitlyn Weaver & Andrew Poje	CAN Piper Gilles & Paul Poirier	USA Madison Hubbell & Zachary Donohue
2015	Lethbridge	CAN Kaitlyn Weaver & Andrew Poje	USA Maia Shibutani & Alex Shibutani	RUS Ekaterina Bobrova & Dmitri Soloviev

Year	Location	Gold	Silver	Bronze
2016	Mississauga	CAN Tessa Virtue & Scott Moir	USA Madison Chock & Evan Bates	CAN Piper Gilles & Paul Poirier

Above: American ice dancing pair **Meryl Davis & Charlie White** only won gold once at Skate Canada, (in 2008). But that hardly tells their story. They are 4-time gold medal winners at Skate America, 5-time Grand Prix final winners, 3-time Four Continents winners, 6-time US National Champions, and Olympic gold medal winners in 2014, (the first Americans to ever win gold in ice dancing in Olympics competition).

NHK Trophy - MEN

Year	Location	Gold	Silver	Bronze
1979	Tokyo	GBR Robin Cousins	JPN Fumio Igarashi	USA David Santee
1980	Sapporo	JPN Fumio Igarashi	USA Robert Wagenhoffer	USA Allen Schramm
1981	Kobe	JPN Fumio Igarashi	FRG Norbert Schramm	FRA Jean-Christophe Simond
1982	Tokyo	USA Scott Hamilton	URS Alexander Fadeev	POL Grzegorz Filipowski
1983	Sapporo	Held as 1984	World Junior	Championships
1984	Tokyo	URS Alexander Fadeev	CAN Brian Orser	USA Brian Boitano
1985	Kobe	USA Brian Boitano	CAN Brian Orser	URS Viktor Petrenko
1986	Tokyo	USA Angelo D'Agostino	JPN Makoto Kano	FRA Philippe Roncoli
1987	Kushiro	USA Christopher Bowman	USA Paul Wylie	JPN Makoto Kano
1988	Tokyo	URS Alexander Fadeev	CZE Petr Barna	CAN Kurt Browning
1989	Kobe	URS Viktor Petrenko	URS Alexander Fadeev	CAN Kurt Browning
1990	Asahikawa	URS Viktor Petrenko	POL Grzegorz Filipowski	URS Viacheslav Zagorodniuk
1991	Hiroshima	POL Grzegorz Filipowski	URS Viacheslav Zagorodniuk	URS Alexei Urmanov
1992	Tokyo	FRA Philippe Candeloro	CAN Elvis Stojko	RUS Alexei Urmanov
1993	Chiba	FRA Philippe Candeloro	UKR Viacheslav Zagorodniuk	RUS Alexei Urmanov
1994	Morioka	USA Todd Eldredge	FRA Philippe Candeloro	UKR Viacheslav Zagorodniuk
1995	Nagoya	CAN Elvis Stojko	RUS Igor Pashkevich	FRA Philippe Candeloro
1996	Osaka	CAN Elvis Stojko	RUS Ilia Kulik	UKR Dmitri Dmitrenko
1997	Nagano	RUS Ilia Kulik	USA Scott Davis	CHN Guo Zhengxin

Year	Location	Gold	Silver	Bronze
1998	Sapporo	RUS Evgeni Plushenko	JPN Takeshi Honda	GER Andrejs Vlascenko
1999	Nagoya	RUS Evgeni Plushenko	USA Timothy Goebel	RUS Ilia Klimkin
2000	Asahikawa	RUS Evgeni Plushenko	RUS Ilia Klimkin	CHN Li Chengjiang
2001	Kumamoto	JPN Takeshi Honda	CAN Jeffrey Buttle	BUL Ivan Dinev
2002	Kyoto	RUS Ilia Klimkin	JPN Takeshi Honda	CHN Li Chengjiang
2003	Asahikawa	CAN Jeffrey Buttle	USA Timothy Goebel	CHN Gao Song
2004	Nagoya	USA Johnny Weir	USA Timothy Goebel	FRA Frédéric Dambier
2005	Osaka	JPN Nobunari Oda	USA Evan Lysacek	JPN Daisuke Takahashi
2006	Nagano	JPN Daisuke Takahashi	JPN Nobunari Oda	JPN Takahiko Kozuka
2007	Sendai	JPN Daisuke Takahashi	CZE Tomáš Verner	USA Stephen Carriere
2008	Tokyo	JPN Nobunari Oda	USA Johnny Weir	FRA Yannick Ponsero
2009	Nagano	FRA Brian Joubert	USA Johnny Weir	CZE Michal Březina
2010	Nagoya	JPN Daisuke Takahashi	USA Jeremy Abbott	FRA Florent Amodio
2011	Sapporo	JPN Daisuke Takahashi	JPN Takahiko Kozuka	USA Ross Miner
2012	Sendai	JPN Yuzuru Hanyu	JPN Daisuke Takahashi	USA Ross Miner
2013	Tokyo	JPN Daisuke Takahashi	JPN Nobunari Oda	USA Jeremy Abbott
2014	Osaka	JPN Daisuke Murakami	RUS Sergei Voronov	JPN Takahito Mura
2015	Nagano	JPN Yuzuru Hanyu	CHN Boyang Jin	JPN Takahito Mura
2016	Sapporo	JPN Yuzuru Hanyu	USA Nathan Chen	JPN Keiji Tanaka

NHK Trophy - PAIRS

Year	Location	Gold	Silver	Bronze
1979	Tokyo	URS Irina Vorobieva & Igor Lisovski	USA Vicki Heasley & Robert Waggenhoffer	USA Sheryl Franks & Michael Botticelli
1980	Sapporo	CAN Barbara Underhill & Paul Martini	USA Maria DiDomenico & Burt Lancon	JPN Toshimi Ito & Takashi Mura
1981	Kobe	USA Kitty Carruthers & Peter Carruthers	GDR Birgit Lorenz & Knut Schubert	USA Maria DiDomenico & Burt Lancon
1982	Tokyo	CAN Barbara Underhill & Paul Martini	URS Irina Vorobieva & Igor Lisovski	URS Marina Avstriskaya & Yuri Kvashnin
1983	Sapporo	Held as 1984	World Junior	Championships
1984	Tokyo	URS Veronika Pershina & Marat Akbarov	GDR Birgit Lorenz & Knut Schubert	CAN Cynthia Coull & Mark Rowsom
1985	Kobe	USA Gillian Wachsman & Todd Waggoner	URS Veronika Pershina & Marat Akbarov	CAN Denise Benning & Lyndon Johnston
1986	Tokyo	URS Elena Valova & Oleg Vasiliev	USA Jill Watson & Peter Oppegard	USA Natalie Seybold & Wayne Seybold
1987	Kushiro	URS Elena Leonova & Gennadi Krasnitski	USA Gillian Wachsman & Todd Waggoner	USA Katy Keely & Joseph Mero
1988	Tokyo	URS Larisa Selezneva & Oleg Makarov	URS Elena Bechke & Denis Petrov	USA Kristi Yamaguchi & Rudy Galindo
1989	Kobe	URS Ekaterina Gordeeva & Sergei Grinkov	URS Larisa Selezneva & Oleg Makarov	CAN Christine Hough & Doug Ladret

Year	Location	Gold	Silver	Bronze
1990	Asahikawa	URS Elena Bechke & Denis Petrov	CAN Isabelle Brasseur & Lloyd Eisler	URS Natalia Mishkutenok & Artur Dmitriev
1991	Hiroshima	URS Evgenia Shishkova & Vadim Naumov	CZE Radka Kovaříková & René Novotný	URS Marina Eltsova & Andrei Bushkov
1992	Tokyo	RUS Evgenia Shishkova & Vadim Naumov	RUS Marina Eltsova & Andrei Bushkov	USA Calla Urbanski & Rocky Marval
1993	Chiba	CAN Isabelle Brasseur & Lloyd Eisler	CZE Radka Kovaříková & René Novotný	JPN Yukiko Kawasaki & Alexei Tikhonov
1994	Morioka	RUS Marina Eltsova & Andrei Bushkov	CZE Radka Kovaříková & René Novotný	GER Mandy Wötzel & Ingo Steuer
1995	Nagoya	RUS Evgenia Shishkova & Vadim Naumov	GER Mandy Wötzel & Ingo Steuer	RUS Natalia Krestianinova & Alexei Torchinski
1996	Osaka	USA Jenni Meno & Todd Sand	RUS Evgenia Shishkova & Vadim Naumov	USA Kyoko Ina & Jason Dungjen
1997	Nagano	CHN Shen Xue & Zhao Hongbo	USA Jenni Meno & Todd Sand	GER Peggy Schwarz & Mirko Müller
1998	Sapporo	RUS Elena Berezhnaya & Anton Sikharulidze	CHN Shen Xue & Zhao Hongbo	CAN Jamie Salé & David Pelletier
1999	Nagoya	RUS Maria Petrova & Alexei Tikhonov	FRA Sarah Abitbol & Stéphane Bernadis	POL Dorota Zagorska & Mariusz Siudek
2000	Asahikawa	CHN Shen Xue & Zhao Hongbo	FRA Sarah Abitbol & Stéphane Bernadis	RUS Maria Petrova & Alexei Tikhonov

Year	Location	Gold	Silver	Bronze
2001	Kumamoto	CHN Shen Xue & Zhao Hongbo	RUS Maria Petrova & Alexei Tikhonov	POL Dorota Zagorska & Mariusz Siudek
2002	Kyoto	CHN Shen Xue & Zhao Hongbo	POL Dorota Zagorska & Mariusz Siudek	CAN Anabelle Langlois & Patrice Archetto
2003	Asahikawa	RUS Maria Petrova & Alexei Tikhonov	CAN Anabelle Langlois & Patrice Archetto	POL Dorota Zagorska & Mariusz Siudek
2004	Nagoya	RUS Maria Petrova & Alexei Tikhonov	CHN Pang Qing & Tong Jian	POL Dorota Zagorska & Mariusz Siudek
2005	Osaka	CHN Zhang Dan & Zhang Hao	GER Aliona Savchenko & Robin Szolkowy	CAN Utako Wakamatsu & Jean-Sébastien Fecteau
2006	Nagano	CHN Shen Xue & Zhao Hongbo	CHN Zhang Dan & Zhang Hao	CAN Valérie Marcoux & Craig Buntin
2007	Sendai	GER Aliona Savchenko & Robin Szolkowy	USA Keauna McLaughlin & Rockne Brubaker	CAN Jessica Dubé & Bryce Davison
2008	Tokyo	CHN Pang Qing & Tong Jian	USA Rena Inoue & John Baldwin	CAN Jessica Dubé & Bryce Davison
2009	Nagano	CHN Pang Qing & Tong Jian	RUS Yuko Kavaguti & Alexander Smirnov	USA Rena Inoue & John Baldwin
2010	Nagoya	CHN Pang Qing & Tong Jian	RUS Vera Bazarova & Yuri Larionov	JPN Narumi Takahashi & Mervin Tran
2011	Sapporo	RUS Yuko Kavaguti & Alexander Smirnov	JPN Narumi Takahashi & Mervin Tran	GER Aliona Savchenko & Robin Szolkowy

Year	Location	Gold	Silver	Bronze
2012	Sendai	RUS Vera Bazarova & Yuri Larionov	CAN Kirsten Moore-Towers & Dylan Moscovitch	USA Marissa Castelli & Simon Shnapir
2013	Tokyo	RUS Tatiana Volosozhar & Maxim Trankov	CHN Peng Cheng & Hao Zhang	CHN Wenjing Sui & Cong Han
2014	Osaka	CAN Meagan Duhamel & Eric Radford	RUS Yuko Kavaguti & Alexander Smirnov	CHN Yu Xiaoyu & Jin Yang
2015	Nagano	CAN Meagan Duhamel & Eric Radford	CHN Yu Xiaoyu & Jin Yang	USA Alexa Scimeca & Chris Knierim
2016	Sapporo	CAN Meagan Duhamel & Eric Radford	CHN Peng Cheng & Jin Yang	CHN Wang Xuehan & Wang Lei

NHK Trophy - LADIES

Year	Location	Gold	Silver	Bronze
1979	Tokyo	JPN Emi Watanabe	USA Lisa-Marie Allen	USA Sandy Lenz
1980	Sapporo	SUI Denise Biellmann	GDR Katarina Witt	USA Melissa Thomas
1981	Kobe	FIN Kristiina Wegelius	USA Vikki de Vries	CAN Charlene Wong
1982	Tokyo	GDR Katarina Witt	USA Rosalynn Sumners	USA Tiffany Chin
1983	Sapporo	Held as 1984	World Junior	Championships
1984	Tokyo	JPN Midori Ito	USA Debi Thomas	JPN Juri Ozawa
1985	Kobe	JPN Midori Ito	CAN Cynthia Coull	JPN Juri Ozawa
1986	Tokyo	GDR Katarina Witt	JPN Midori Ito	JPN Juri Ozawa
1987	Kushiro	GDR Katarina Witt	JPN Midori Ito	USA Tonya Harding
1988	Tokyo	JPN Midori Ito	USA Kristi Yamaguchi	FRG Marina Kielmann
1989	Kobe	JPN Midori Ito	USA Kristi Yamaguchi	USA Tonia Kwiatkowski
1990	Asahikawa	JPN Midori Ito	USA Tonya Harding	URS Larisa Zamotina
1991	Hiroshima	JPN Midori Ito	FRA Surya Bonaly	CHN Chen Lu
1992	Tokyo	FRA Surya Bonaly	JPN Kumiko Koiwai	JPN Yuka Sato
1993	Chiba	FRA Surya Bonaly	JPN Yuka Sato	CHN Chen Lu
1994	Morioka	CHN Chen Lu	FRA Surya Bonaly	JPN Junko Yaginuma
1995	Nagoya	CHN Chen Lu	JPN Hanae Yokoya	RUS Olga Markova
1996	Osaka	RUS Maria Butyrskaya	USA Tonia Kwiatkowski	AZE Yulia Vorobieva
1997	Nagano	GER Tanja Szewczenko	RUS Maria Butyrskaya	CHN Chen Lu

Year	Location	Gold	Silver	Bronze
1998	Sapporo	UZB Tatiana Malinina	RUS Irina Slutskaya	JPN Fumie Suguri
1999	Nagoya	RUS Maria Butyrskaya	RUS Viktoria Volchkova	UZB Tatiana Malinina
2000	Asahikawa	RUS Irina Slutskaya	RUS Maria Butyrskaya	UZB Tatiana Malinina
2001	Kumamoto	UZB Tatiana Malinina	JPN Yoshie Onda	UKR Elena Liashenko
2002	Kyoto	JPN Yoshie Onda	RUS Irina Slutskaya	JPN Shizuka Arakawa
2003	Asahikawa	JPN Fumie Suguri	UKR Elena Liashenko	JPN Yoshie Onda
2004	Nagoya	JPN Shizuka Arakawa	JPN Miki Ando	RUS Elena Sokolova
2005	Osaka	JPN Yukari Nakano	JPN Fumie Suguri	UKR Elena Liashenko
2006	Nagano	JPN Mao Asada	JPN Fumie Suguri	JPN Yukari Nakano
2007	Sendai	ITA Carolina Kostner	SUI Sarah Meier	JPN Nana Takeda
2008	Tokyo	JPN Mao Asada	JPN Akiko Suzuki	JPN Yukari Nakano
2009	Nagano	JPN Miki Ando	RUS Alena Leonova	USA Ashley Wagner
2010	Nagoya	ITA Carolina Kostner	USA Rachael Flatt	JPN Kanako Murakami
2011	Sapporo	JPN Akiko Suzuki	JPN Mao Asada	RUS Alena Leonova
2012	Sendai	JPN Mao Asada	JPN Akiko Suzuki	USA Mirai Nagasu
2013	Tokyo	JPN Mao Asada	RUS Elena Radionova	JPN Akiko Suzuki
2014	Osaka	USA Gracie Gold	RUS Alena Leonova	JPN Satoko Miyahara
2015	Nagano	JPN Satoko Miyahara	USA Rachael Flatt	JPN Mao Asada
2016	Sapporo	RUS Anna Pogorilaya	JPN Satoko Miyahara	RUS Maria Sotskova

NHK Trophy - ICE DANCING

Year	Location	Gold	Silver	Bronze
1979	Tokyo	URS Irina Moiseeva & Andrei Minenkov	GBR Jayne Torvill & Christopher Dean	URS Natalia Karamysheva & Rostislav Sinitsyn
1980	Sapporo	USA Carol Fox & Richard Dalley	GBR Karen Barber & Nicholas Slater	GBR Lillian Heming & Murray Carey
1981	Kobe	GBR Karen Barber & Nicholas Slater	URS Natalia Karamysheva & Rostislav Sinitsyn	CZE Jana Berankova & Jan Bartak
1982	Tokyo	URS Elena Batanova & Alexei Soloviev	USA Carol Fox & Richard Dalley	GBR Wendy Sessions & Stephen Williams
1983	Sapporo	Held as 1984	World Junior	Championships
1984	Tokyo	GBR Karen Barber & Nicholas Slater	URS Elena Batanova & Alexei Soloviev	CAN John Thomas & Kelly Johnson
1985	Kobe	URS Marina Klimova & Sergei Ponomarenko	CAN Karyn Garossino & Rod Garossino	GBR Sharon Jones & Paul Askham
1986	Tokyo	URS Natalia Bestemianova & Andrei Bukin	USA Suzanne Semanick & Scott Gregory	AUT Kathrin Beck & Christoff Beck
1987	Kushiro	URS Natalia Bestemianova & Andrei Bukin	URS Svetlana Liapina & Gorsha Sur	USA Susan Wynne & Joseph Druar
1988	Tokyo	URS Marina Klimova & Sergei Ponomarenko	URS Maya Usova & Alexander Zhulin	USA April Sargent & Russ Witherby
1989	Kobe	URS Marina Klimova & Sergei Ponomarenko	URS Pasha Grishuk & Evgeni Platov	CAN Jo-Anne Borlase & Martin Smith

Year	Location	Gold	Silver	Bronze
1990	Asahikawa	URS Maya Usova & Alexander Zhulin	HUN Klára Engi & Attila Tóth	ITA Stefania Calegari & Pasquale Camerlengo
1991	Hiroshima	URS Maya Usova & Alexander Zhulin	URS Pasha Grishuk & Evgeni Platov	ITA Stefania Calegari & Pasquale Camerlengo
1992	Tokyo	RUS Maya Usova & Alexander Zhulin	RUS Anjelika Krylova & Vladimir Fedorov	FRA Sophie Moniotte & Pascal Lavanchy
1993	Chiba	RUS Oksana Grishuk & Evgeny Platov	UKR Irina Romanova & Igor Yaroshenko	UZB Aliki Stergiadu & Juris Razgulajevs
1994	Morioka	FRA Sophie Moniotte & Pascal Lavanchy	BLR Tatiana Navka & Samvel Gezalian	FRA Marina Anissina & Gwendal Peizerat
1995	Nagoya	FRA Marina Anissina & Gwendal Peizerat	CAN Shae-Lynn Bourne & Viktor Kraatz	RUS Anna Semenovich & Vladimir Fedorov
1996	Osaka	FRA Sophie Moniotte & Pascal Lavanchy	FRA Marina Anissina & Gwendal Peizerat	UKR Irina Romanova & Igor Yaroshenko
1997	Nagano	RUS Pasha Grishuk & Evgeni Platov	CAN Shae-Lynn Bourne & Viktor Kraatz	ITA Barbara Fusar-Poli & Maurizio Margaglio
1998	Sapporo	FRA Marina Anissina & Gwendal Peizerat	RUS Irina Lobacheva & Ilia Averbukh	LTU Margarita Drobiazko & Povilas Vanagas
1999	Nagoya	FRA Marina Anissina & Gwendal Peizerat	RUS Irina Lobacheva & Ilia Averbukh	LTU Margarita Drobiazko & Povilas Vanagas
2000	Asahikawa	FRA Marina Anissina & Gwendal Peizerat	LTU Margarita Drobiazko & Povilas Vanagas	GER Kati Winkler & René Lohse

Greg Fox

Year	Location	Gold	Silver	Bronze
2001	Kumamoto	FRA Marina Anissina & Gwendal Peizerat	LTU Margarita Drobiazko & Povilas Vanagas	BUL Albena Denkova & Maxim Staviski
2002	Kyoto	RUS Irina Lobacheva & Ilia Averbukh	GER Kati Winkler & René Lohse	ISR Galit Chait & Sergei Sakhnovski
2003	Asahikawa	BUL Albena Denkova & Maxim Staviski	UKR Elena Grushina & Ruslan Goncharov	ISR Galit Chait & Sergei Sakhnovski
2004	Nagoya	BUL Albena Denkova & Maxim Staviski	RUS Tatiana Navka & Roman Kostomarov	FRA Isabelle Delobel & Olivier Schoenfelder
2005	Osaka	CAN Marie-France Dubreuil & Patrice Lauzon	BUL Albena Denkova & Maxim Staviski	ARM Anastasia Grebenkina & Vazgen Azrojan
2006	Nagano	CAN Marie-France Dubreuil & Patrice Lauzon	RUS Jana Khokhlova & Sergei Novitski	USA Melissa Gregory & Denis Petukhov
2007	Sendai	FRA Isabelle Delobel & Olivier Schoenfelder	CAN Tessa Virtue & Scott Moir	RUS Jana Khokhlova & Sergei Novitski
2008	Tokyo	ITA Federica Faiella & Massimo Scali	FRA Nathalie Péchalat & Fabian Bourzat	USA Emily Samuelson & Evan Bates
2009	Nagano	USA Meryl Davis & Charlie White	GBR Sinead Kerr & John Kerr	CAN Vanessa Crone & Paul Poirier
2010	Nagoya	USA Meryl Davis & Charlie White	CAN Kaitlyn Weaver & Andrew Poje	USA Maia Shibutani & Alex Shibutani
2011	Sapporo	USA Maia Shibutani & Alex Shibutani	CAN Kaitlyn Weaver & Andrew Poje	RUS Elena Ilinykh & Nikita Katsalapov

Year	Location	Gold	Silver	Bronze
2012	Sendai	USA Meryl Davis & Charlie White	RUS Elena Ilinykh & Nikita Katsalapov	USA Maia Shibutani & Alex Shibutani
2013	Tokyo	USA Meryl Davis & Charlie White	ITA Anna Cappellini & Luca Lanotte	USA Maia Shibutani & Alex Shibutani
2014	Osaka	CAN Kaitlyn Weaver & Andrew Poje	RUS Ksenia Monko & Kirill Khaliavin	USA Kaitlin Hawayek & Jean-Luc Baker
2015	Nagano	USA Maia Shibutani & Alex Shibutani	RUS Ekaterina Bobrova & Dmitri Soloviev	USA Madison Hubbell & Zachary Donohue
2016	Sapporo	CAN Tessa Virtue & Scott Moir	FRA Gabriella Papadakis & Guillaume Cizeron	ITA Anna Cappellini & Luca Lanotte

Cup of China - MEN

Year	Location	Gold	Silver	Bronze
2003	Beijing	USA Timothy Goebel	FRA Brian Joubert	CHN Li Chengjiang
2004	Beijing	CAN Jeffrey Buttle	CHN Li Chengjiang	GER Stefan Lindemann
2005	Beijing	CAN Emanuel Sandhu	SUI Stéphane Lambiel	RUS Andrei Griazev
2006	Nanjing	USA Evan Lysacek	BLR Sergei Davydov	CAN Emanuel Sandhu
2007	Harbin	USA Johnny Weir	USA Evan Lysacek	SUI Stéphane Lambiel
2008	Beijing	USA Jeremy Abbott	USA Stephen Carriere	CZE Tomáš Verner
2009	Beijing	JPN Nobunari Oda	USA Evan Lysacek	RUS Sergei Voronov
2010	Beijing	JPN Takahiko Kozuka	USA Brandon Mroz	CZE Tomáš Verner
2011	Shanghai	USA Jeremy Abbott	JPN Nobunari Oda	CHN Song Nan
2012	Shanghai	JPN Tatsuki Machida	JPN Daisuke Takahashi	RUS Sergei Voronov
2013	Beijing	CHN Yan Han	RUS Maxim Kovtun	JPN Takahiko Kozuka
2014	Shanghai	RUS Maxim Kovtun	JPN Yuzuru Hanyu	USA Richard Dornbush
2015	Beijing	ESP Javier Fernández	CHN Jin Boyang	CHN Yan Han
2016	Beijing	CAN Patrick Chan	CHN Jin Boyang	RUS Sergei Voronov

Cup of China - PAIRS

Year	Location	Gold	Silver	Bronze
2003	Beijing	CHN Shen Xue & Zhao Hongbo	CHN Pang Qing & Tong Jian	RUS Maria Petrova & Alexei Tikhonov
2004	Beijing	CHN Shen Xue & Zhao Hongbo	CHN Zhang Dan & Zhang Hao	CAN Valérie Marcoux & Craig Buntin

Year	Location	Gold	Silver	Bronze
2005	Beijing	RUS Maria Petrova & Alexei Tikhonov	CHN Pang Qing & Tong Jian	POL Dorota Zagórska & Mariusz Siudek
2006	Nanjing	CHN Shen Xue & Zhao Hongbo	CHN Pang Qing & Tong Jian	GER Aliona Savchenko & Robin Szolkowy
2007	Harbin	CHN Pang Qing & Tong Jian	USA Keauna McLaughlin & Rockne Brubaker	CAN Jessica Miller & Ian Moram
2008	Beijing	CHN Zhang Dan & Zhang Hao	UKR Tatiana Volosozhar & Stanislav Morozov	CHN Pang Qing & Tong Jian
2009	Beijing	CHN Shen Xue & Zhao Hongbo	CHN Zhang Dan & Zhang Hao	UKR Tatiana Volosozhar & Stanislav Morozov
2010	Beijing	CHN Pang Qing & Tong Jian	CHN Sui Wenjing & Han Cong	USA Caitlin Yankowskas & John Coughlin
2011	Shanghai	RUS Yuko Kavaguti & Alexander Smirnov	CHN Zhang Dan & Zhang Hao	CAN Kirsten Moore-Towers & Dylan Moscovitch
2012	Shanghai	CHN Pang Qing & Tong Jian	RUS Yuko Kavaguti & Alexander Smirnov	RUS Ksenia Stolbova & Fedor Klimov
2013	Beijing	GER Aliona Savchenko & Robin Szolkowy	CHN Pang Qing & Tong Jian	CHN Peng Cheng & Zhang Hao
2014	Shanghai	CHN Peng Cheng & Zhang Hao	CHN Yu Xiaoyu & Jin Yang	CHN Wang Xuehan & Wang Lei
2015	Beijing	RUS Yuko Kavaguti & Alexander Smirnov	CHN Sui Wenjing & Han Cong	CHN Yu Xiaoyu & Jin Yang
2016	Beijing	CHN Yu Xiaoyu & Zhang Hao	CHN Peng Cheng & Jin Yang	CAN Lubov Ilyushechkina & Dylan Moscovitch

Greg Fox

Cup of China - LADIES

Year	Location	Gold	Silver	Bronze
2003	Beijing	UKR Elena Liashenko	JPN Yoshie Onda	JPN Fumie Suguri
2004	Beijing	RUS Irina Slutskaya	RUS Viktoria Volchkova	CAN Joannie Rochette
2005	Beijing	RUS Irina Slutskaya	JPN Mao Asada	JPN Shizuka Arakawa
2006	Nanjing	HUN Júlia Sebestyén	JPN Yukari Nakano	USA Emily Hughes
2007	Harbin	KOR Kim Yuna	USA Caroline Zhang	ITA Carolina Kostner
2008	Beijing	KOR Kim Yuna	JPN Miki Ando	FIN Laura Lepistö
2009	Beijing	JPN Akiko Suzuki	FIN Kiira Korpi	CAN Joannie Rochette
2010	Beijing	JPN Miki Ando	JPN Akiko Suzuki	RUS Alena Leonova
2011	Shanghai	ITA Carolina Kostner	USA Mirai Nagasu	RUS Adelina Sotnikova
2012	Shanghai	JPN Mao Asada	RUS Yulia Lipnitskaya	FIN Kiira Korpi
2013	Beijing	RUS Anna Pogorilaya	RUS Adelina Sotnikova	ITA Carolina Kostner
2014	Shanghai	RUS Elizaveta Tuktamysheva	RUS Yulia Lipnitskaya	JPN Kanako Murakami
2015	Beijing	JPN Mao Asada	JPN Rika Hongo	RUS Elena Radionova
2016	Beijing	RUS Elena Radionova	CAN Kaetlyn Osmond	RUS Elizaveta Tuktamysheva

Cup of China - ICE DANCING

Year	Location	Gold	Silver	Bronze
2003	Beijing	RUS Tatiana Navka & Roman Kostomarov	UKR Elena Grushina & Ruslan Goncharov	FRA Isabelle Delobel & Olivier Schoenfelder
2004	Beijing	USA Tanith Belbin & Benjamin Agosto	ISR Galit Chait & Sergei Sakhnovski	CAN Marie-France Dubreuil & Patrice Lauzon

Year	Location	Gold	Silver	Bronze
2005	Beijing	RUS Tatiana Navka & Roman Kostomarov	ISR Galit Chait & Sergei Sakhnovski	CAN Megan Wing & Aaron Lowe
2006	Nanjing	RUS Oksana Domnina & Maxim Shabalin	USA Tanith Belbin & Benjamin Agosto	RUS Jana Khokhlova & Sergei Novitski
2007	Harbin	USA Tanith Belbin & Benjamin Agosto	RUS Oksana Domnina & Maxim Shabalin	ITA Federica Faiella & Massimo Scali
2008	Beijing	RUS Oksana Domnina & Maxim Shabalin	USA Tanith Belbin & Benjamin Agosto	RUS Jana Khokhlova & Sergei Novitski
2009	Beijing	USA Tanith Belbin & Benjamin Agosto	RUS Jana Khokhlova & Sergei Novitski	ITA Federica Faiella & Massimo Scali
2010	Beijing	FRA Nathalie Péchalat & Fabian Bourzat	RUS Ekaterina Bobrova & Dmitri Soloviev	ITA Federica Faiella & Massimo Scali
2011	Shanghai	RUS Ekaterina Bobrova & Dmitri Soloviev	USA Maia Shibutani & Alex Shibutani	FRA Pernelle Carron & Lloyd Jones
2012	Shanghai	FRA Nathalie Péchalat & Fabian Bourzat	RUS Ekaterina Bobrova & Dmitri Soloviev	CAN Kaitlyn Weaver & Andrew Poje
2013	Beijing	FRA Nathalie Péchalat & Fabian Bourzat	RUS Ekaterina Bobrova & Dmitri Soloviev	USA Madison Chock & Evan Bates
2014	Shanghai	FRA Gabriella Papadakis & Guillaume Cizeron	USA Maia Shibutani & Alex Shibutani	ITA Anna Cappellini & Luca Lanotte
2015	Beijing	ITA Anna Cappellini & Luca Lanotte	USA Madison Chock & Evan Bates	RUS Elena Ilinykh & Ruslan Zhiganshin
2016	Beijing	USA Maia Shibutani & Alex Shibutani	CAN Kaitlyn Weaver & Andrew Poje	RUS Alexandra Stepanova & Ivan Bukin

Greg Fox

Trophée de France - MEN

Year	Location	Gold	Silver	Bronze
f1987	Paris	CZE Petr Barna	USA Angelo D'Agostino	GBR Paul Robinson
1988	Paris	USA Paul Wylie	POL Grzegorz Filipowski	CAN Michael Slipchuk
1989	Paris	URS Viacheslav Zagorodniuk	POL Grzegorz Filipowski	CAN Norm Proft
1990	Paris	USA Christopher Bowman	URS Viacheslav Zagorodniuk	CAN Elvis Stojko
1991	Albertville	CAN Kurt Browning	URS Viacheslav Zagorodniuk	URS Alexei Urmanov
1992	Paris	USA Mark Mitchell	FRA Éric Millot	CAN Sébastien Britten
1993	Paris	USA Todd Eldredge	FRA Philippe Candeloro	UKR Viacheslav Zagorodniuk
1994	Lyon	FRA Philippe Candeloro	FRA Éric Millot	USA Michael Chack
1995	Bordeaux	RUS Ilia Kulik	FRA Éric Millot	CAN Elvis Stojko
1996	Paris	USA Todd Eldredge	UKR Viacheslav Zagorodniuk	USA Michael Weiss
1997	Paris	RUS Alexei Yagudin	FRA Philippe Candeloro	AZE Igor Pashkevich
1998	Paris	RUS Alexei Yagudin	USA Michael Weiss	CAN Emanuel Sandhu
1999	Paris	RUS Alexei Yagudin	FRA Vincent Restencourt	BUL Ivan Dinev
2000	Paris	RUS Alexei Yagudin	FRA Stanick Jeannette	RUS Roman Serov
2001	Paris	RUS Alexei Yagudin	USA Todd Eldredge	GER Andrejs Vlascenko
2002	Paris	USA Michael Weiss	CHN Zhang Min	JPN Takeshi Honda
2003	Paris	RUS Evgeni Plushenko	BEL Kevin van der Perren	USA Michael Weiss
2004	Paris	USA Johnny Weir	FRA Brian Joubert	CAN Emanuel Sandhu

Year	Location	Gold	Silver	Bronze
2005	Paris	CAN Jeffrey Buttle	FRA Brian Joubert	ROM Gheorghe Chiper
2006	Paris	FRA Brian Joubert	FRA Alban Préaubert	RUS Sergei Dobrin
2007	Paris	CAN Patrick Chan	RUS Sergei Voronov	FRA Alban Préaubert
2008	Paris	CAN Patrick Chan	JPN Takahiko Kozuka	FRA Alban Préaubert
2009	Paris	JPN Nobunari Oda	CZE Tomáš Verner	USA Adam Rippon
2010	Paris	JPN Takahiko Kozuka	FRA Florent Amodio	USA Brandon Mroz
2011	Paris	CAN Patrick Chan	CHN Song Nan	CZE Michal Březina
2012	Paris	JPN Takahito Mura	USA Jeremy Abbott	FRA Florent Amodio
2013	Paris	CAN Patrick Chan	JPN Yuzuru Hanyu	USA Jason Brown
2014	Bordeaux	RUS Maxim Kovtun	JPN Tatsuki Machida	KAZ Denis Ten
2015	Bordeaux	JPN Shoma Uno	RUS Maxim Kovtun	JPN Daisuke Murakami

Trophée de France - PAIRS

Year	Location	Gold	Silver	Bronze
1987	Paris	USA Natalie Seybold & Wayne Seybold	URS Yulia Bistrova & Alexander Tarasov	CAN Laurene Collin & John Penticost
1988	Paris	URS Elena Bechke & Denis Petrov	GDR Mandy Wötzel & Axel Rauschenbach	USA Katy Keely & Joseph Mero
1989	Paris	GDR Mandy Wötzel & Axel Rauschenbach	CAN Isabelle Brasseur & Lloyd Eisler	CZE Radka Kovaříková & René Novotný
1990	Paris	URS Elena Bechke & Denis Petrov	URS Evgenia Chernysheva & Dmitri Sukhanov	CAN Michelle Menzies & Kevin Wheeler

Year	Location	Gold	Silver	Bronze
1991	Albertville	URS Natalia Mishkutionok & Artur Dmitriev	CZE Radka Kovaříková & René Novotný	URS Elena Bechke & Denis Petrov
1992	Paris	RUS Evgenia Shishkova & Vadim Naumov	CZE Radka Kovaříková & René Novotný	USA Karen Courtland & Todd Reynolds
1993	Paris	RUS Natalia Mishkutionok & Artur Dmitriev	RUS Marina Eltsova & Andrei Bushkov	USA Jenni Meno & Todd Sand
1994	Lyon	RUS Marina Eltsova & Andrei Bushkov	LAT Elena Berezhnaya & Oleg Shliakhov	GER Mandy Wötzel & Ingo Steuer
1995	Bordeaux	LAT Elena Berezhnaya & Oleg Shliakhov	RUS Oksana Kazakova & Artur Dmitriev	USA Jenni Meno & Todd Sand
1996	Paris	RUS Oksana Kazakova & Artur Dmitriev	USA Jenni Meno & Todd Sand	RUS Elena Berezhnaya & Anton Sikharulidze
1997	Paris	RUS Elena Berezhnaya & Anton Sikharulidze	GER Mandy Wötzel & Ingo Steuer	CHN Shen Xue & Zhao Hongbo
1998	Paris	FRA Sarah Abitbol & Stéphane Bernadis	USA Kyoko Ina & John Zimmerman	RUS Marina Eltsova & Andrei Bushkov
1999	Paris	FRA Sarah Abitbol & Stéphane Bernadis	RUS Tatiana Totmianina & Maxim Marinin	POL Dorota Zagórska & Mariusz Siudek
2000	Paris	RUS Elena Berezhnaya & Anton Sikharulidze	CAN Jamie Salé & David Pelletier	USA Kyoko Ina & John Zimmerman
2001	Paris	RUS Elena Berezhnaya & Anton Sikharulidze	USA Kyoko Ina & John Zimmerman	FRA Sarah Abitbol & Stéphane Bernadis

Year	Location	Gold	Silver	Bronze
2002	Paris	RUS Tatiana Totmianina & Maxim Marinin	FRA Sarah Abitbol & Stéphane Bernadis	CHN Pang Qing & Tong Jian
2003	Paris	CHN Zhang Dan & Zhang Hao	RUS Tatiana Totmianina & Maxim Marinin	USA Tiffany Scott & Philip Dulebohn
2004	Paris	CHN Shen Xue & Zhao Hongbo	RUS Maria Petrova & Alexei Tikhonov	CHN Pang Qing & Tong Jian
2005	Paris	RUS Tatiana Totmianina & Maxim Marinin	CHN Pang Qing & Tong Jian	CAN Valérie Marcoux & Craig Buntin
2006	Paris	RUS Maria Petrova & Alexei Tikhonov	USA Rena Inoue & John Baldwin	RUS Julia Obertas & Sergei Slavnov
2007	Paris	CHN Zhang Dan & Zhang Hao	CHN Pang Qing & Tong Jian	RUS Maria Mukhortova & Maxim Trankov
2008	Paris	GER Aliona Savchenko & Robin Szolkowy	RUS Maria Mukhortova & Maxim Trankov	CAN Meagan Duhamel & Craig Buntin
2009	Paris	RUS Maria Mukhortova & Maxim Trankov	CAN Jessica Dubé & Bryce Davison	GER Aliona Savchenko & Robin Szolkowy
2010	Paris	GER Aliona Savchenko & Robin Szolkowy	RUS Vera Bazarova & Yuri Larionov	GER Maylin Hausch & Daniel Wende
2011	Paris	RUS Tatiana Volosozhar & Maxim Trankov	RUS Vera Bazarova & Yuri Larionov	CAN Meagan Duhamel & Eric Radford

Year	Location	Gold	Silver	Bronze
2012	Paris	RUS Yuko Kavaguti & Alexander Smirnov	CAN Meagan Duhamel & Eric Radford	ITA Stefania Berton & Ondřej Hotárek
2013	Paris	CHN Pang Qing & Tong Jian	CAN Meagan Duhamel & Eric Radford	USA Caydee Denney & John Coughlin
2014	Bordeaux	RUS Ksenia Stolbova & Fedor Klimov	CHN Sui Wenjing & Han Cong	CHN Wang Xuehan & Wang Lei
2015	Bordeaux	RUS Tatiana Volosozhar & Maxim Trankov	FRA Vanessa James & Morgan Cipres	CAN Julianne Seguin & Charlie Bilodeau

Trophée de France - LADIES

Year	Location	Gold	Silver	Bronze
1987	Paris	USA Jill Trenary	FRA Agnès Gosselin	FRG Patricia Neske
1988	Paris	FRG Claudia Leistner	URS Natalia Gorbenko	GDR Evelyn Großmann
1989	Paris	FRA Surya Bonaly	USA Holly Cook	FRA Laetitia Hubert
1990	Paris	FRA Surya Bonaly	CZE Lenka Kulovaná	USA Nancy Kerrigan
1991	Albertville	JPN Midori Ito	USA Kristi Yamaguchi	USA Nancy Kerrigan
1992	Paris	FRA Surya Bonaly	CAN Karen Preston	FRA Laetitia Hubert
1993	Paris	FRA Surya Bonaly	FIN Mila Kajas	CAN Lisa Sargeant
1994	Lyon	FRA Surya Bonaly	USA Tonia Kwiatkowski	USA Michelle Kwan

Year	Location	Gold	Silver	Bronze
1995	Bordeaux	CAN Josée Chouinard	CHN Chen Lu	FRA Surya Bonaly
1996	Paris	USA Michelle Kwan	RUS Maria Butyrskaya	USA Tara Lipinski
1997	Paris	FRA Laetitia Hubert	USA Tara Lipinski	FRA Vanessa Gusmeroli
1998	Paris	RUS Maria Butyrskaya	USA Nicole Bobek	FRA Vanessa Gusmeroli
1999	Paris	RUS Maria Butyrskaya	RUS Viktoria Volchkova	USA Sarah Hughes
2000	Paris	RUS Maria Butyrskaya	RUS Viktoria Volchkova	USA Jennifer Kirk
2001	Paris	RUS Maria Butyrskaya	USA Sarah Hughes	USA Sasha Cohen
2002	Paris	USA Sasha Cohen	JPN Yoshie Onda	FIN Alisa Drei
2003	Paris	USA Sasha Cohen	JPN Shizuka Arakawa	HUN Júlia Sebestyén
2004	Paris	CAN Joannie Rochette	ITA Carolina Kostner	HUN Júlia Sebestyén
2005	Paris	JPN Mao Asada	USA Sasha Cohen	JPN Shizuka Arakawa
2006	Paris	KOR Kim Yuna	JPN Miki Ando	USA Kimmie Meissner
2007	Paris	JPN Mao Asada	USA Kimmie Meissner	USA Ashley Wagner
2008	Paris	CAN Joannie Rochette	JPN Mao Asada	USA Caroline Zhang
2009	Paris	KOR Kim Yuna	JPN Mao Asada	JPN Yukari Nakano
2010	Paris	FIN Kiira Korpi	USA Mirai Nagasu	USA Alissa Czisny
2011	Paris	RUS Elizaveta Tuktamysheva	ITA Carolina Kostner	USA Alissa Czisny
2012	Paris	USA Ashley Wagner	RUS Elizaveta Tuktamysheva	RUS Yulia Lipnitskaya
2013	Paris	USA Ashley Wagner	RUS Adelina Sotnikova	RUS Anna Pogorilaya
2014	Bordeaux	RUS Elena Radionova	RUS Yulia Lipnitskaya	USA Ashley Wagner
2015	Bordeaux	USA Gracie Gold	RUS Yulia Lipnitskaya	ITA Roberta Rodeghiero

Trophée de France - ICE DANCING

Year	Location	Gold	Silver	Bronze
1987	Paris	ITA Lia Trovati & Roberto Pelizzola	USA Susan Wynne & Joseph Druar	FRA Corinne Paliard & Didier Courtois
1988	Paris	USA Susan Wynne & Joseph Druar	GBR Sharon Jones & Paul Askham	URS Oksana Grishuk & Alexandr Chichkov
1989	Paris	URS Anjelika Krylova & Vladimir Leliukh	USA April Sargeant-Thomas & Russ Witherby	FIN Susanna Rahkamo & Petri Kokko
1990	Paris	ITA Stefania Calegari & Pasquale Camerlengo	FRA Sophie Moniotte & Pascal Lavanchy	URS Anjelika Krylova & Vladimir Leliukh
1991	Albertville	URS Anjelika Krylova & Vladimir Fedorov	FRA Dominique Yvon & Frédéric Palluel	CZE Kateřina Mrázová & Martin Šimeček
1992	Paris	FRA Sophie Moniotte & Pascal Lavanchy	UKR Irina Romanova & Igor Yaroshenko	RUS Elena Kustarova & Oleg Ovsyannikov
1993	Paris	RUS Irina Lobacheva & Ilia Averbukh	USA Elizabeth Punsalan & Jerod Swallow	FRA Marina Anissina & Gwendal Peizerat
1994	Lyon	FRA Marina Anissina & Gwendal Peizerat	USA Elizabeth Punsalan & Jerod Swallow	CZE Kateřina Mrázová & Martin Šimeček
1995	Bordeaux	RUS Oksana Grishuk & Evgeni Platov	FRA Marina Anissina & Gwendal Peizerat	UKR Irina Romanova & Igor Yaroshenko
1996	Paris	FRA Marina Anissina & Gwendal Peizerat	USA Elizabeth Punsalan & Jerod Swallow	UKR Irina Romanova & Igor Yaroshenko

Year	Location	Gold	Silver	Bronze
1997	Paris	RUS Oksana Grishuk & Evgeni Platov	FRA Marina Anissina & Gwendal Peizerat	UKR Irina Romanova & Igor Yaroshenko
1998	Paris	FRA Marina Anissina & Gwendal Peizerat	ITA Barbara Fusar-Poli & Maurizio Margaglio	LTU Margarita Drobiazko & Povilas Vanagas
1999	Paris	FRA Marina Anissina & Gwendal Peizerat	ITA Barbara Fusar-Poli & Maurizio Margaglio	LTU Margarita Drobiazko & Povilas Vanagas
2000	Paris	FRA Marina Anissina & Gwendal Peizerat	RUS Irina Lobacheva & Ilia Averbukh	GER Kati Winkler & René Lohse
2001	Paris	FRA Marina Anissina & Gwendal Peizerat	CAN Shae-Lynn Bourne & Victor Kraatz	LTU Margarita Drobiazko & Povilas Vanagas
2002	Paris	UKR Elena Grushina & Ruslan Goncharov	FRA Isabelle Delobel & Olivier Schoenfelder	USA Tanith Belbin & Benjamin Agosto
2003	Paris	BUL Albena Denkova & Maxim Staviski	CAN Marie-France Dubreuil & Patrice Lauzon	FRA Isabelle Delobel & Olivier Schoenfelder
2004	Paris	RUS Tatiana Navka & Roman Kostomarov	BUL Albena Denkova & Maxim Staviski	FRA Isabelle Delobel & Olivier Schoenfelder
2005	Paris	UKR Elena Grushina & Ruslan Goncharov	FRA Isabelle Delobel & Olivier Schoenfelder	ITA Federica Faiella & Massimo Scali
2006	Paris	BUL Albena Denkova & Maxim Staviski	FRA Isabelle Delobel & Olivier Schoenfelder	ITA Federica Faiella & Massimo Scali
2007	Paris	FRA Isabelle Delobel & Olivier Schoenfelder	RUS Jana Khokhlova & Sergei Novitski	USA Meryl Davis & Charlie White

Greg Fox

Year	Location	Gold	Silver	Bronze
2008	Paris	FRA Isabelle Delobel & Olivier Schoenfelder	ITA Federica Faiella & Massimo Scali	GBR Sinead Kerr & John Kerr
2009	Paris	CAN Tessa Virtue & Scott Moir	FRA Nathalie Péchalat & Fabian Bourzat	GBR Sinead Kerr & John Kerr
2010	Paris	FRA Nathalie Péchalat & Fabian Bourzat	RUS Ekaterina Riazanova & Ilia Tkachenko	USA Madison Chock & Greg Zuerlein
2011	Paris	CAN Tessa Virtue & Scott Moir	FRA Nathalie Péchalat & Fabian Bourzat	ITA Anna Cappellini & Luca Lanotte
2012	Paris	FRA Nathalie Péchalat & Fabian Bourzat	ITA Anna Cappellini & Luca Lanotte	RUS Ekaterina Riazanova & Ilia Tkachenko
2013	Paris	CAN Tessa Virtue & Scott Moir	RUS Elena Ilinykh & Nikita Katsalapov	FRA Nathalie Péchalat & Fabian Bourzat
2014	Bordeaux	FRA Gabriella Papadakis & Guillaume Cizeron	CAN Piper Gilles & Paul Poirier	USA Madison Hubbell & Zachary Donohue
2015	Bordeaux	USA Madison Hubbell & Zachary Donohue	CAN Piper Gilles & Paul Poirier	RUS Alexandra Stepanova & Ivan Bukin

Cup of Russia-Rostelecom Cup
MEN

Year	Location	Gold	Silver	Bronze
1996	St. Petersburg	RUS Alexei Urmanov	RUS Alexei Yagudin	USA Michael Weiss
1997	St. Petersburg	RUS Alexei Yagudin	RUS Evgeni Plushenko	UKR Viacheslav Zagorodniuk
1998	Moscow	RUS Alexei Urmanov	RUS Evgeni Plushenko	RUS Alexander Abt
1999	St. Petersburg	RUS Evgeni Plushenko	RUS Alexander Abt	CHN Guo Zhengxin
2000	St. Petersburg	RUS Evgeni Plushenko	RUS Ilia Klimkin	USA Matthew Savoie
2001	St. Petersburg	RUS Evgeni Plushenko	RUS Roman Serov	BUL Ivan Dinev
2002	Moscow	RUS Evgeni Plushenko	CHN Li Chengjiang	RUS Alexander Abt
2003	Moscow	RUS Evgeni Plushenko	CHN Li Chengjiang	FRA Frédéric Dambier
2004	Moscow	RUS Evgeni Plushenko	USA Johnny Weir	CHN Zhang Min
2005	St. Petersburg	RUS Evgeni Plushenko	SUI Stéphane Lambiel	USA Johnny Weir
2006	Moscow	FRA Brian Joubert	USA Johnny Weir	RUS Ilia Klimkin
2007	Moscow	USA Johnny Weir	SUI Stéphane Lambiel	RUS Andrei Griazev
2008	Moscow	FRA Brian Joubert	CZE Tomáš Verner	FRA Alban Préaubert
2009	Moscow	RUS Evgeni Plushenko	JPN Takahiko Kozuka	RUS Artem Borodulin
2010	Moscow	CZE Tomáš Verner	CAN Patrick Chan	USA Jeremy Abbott
2011	Moscow	JPN Yuzuru Hanyu	ESP Javier Fernández	USA Jeremy Abbott
2012	Moscow	CAN Patrick Chan	JPN Takahiko Kozuka	CZE Michal Březina
2013	Moscow	JPN Tatsuki Machida	RUS Maxim Kovtun	ESP Javier Fernández
2014	Moscow	ESP Javier Fernández	RUS Sergei Voronov	CZE Michal Březina
2015	Moscow	ESP Javier Fernández	RUS Adian Pitkeev	USA Ross Miner
2016	Moscow	ESP Javier Fernández	JPN Shoma Uno	ISR Alexei Bychenko

Greg Fox

Cup of Russia-Rostelecom Cup
PAIRS

Year	Location	Gold	Silver	Bronze
1996	St. Petersburg	GER Mandy Wötzel & Ingo Steuer	RUS Marina Eltsova & Andrei Bushkov	RUS Oksana Kazakova & Artur Dmitriev
1997	St. Petersburg	RUS Marina Eltsova & Andrei Bushkov	RUS Evgenia Shishkova & Vadim Naumov	CAN Marie-Claude Savard-Gagnon & Luc Bradet
1998	Moscow	RUS Elena Berezhnaya & Anton Sikharulidze	CHN Shen Xue & Zhao Hongbo	USA Kyoko Ina & John Zimmerman
1999	St. Petersburg	RUS Maria Petrova & Alexei Tikhonov	CHN Shen Xue & Zhao Hongbo	RUS Tatiana Totmianina & Maxim Marinin
2000	St. Petersburg	RUS Elena Berezhnaya & Anton Sikharulidze	CHN Shen Xue & Zhao Hongbo	POL Dorota Zagórska & Mariusz Siudek
2001	St. Petersburg	RUS Elena Berezhnaya & Anton Sikharulidze	RUS Maria Petrova & Alexei Tikhonov	FRA Sarah Abitbol & Stéphane Bernadis
2002	Moscow	CHN Shen Xue & Zhao Hongbo	RUS Maria Petrova & Alexei Tikhonov	RUS Julia Obertas & Sergei Slavnov
2003	Moscow	RUS Tatiana Totmianina & Maxim Marinin	CHN Pang Qing & Tong Jian	CHN Zhang Dan & Zhang Hao
2004	Moscow	CHN Zhang Dan & Zhang Hao	RUS Julia Obertas & Sergei Slavnov	GER Aliona Savchenko & Robin Szolkowy
2005	St. Petersburg	RUS Tatiana Totmianina & Maxim Marinin	RUS Julia Obertas & Sergei Slavnov	POL Dorota Zagórska & Mariusz Siudek

Year	Location	Gold	Silver	Bronze
2006	Moscow	GER Aliona Savchenko & Robin Szolkowy	RUS Maria Petrova & Alexei Tikhonov	RUS Yuko Kawaguchi & Alexander Smirnov
2007	Moscow	CHN Zhang Dan & Zhang Hao	GER Aliona Savchenko & Robin Szolkowy	RUS Yuko Kawaguchi & Alexander Smirnov
2008	Moscow	CHN Zhang Dan & Zhang Hao	RUS Yuko Kawaguchi & Alexander Smirnov	UKR Tatiana Volosozhar & Stanislav Morozov
2009	Moscow	CHN Pang Qing & Tong Jian	RUS Yuko Kavaguti & Alexander Smirnov	USA Keauna McLaughlin & Rockne Brubaker
2010	Moscow	RUS Yuko Kavaguti & Alexander Smirnov	JPN Narumi Takahashi & Mervin Tran	USA Amanda Evora & Mark Ladwig
2011	Moscow	GER Aliona Savchenko & Robin Szolkowy	RUS Yuko Kavaguti & Alexander Smirnov	ITA Stefania Berton & Ondřej Hotárek
2012	Moscow	RUS Tatiana Volosozhar & Maxim Trankov	RUS Vera Bazarova & Yuri Larionov	USA Caydee Denney & John Coughlin
2013	Moscow	GER Aliona Savchenko & Robin Szolkowy	RUS Vera Bazarova & Yuri Larionov	CAN Kirsten Moore-Towers & Dylan Moscovitch
2014	Moscow	RUS Ksenia Stolbova & Fedor Klimov	RUS Evgenia Tarasova & Vladimir Morozov	RUS Kristina Astakhova & Alexei Rogonov
2015	Moscow	RUS Ksenia Stolbova & Fedor Klimov	RUS Yuko Kavaguti & Alexander Smirnov	CHN Cheng Peng & Hao Zhang
2016	Moscow	GER Aliona Savchenko & Bruno Massot	RUS Natalja Zabijako & Alexander Enbert	RUS Kristina Astakhova & Alexei Rogonov

Cup of Russia-Rostelecom Cup
LADIES

Year	Location	Gold	Silver	Bronze
1996	St. Petersburg	RUS Irina Slutskaya	AUT Julia Lautowa	RUS Olga Markova
1997	St. Petersburg	RUS Irina Slutskaya	RUS Elena Sokolova	RUS Olga Markova
1998	Moscow	RUS Elena Sokolova	RUS Julia Soldatova	RUS Irina Slutskaya
1999	St. Petersburg	RUS Irina Slutskaya	RUS Julia Soldatova	RUS Elena Sokolova
2000	St. Petersburg	RUS Irina Slutskaya	RUS Elena Sokolova	USA Sarah Hughes
2001	St. Petersburg	RUS Irina Slutskaya	RUS Viktoria Volchkova	USA Angela Nikodinov
2002	Moscow	RUS Viktoria Volchkova	USA Sasha Cohen	RUS Irina Slutskaya
2003	Moscow	UKR Elena Liashenko	ITA Carolina Kostner	UKR Galina Maniachenko
2004	Moscow	RUS Irina Slutskaya	JPN Shizuka Arakawa	HUN Júlia Sebestyén
2005	St. Petersburg	RUS Irina Slutskaya	JPN Miki Ando	JPN Yoshie Onda
2006	Moscow	SUI Sarah Meier	HUN Júlia Sebestyén	JPN Yoshie Onda
2007	Moscow	KOR Kim Yuna	JPN Yukari Nakano	CAN Joannie Rochette
2008	Moscow	ITA Carolina Kostner	USA Rachael Flatt	JPN Fumie Suguri
2009	Moscow	JPN Miki Ando	USA Ashley Wagner	RUS Alena Leonova
2010	Moscow	JPN Miki Ando	JPN Akiko Suzuki	USA Ashley Wagner
2011	Moscow	JPN Mao Asada	RUS Alena Leonova	RUS Adelina Sotnikova
2012	Moscow	FIN Kiira Korpi	USA Gracie Gold	USA Agnes Zawadzki
2013	Moscow	RUS Yulia Lipnitskaya	ITA Carolina Kostner	USA Mirai Nagasu
2014	Moscow	JPN Rika Hongo	RUS Anna Pogorilaya	CAN Alaine Chartrand
2015	Moscow	RUS Elena Radionova	RUS Evgenia Medvedeva	RUS Adelina Sotnikova
2016	Moscow	RUS Anna Pogorilaya	RUS Elena Radionova	USA Courtney Hicks

Cup of Russia-Rostelecom Cup
ICE DANCING

Year	Location	Gold	Silver	Bronze
1996	St. Petersburg	RUS Anjelika Krylova & Oleg Ovsyannikov	RUS Irina Lobacheva & Ilia Averbukh	USA Elizabeth Punsalan & Jerod Swallow
1997	St. Petersburg	RUS Anjelika Krylova & Oleg Ovsyannikov	RUS Irina Lobacheva & Ilia Averbukh	BLR Tatiana Navka & Nikolai Morozov
1998	Moscow	RUS Anjelika Krylova & Oleg Ovsyannikov	RUS Irina Lobacheva & Ilia Averbukh	RUS Tatiana Navka & Roman Kostomarov
1999	St. Petersburg	ITA Barbara Fusar-Poli & Maurizio Margaglio	CAN Shae-Lynn Bourne & Viktor Kraatz	POL Sylwia Nowak & Sebastien Kolasinski
2000	St. Petersburg	ITA Barbara Fusar-Poli & Maurizio Margaglio	RUS Irina Lobacheva & Ilia Averbukh	ISR Galit Chait & Sergei Sakhnovski
2001	St. Petersburg	ITA Barbara Fusar-Poli & Maurizio Margaglio	ISR Galit Chait & Sergei Sakhnovski	UKR Elena Grushina & Ruslan Goncharov
2002	Moscow	RUS Irina Lobacheva & Ilia Averbukh	RUS Tatiana Navka & Roman Kostomarov	BUL Albena Denkova & Maxim Staviski
2003	Moscow	RUS Tatiana Navka & Roman Kostomarov	USA Tanith Belbin & Benjamin Agosto	ISR Galit Chait & Sergei Sakhnovski
2004	Moscow	RUS Tatiana Navka & Roman Kostomarov	UKR Elena Grushina & Ruslan Goncharov	ITA Federica Faiella & Massimo Scali
2005	St. Petersburg	RUS Tatiana Navka & Roman Kostomarov	ISR Galit Chait & Sergei Sakhnovski	RUS Oksana Domnina & Maxim Shabalin

Greg Fox

Year	Location	Gold	Silver	Bronze
2006	Moscow	USA Tanith Belbin & Benjamin Agosto	RUS Oksana Domnina & Maxim Shabalin	FRA Isabelle Delobel & Olivier Schoenfelder
2007	Moscow	RUS Oksana Domnina & Maxim Shabalin	FRA Nathalie Péchalat & Fabian Bourzat	UKR Anna Zadorozhniuk & Sergei Verbillo
2008	Moscow	RUS Jana Khokhlova & Sergei Novitski	RUS Oksana Domnina & Maxim Shabalin	USA Meryl Davis & Charlie White
2009	Moscow	USA Meryl Davis & Charlie White	ITA Anna Cappellini & Luca Lanotte	RUS Ekaterina Rubleva & Ivan Shefer
2010	Moscow	RUS Ekaterina Bobrova & Dmitri Soloviev	HUN Nóra Hoffmann & Maxim Zavozin	RUS Elena Ilinykh & Nikita Katsalapov
2011	Moscow	USA Meryl Davis & Charlie White	CAN Kaitlyn Weaver & Andrew Poje	RUS Ekaterina Bobrova & Dmitri Soloviev
2012	Moscow	CAN Tessa Virtue & Scott Moir	RUS Elena Ilinykh & Nikita Katsalapov	RUS Victoria Sinitsina & Ruslan Zhiganshin
2013	Moscow	RUS Ekaterina Bobrova & Dmitri Soloviev	CAN Kaitlyn Weaver & Andrew Poje	USA Madison Chock & Evan Bates
2014	Moscow	USA Madison Chock & Evan Bates	RUS Elena Ilinykh & Ruslan Zhiganshin	GBR Penny Coomes & Nicholas Buckland
2015	Moscow	CAN Kaitlyn Weaver & Andrew Poje	ITA Anna Cappellini & Luca Lanotte	RUS Viktoria Sinitsina & Nikita Katsalapov
2016	Moscow	RUS Ekaterina Bobrova & Dmitri Soloviev	USA Madison Chock & Evan Bates	CAN Kaitlyn Weaver & Andrew Poje

Bofrost Cup on Ice- MEN

(As previously noted, this event was discontinued after 2004, being replaced in the Grand Prix series by the Cup of China event).

Year	Location	Gold	Silver	Bronze
1986	Frankfurt	CZE Petr Barna	ITA Alessandro Riccitelli	CHN Zhang Shubin
1987	W. Germany	USA Christopher Bowman	URS Vladimir Petrenko	JPN Makoto Kano
1988		NO	COMPETITION	HELD
1989	Gelsenkirchen	CZE Petr Barna	URS Viktor Petrenko	USA Paul Wylie
1990	Gelsenkirchen	CAN Kurt Browning	USA Todd Eldredge	GER Ronny Winkler
1991	Gelsenkirchen	USA Mark Mitchell	GER Mirko Eichhorn	GER Daniel Weiss
1992	Gelsenkirchen	USA Todd Eldredge	RUS Alexei Urmanov	UKR Viacheslav Zagorodniuk
1993	Gelsenkirchen	UKR Viktor Petrenko	USA Scott Davis	CAN Sébastien Britten
1994	Gelsenkirchen	CAN Elvis Stojko	USA Shepherd Clark	UKR Dmitri Dmitrenko
1995	Gelsenkirchen	UKR Viacheslav Zagorodniuk	RUS Alexei Urmanov	USA Todd Eldredge
1996	Gelsenkirchen	RUS Alexei Urmanov	UKR Dmitri Dmitrenko	RUS Alexei Yagudin
1997	Gelsenkirchen	CAN Elvis Stojko	AZE Igor Pashkevich	RUS Alexander Abt
1998	Gelsenkirchen	RUS Alexei Yagudin	RUS Alexander Abt	GER Andrejs Vlascenko
1999	Gelsenkirchen	RUS Evgeni Plushenko	CHN Guo Zhengxin	USA Matthew Savoie
2000	Gelsenkirchen	RUS Evgeni Plushenko	USA Timothy Goebel	CHN Li Chengjiang
2001	Gelsenkirchen	RUS Evgeni Plushenko	USA Timothy Goebel	CHN Li Chengjiang
2002	Gelsenkirchen	RUS Evgeni Plushenko	RUS Alexander Abt	CHN Li Chengjiang
2003	Gelsenkirchen	GER Stefan Lindemann	CAN Jeffrey Buttle	GER Silvio Smalun
2004	Gelsenkirchen	GER Stefan Lindemann	CAN Ben Ferreira	USA Matthew Savoie

Greg Fox

Bofrost Cup on Ice - PAIRS

Year	Location	Gold	Silver	Bronze
1986	Frankfurt	CAN Melanie Gaylor & Lee Barkell	GBR Colette May & Carl Nelson	FRG Kerstin Kiminus & Stefan Pfrengle
1987	W. Germany	USA Jill Watson & Peter Oppegard	CAN Laurene Collin & John Penticost	GDR Brigitte Groh & Holger Maletz
1988		NO COMPETITION HELD		
1989	Gelsenkirchen	URS Elena Bechke & Denis Petrov	GDR Peggy Schwarz & Alexander König	USA Calla Urbanski & Mark Naylor
1990	Gelsenkirchen	URS Natalia Mishkutionok & Artur Dmitriev	CAN Christine Hough & Doug Ladret	CZE Radka Kovaříková & René Novotný
1991	Gelsenkirchen	CAN Isabelle Brasseur & Lloyd Eisler	URS Evgenia Shishkova & Vadim Naumov	CZE Radka Kovaříková & René Novotný
1992	Gelsenkirchen	GER Mandy Wötzel & Ingo Steuer	USA Kyoko Ina & Jason Dungjen	RUS Oksana Kazakova & Dmitri Sukhanov
1993	Gelsenkirchen	RUS Evgenia Shishkova & Vadim Naumov	GER Mandy Wötzel & Ingo Steuer	USA Kyoko Ina & Jason Dungjen
1994	Gelsenkirchen	GER Mandy Wötzel & Ingo Steuer	RUS Oksana Kazakova & Dmitri Sukhanov	USA Stephanie Stiegler & Lance Travis
1995	Gelsenkirchen	RUS Marina Eltsova & Andrei Bushkov	GER Mandy Wötzel & Ingo Steuer	LAT Elena Berezhnaya & Oleg Shliakhov
1996	Gelsenkirchen	GER Mandy Wötzel & Ingo Steuer	RUS Marina Eltsova & Andrei Bushkov	USA Kyoko Ina & Jason Dungjen

Year	Location	Gold	Silver	Bronze
1997	Gelsenkirchen	GER Mandy Wötzel & Ingo Steuer	RUS Elena Berezhnaya & Anton Sikharulidze	UKR Evgenia Filonenko & Igor Marchenko
1998	Gelsenkirchen	RUS Maria Petrova & Alexei Tikhonov	GER Peggy Schwarz & Mirko Müller	USA Tiffany Stiegler & Johnnie Stiegler
1999	Gelsenkirchen	RUS Maria Petrova & Alexei Tikhonov	CAN Jamie Salé & David Pelletier	CHN Shen Xue & Zhao Hongbo
2000	Gelsenkirchen	FRA Sarah Abitbol & Stéphane Bernadis	RUS Maria Petrova & Alexei Tikhonov	RUS Tatiana Totmianina & Maxim Marinin
2001	Gelsenkirchen	CHN Shen Xue & Zhao Hongbo	USA Kyoko Ina & John Zimmerman	RUS Maria Petrova & Alexei Tikhonov
2002	Gelsenkirchen	CHN Shen Xue & Zhao Hongbo	RUS Julia Obertas & Alexei Sokolov	POL Dorota Zagórska & Mariusz Siudek
2003	Gelsenkirchen	CAN Valérie Marcoux & Craig Buntin	RUS Julia Obertas & Sergei Slavnov	CAN Elizabeth Putnam & Sean Wirtz
2004	Gelsenkirchen	RUS Viktoria Borzenkova & Andrei Chuvilaev	CAN Valérie Marcoux & Craig Buntin	GER Rebecca Handke & Daniel Wende

Bofrost Cup on Ice- LADIES

Year	Location	Gold	Silver	Bronze
1986	Frankfurt	CAN Dianne Takeuchi	CHN Caishu Fu	FRG Cornelia Renner
1987	W. Germany	JPN Midori Ito	USA Jill Trenary	URS Natalia Gorbenko
1988		NO	COMPETITION	HELD
1989	Gelsenkirchen	USA Tonya Harding	FRG Marina Kielmann	FRG Patricia Neske
1990	Gelsenkirchen	USA Kristi Yamaguchi	GER Evelyn Großmann	CAN Karen Preston

Year	Location	Gold	Silver	Bronze
1991	Gelsenkirchen	USA Nancy Kerrigan	GER Marina Kielmann	FRA Laetitia Hubert
1992	Gelsenkirchen	FRA Surya Bonaly	CAN Tanya Bingert	GER Marina Kielmann
1993	Gelsenkirchen	GER Tanja Szewczenko	UKR Oksana Baiul	JPN Rena Inoue
1994	Gelsenkirchen	GER Marina Kielmann	UKR Elena Liashenko	GER Tanja Szewczenko
1995	Gelsenkirchen	USA Michelle Kwan	RUS Maria Butyrskaya	USA Nicole Bobek
1996	Gelsenkirchen	RUS Irina Slutskaya	USA Tara Lipinski	FRA Vanessa Gusmeroli
1997	Gelsenkirchen	GER Tanja Szewczenko	RUS Irina Slutskaya	UKR Elena Liashenko
1998	Gelsenkirchen	RUS Elena Sokolova	UKR Yulia Lavrenchuk	RUS Maria Butyrskaya
1999	Gelsenkirchen	RUS Maria Butyrskaya	UKR Elena Liashenko	RUS Irina Slutskaya
2000	Gelsenkirchen	RUS Maria Butyrskaya	USA Sarah Hughes	UZB Tatiana Malinina
2001	Gelsenkirchen	RUS Maria Butyrskaya	JPN Yoshie Onda	USA Angela Nikodinov
2002	Gelsenkirchen	JPN Yoshie Onda	JPN Fumie Suguri	FIN Susanna Pöykiö
2003	Gelsenkirchen	CAN Joannie Rochette	FIN Susanna Pöykiö	HUN Júlia Sebestyén
2004	Gelsenkirchen	USA Jane Bugaeva	GER Constanze Paulinus	CAN Annie Bellemare

Bofrost Cup on Ice- ICE DANCING

Year	Location	Gold	Silver	Bronze
1986	Frankfurt	ITA Lia Trovati & Roberto Pelizzola	GBR Elizabeth Coates & Alan Abretti	FRA Dominique Yvon & Frédéric Palluel
1987	W. Germany	URS Marina Klimova & Sergei Ponomarenko	FRG Antonia Becherer & Ferdinand Becherer	ITA Michela Malingambi & Andrea Gilardi
1988		NO	COMPETITION	HELD
1989	Gelsenkirchen	URS Maya Usova & Alexander Zhulin	USA Suzanne Semanick & Ron Kravette	FRG Andrea Weppelmann & Hendryk Schamberger

Year	Location	Gold	Silver	Bronze
1990	Gelsenkirchen	URS Irina Romanova & Igor Yaroshenko	USA April Sargent & Russ Witherby	ITA Anna Croci & Luca Mantovani
1991	Gelsenkirchen	URS Tatiana Navka & Samuel Gezalian	CZE Kateřina Mrázová & Martin Šimeček	USA April Sargent-Thomas & Russ Witherby
1992	Gelsenkirchen	RUS Anjelika Krylova & Vladimir Fedorov	ITA Stefania Calegari & Pasquale Camerlengo	GER Jennifer Goolsbee & Hendryk Schamberger
1993	Gelsenkirchen	UKR Irina Romanova & Igor Yaroshenko	CZE Kateřina Mrázová & Martin Šimeček	RUS Elena Kustarova & Oleg Ovsyannikov
1994	Gelsenkirchen	FRA Marina Anissina & Gwendal Peizerat	LTU Margarita Drobiazko & Povilas Vanagas	CAN Jennifer Boyce & Michel Brunet
1995	Gelsenkirchen	RUS Anjelika Krylova & Oleg Ovsyannikov	UKR Irina Romanova & Igor Yaroshenko	RUS Irina Lobacheva & Ilia Averbukh
1996	Gelsenkirchen	RUS Anjelika Krylova & Oleg Ovsyannikov	CAN Shae-Lynn Bourne & Viktor Kraatz	FRA Sophie Moniotte & Pascal Lavanchy
1997	Gelsenkirchen	RUS Anjelika Krylova & Oleg Ovsyannikov	FRA Marina Anissina & Gwendal Peizerat	UKR Irina Romanova & Igor Yaroshenko
1998	Gelsenkirchen	RUS Anjelika Krylova & Oleg Ovsyannikov	CAN Shae-Lynn Bourne & Viktor Kraatz	GER Kati Winkler & René Lohse
1999	Gelsenkirchen	CAN Shae-Lynn Bourne & Viktor Kraatz	GER Kati Winkler & René Lohse	BUL Albena Denkova & Maxim Staviski
2000	Gelsenkirchen	ITA Barbara Fusar-Poli & Maurizio Margaglio	LTU Margarita Drobiazko & Povilas Vanagas	CAN Shae-Lynn Bourne & Viktor Kraatz

Year	Location	Gold	Silver	Bronze
2001	Gelsenkirchen	ITA Barbara Fusar-Poli & Maurizio Margaglio	CAN Marie-France Dubreuil & Patrice Lauzon	RUS Natalia Romaniuta & Daniil Barantsev
2002	Gelsenkirchen	BUL Albena Denkova & Maxim Staviski	ISR Galit Chait & Sergei Sakhnovsky	GER Kati Winkler & René Lohse
2003	Gelsenkirchen	CAN Marie-France Dubreuil & Patrice Lauzon	GER Kati Winkler & René Lohse	ITA Federica Faiella & Massimo Scali
2004	Gelsenkirchen	BUL Albena Denkova & Maxim Staviski	FRA Isabelle Delobel & Olivier Schoenfelder	RUS Ekaterina Rubleva & Ivan Shefer

Grand Prix of Figure Skating Final - MEN

Year	Location	Gold	Silver	Bronze
1995/1996	FRA Paris	RUS Alexei Urmanov	CAN Elvis Stojko	FRA Éric Millot
1996/1997	CAN Hamilton	CAN Elvis Stojko	USA Todd Eldredge	RUS Alexei Urmanov
1997/1998	GER Munich	RUS Ilia Kulik	CAN Elvis Stojko	USA Todd Eldredge
1998/1999	RUS Saint Petersburg	RUS Alexei Yagudin	RUS Alexei Urmanov	RUS Evgeni Plushenko
1999/2000	FRA Lyon	RUS Evgeni Plushenko	CAN Elvis Stojko	USA Timothy Goebel
2000/2001	JPN Tokyo	RUS Evgeni Plushenko	RUS Alexei Yagudin	USA Matthew Savoie
2001/2002	CAN Kitchener	RUS Alexei Yagudin	RUS Evgeni Plushenko	USA Timothy Goebel
2002/2003	RUS Saint Petersburg	RUS Evgeni Plushenko	RUS Ilia Klimkin	FRA Brian Joubert
2003/2004	USA Colorado Springs	CAN Emanuel Sandhu	RUS Evgeni Plushenko	USA Michael Weiss
2004/2005	CHN Beijing	RUS Evgeni Plushenko	CAN Jeffrey Buttle	CHN Li Chengjiang
2005/2006	JPN Tokyo	SUI Stéphane Lambiel	CAN Jeffrey Buttle	JPN Daisuke Takahashi
2006/2007	RUS Saint Petersburg	FRA Brian Joubert	JPN Daisuke Takahashi	JPN Nobunari Oda
2007/2008	ITA Turin	SUI Stéphane Lambiel	JPN Daisuke Takahashi	USA Evan Lysacek
2008/2009	KOR Goyang	USA Jeremy Abbott	JPN Takahiko Kozuka	USA Johnny Weir
2009/2010	JPN Tokyo	USA Evan Lysacek	JPN Nobunari Oda	USA Johnny Weir
2010/2011	CHN Beijing	CAN Patrick Chan	JPN Nobunari Oda	JPN Takahiko Kozuka
2011/2012	CAN Quebec City	CAN Patrick Chan	JPN Daisuke Takahashi	ESP Javier Fernández
2012/2013	RUS Sochi	JPN Daisuke Takahashi	JPN Yuzuru Hanyu	CAN Patrick Chan
2013/2014	JPN Fukuoka	JPN Yuzuru Hanyu	CAN Patrick Chan	JPN Nobunari Oda
2014/2015	ESP Barcelona	JPN Yuzuru Hanyu	ESP Javier Fernández	RUS Sergei Voronov
2015/2016	ESP Barcelona	JPN Yuzuru Hanyu	ESP Javier Fernández	JPN Shoma Uno
2016/2017	FRA Marseille	JPN Yuzuru Hanyu	USA Nathan Chen	JPN Shoma Uno

Grand Prix of Figure Skating Final - PAIRS

Year	Location	Gold	Silver	Bronze
1995/ 1996	FRA Paris	RUS Evgenia Shishkova & Vadim Naumov	RUS Marina Eltsova & Andrei Bushkov	GER Mandy Wötzel & Ingo Steuer
1996/ 1997	CAN Hamilton	GER Mandy Wötzel & Ingo Steuer	RUS Oksana Kazakova & Artur Dmitriev	RUS Marina Eltsova & Andrei Bushkov
1997/ 1998	GER Munich	RUS Elena Berezhnaya & Anton Sikharulidze	GER Mandy Wötzel & Ingo Steuer	RUS Oksana Kazakova & Artur Dmitriev
1998/ 1999	RUS Saint Petersburg	CHN Shen Xue & Zhao Hongbo	RUS Elena Berezhnaya & Anton Sikharulidze	RUS Maria Petrova & Alexei Tikhonov
1999/ 2000	FRA Lyon	CHN Shen Xue & Zhao Hongbo	FRA Sarah Abitbol & Stéphane Bernadis	RUS Elena Berezhnaya & Anton Sikharulidze
2000/ 2001	JPN Tokyo	CAN Jamie Salé & David Pelletier	RUS Elena Berezhnaya & Anton Sikharulidze	CHN Shen Xue & Zhao Hongbo
2001/ 2002	CAN Kitchener	CAN Jamie Salé & David Pelletier	RUS Elena Berezhnaya & Anton Sikharulidze	CHN Shen Xue & Zhao Hongbo
2002/ 2003	RUS Saint Petersburg	RUS Tatiana Totmianina & Maxim Marinin	CHN Shen Xue & Zhao Hongbo	RUS Maria Petrova & Alexei Tikhonov
2003/ 2004	USA Colorado Springs	CHN Shen Xue & Zhao Hongbo	RUS Tatiana Totmianina & Maxim Marinin	RUS Maria Petrova & Alexei Tikhonov
2004/ 2005	CHN Beijing	CHN Shen Xue & Zhao Hongbo	RUS Maria Petrova & Alexei Tikhonov	CHN Pang Qing & Tong Jian

Year	Location	Gold	Silver	Bronze
2005/ 2006	JPN Tokyo	RUS Tatiana Totmianina & Maxim Marinin	CHN Zhang Dan & Zhang Hao	GER Aliona Savchenko & Robin Szolkowy
2006/ 2007	RUS Saint Petersburg	CHN Shen Xue & Zhao Hongbo	GER Aliona Savchenko & Robin Szolkowy	CHN Zhang Dan & Zhang Hao
2007/ 2008	ITA Turin	GER Aliona Savchenko & Robin Szolkowy	CHN Zhang Dan & Zhang Hao	CHN Pang Qing & Tong Jian
2008/ 2009	KOR Goyang	CHN Pang Qing & Tong Jian	CHN Zhang Dan & Zhang Hao	GER Aliona Savchenko & Robin Szolkowy
2009/ 2010	JPN Tokyo	CHN Shen Xue & Zhao Hongbo	CHN Pang Qing & Tong Jian	GER Aliona Savchenko & Robin Szolkowy
2010/ 2011	CHN Beijing	GER Aliona Savchenko & Robin Szolkowy	CHN Pang Qing & Tong Jian	CHN Sui Wenjing & Han Cong
2011/ 2012	CAN Quebec City	GER Aliona Savchenko & Robin Szolkowy	RUS Tatiana Volosozhar & Maxim Trankov	RUS Yuko Kavaguti & Alexander Smirnov
2012/ 2013	RUS Sochi	RUS Tatiana Volosozhar & Maxim Trankov	RUS Vera Bazarova & Yuri Larionov	CHN Pang Qing & Tong Jian
2013/ 2014	JPN Fukuoka	GER Aliona Savchenko & Robin Szolkowy	RUS Tatiana Volosozhar & Maxim Trankov	CHN Pang Qing & Tong Jian
2014/ 2015	ESP Barcelona	CAN Meagan Duhamel & Eric Radford	RUS Ksenia Stolbova & Fedor Klimov	CHN Sui Wenjing & Han Cong
2015/ 2016	ESP Barcelona	RUS Ksenia Stolbova & Fedor Klimov	CAN Meagan Duhamel & Eric Radford	RUS Yuko Kavaguti & Alexander Smirnov
2016/ 2017	FRA Marseille	RUS Evgenia Tarasova & Vladimir Morozov	CHN Yu Xiaoyu & Zhang Hao	CAN Meagan Duhamel & Eric Radford

Grand Prix of Figure Skating Final - LADIES

Year	Location	Gold	Silver	Bronze
1995/ 1996	FRA Paris	USA Michelle Kwan	RUS Irina Slutskaya	CAN Josée Chouinard
1996/ 1997	CAN Hamilton	USA Tara Lipinski	USA Michelle Kwan	RUS Irina Slutskaya
1997/ 1998	GER Munich	USA Tara Lipinski	GER Tanja Szewczenko	RUS Maria Butyrskaya
1998/ 1999	RUS Saint Petersburg	UZB Tatiana Malinina	RUS Maria Butyrskaya	RUS Irina Slutskaya
1999/ 2000	FRA Lyon	RUS Irina Slutskaya	USA Michelle Kwan	RUS Maria Butyrskaya
2000/ 2001	JPN Tokyo	RUS Irina Slutskaya	USA Michelle Kwan	USA Sarah Hughes
2001/ 2002	CAN Kitchener	RUS Irina Slutskaya	USA Michelle Kwan	USA Sarah Hughes
2002/ 2003	RUS Saint Petersburg	USA Sasha Cohen	RUS Irina Slutskaya	RUS Viktoria Volchkova
2003/ 2004	USA Colorado Springs	JPN Fumie Suguri	USA Sasha Cohen	JPN Shizuka Arakawa
2004/ 2005	CHN Beijing	RUS Irina Slutskaya	JPN Shizuka Arakawa	CAN Joannie Rochette
2005/ 2006	JPN Tokyo	JPN Mao Asada	RUS Irina Slutskaya	JPN Yukari Nakano
2006/ 2007	RUS Saint Petersburg	KOR Kim Yuna	JPN Mao Asada	SUI Sarah Meier
2007/ 2008	ITA Turin	KOR Kim Yuna	JPN Mao Asada	ITA Carolina Kostner
2008/ 2009	KOR Goyang	JPN Mao Asada	KOR Kim Yuna	ITA Carolina Kostner
2009/ 2010	JPN Tokyo	KOR Kim Yuna	JPN Miki Ando	JPN Akiko Suzuki
2010/ 2011	CHN Beijing	USA Alissa Czisny	ITA Carolina Kostner	JPN Kanako Murakami
2011/ 2012	CAN Quebec City	ITA Carolina Kostner	JPN Akiko Suzuki	RUS Alena Leonova
2012/ 2013	RUS Sochi	JPN Mao Asada	USA Ashley Wagner	JPN Akiko Suzuki
2013/ 2014	JPN Fukuoka	JPN Mao Asada	RUS Yulia Lipnitskaya	USA Ashley Wagner
2014/ 2015	ESP Barcelona	RUS Elizaveta Tuktamysheva	RUS Elena Radionova	USA Ashley Wagner
2015/ 2016	ESP Barcelona	RUS Evgenia Medvedeva	JPN Satoko Miyahara	RUS Elena Radionova
2016/ 2017	FRA Marseille	RUS Evgenia Medvedeva	JPN Satoko Miyahara	RUS Anna Pogorilaya

Grand Prix of Figure Skating Final - ICE DANCING

Year	Location	Gold	Silver	Bronze
1995/ 1996	FRA Paris	RUS Oksana Grishuk & Evgeni Platov	RUS Anjelika Krylova & Oleg Ovsyannikov	FRA Marina Anissina & Gwendal Peizerat
1996/ 1997	CAN Hamilton	CAN Shae-Lynn Bourne & Viktor Kraatz	RUS Anjelika Krylova & Oleg Ovsyannikov	FRA Marina Anissina & Gwendal Peizerat
1997/ 1998	GER Munich	RUS Oksana Grishuk & Evgeni Platov	CAN Shae-Lynn Bourne & Viktor Kraatz	FRA Marina Anissina & Gwendal Peizerat
1998/ 1999	RUS Saint Petersburg	RUS Anjelika Krylova & Oleg Ovsyannikov	FRA Marina Anissina & Gwendal Peizerat	RUS Irina Lobacheva & Ilia Averbukh
1999/ 2000	FRA Lyon	FRA Marina Anissina & Gwendal Peizerat	ITA Barbara Fusar-Poli & Maurizio Margaglio	LTU Margarita Drobiazko & Povilas Vanagas
2000/ 2001	JPN Tokyo	ITA Barbara Fusar-Poli & Maurizio Margaglio	RUS Irina Lobacheva & Ilia Averbukh	LTU Margarita Drobiazko & Povilas Vanagas
2001/ 2002	CAN Kitchener	CAN Shae-Lynn Bourne & Viktor Kraatz	FRA Marina Anissina & Gwendal Peizerat	LTU Margarita Drobiazko & Povilas Vanagas
2002/ 2003	RUS Saint Petersburg	RUS Irina Lobacheva & Ilia Averbukh	RUS Tatiana Navka & Roman Kostomarov	BUL Albena Denkova & Maxim Staviyski
2003/ 2004	USA Colorado Springs	RUS Tatiana Navka & Roman Kostomarov	BUL Albena Denkova & Maxim Staviyski	USA Tanith Belbin & Benjamin Agosto
2004/ 2005	CHN Beijing	RUS Tatiana Navka & Roman Kostomarov	USA Tanith Belbin & Benjamin Agosto	BUL Albena Denkova & Maxim Staviyski

Greg Fox

Year	Location	Gold	Silver	Bronze
2005/ 2006	JPN Tokyo	RUS Tatiana Navka & Roman Kostomarov	UKR Elena Grushina & Ruslan Goncharov	CAN Marie-FRA Dubreuil & Patrice Lauzon
2006/ 2007	RUS Saint Petersburg	BUL Albena Denkova & Maxim Staviski	CAN Marie-FRA Dubreuil & Patrice Lauzon	RUS Oksana Domnina & Maxim Shabalin
2007/ 2008	ITA Turin	RUS Oksana Domnina & Maxim Shabalin	USA Tanith Belbin & Benjamin Agosto	FRA Isabelle Delobel & Olivier Schoenfelder
2008/ 2009	KOR Goyang	FRA Isabelle Delobel & Olivier Schoenfelder	RUS Oksana Domnina & Maxim Shabalin	USA Meryl Davis & Charlie White
2009/ 2010	JPN Tokyo	USA Meryl Davis & Charlie White	CAN Tessa Virtue & Scott Moir	FRA Nathalie Péchalat & Fabian Bourzat
2010/ 2011	CHN Beijing	USA Meryl Davis & Charlie White	FRA Nathalie Péchalat & Fabian Bourzat	CAN Vanessa Crone & Paul Poirier
2011/ 2012	CAN Quebec City	USA Meryl Davis & Charlie White	CAN Tessa Virtue & Scott Moir	FRA Nathalie Péchalat & Fabian Bourzat
2012/ 2013	RUS Sochi	USA Meryl Davis & Charlie White	CAN Tessa Virtue & Scott Moir	FRA Nathalie Péchalat & Fabian Bourzat
2013/ 2014	JPN Fukuoka	USA Meryl Davis & Charlie White	CAN Tessa Virtue & Scott Moir	FRA Nathalie Péchalat & Fabian Bourzat
2014/ 2015	ESP Barcelona	CAN Kaitlyn Weaver & Andrew Poje	USA Madison Chock & Evan Bates	FRA Gabriella Papadakis & Guillaume Cizeron
2015/ 2016	ESP Barcelona	CAN Kaitlyn Weaver & Andrew Poje	USA Madison Chock & Evan Bates	ITA Anna Cappellini & Luca Lanotte
2016/ 2017	FRA Marseille	CAN Tessa Virtue & Scott Moir	FRA Gabriella Papadakis & Guillaume Cizeron	USA Maia Shibutani & Alex Shibutani

ISU Challenger Series

Above: **Matteo Guarise** and **Nicole Della Monica** are Italian pairs skaters who have won numerous medals in the ISU Challenger Series, (most recently the silver medal in the Finlandia Trophy, [see page 223]). They are also 2-time gold medallists and 3-time silver medallists in the Italian National Championships.

The ISU Challenger Series was created by the International Skating Union as a group of senior-level events ranking below the ISU Grand Prix of Figure Skating series. The ISU Council established the series in 2014, incorporating ten separate events across North America and Europe. The three of those competitions included in this book....**The Nebelhorn Trophy**, the **Ondrej Nepela Memorial**, and the **Finlandia Trophy** ... are considered to be amongst the core group events of the ISU Challenger Series.

Nebelhorn Trophy

The Nebelhorn Trophy is a competition organized by the Deutsche Eislauf-Union, (the German Ice Skating Union) and held annually in Oberstdorf, Germany. It gets its name from the Nebelhorn, a 7,297 ft mountain in the Allgäu Alps that is close by village of Oberstdorf. Held annually since 1969, it became part of the ISU Challenger Series in the 2014–15 season.

Nebelhorn Trophy - MEN

Year	Gold	Silver	Bronze
1969	AUT Günter Anderl		
1970	FRG Klaus Grimmelt		
1971	FRG Erich Reifschneider		
1972	USA Robert Bradshaw		
1973	USA John Carlow	USA Charles Tickner	LUX Paul Cechmanek
1974	USA David Santee	CAN Kevin Robertson	LUX Paul Cechmanek

Year	Gold	Silver	Bronze
1975	CAN Ted Barton	USA Ken Newfield	FRG Harald Kuhn
1976	JPN Fumio Igarashi	USA Scott Hamilton	FRG Rudi Cerne
1977	USA Robert Wagenhoffer	FRG Kurt Kurzinger	FRG Gerd-Walter Gräbner
1978	USA Allen Schramm	USA Mark Cockerell	CAN Gary Beacom
1979	CAN Gordon Forbes	URS Vladimir Rashchetnov	USA Brian Boitano
1980	USA Tom Dickson	CAN Brian Orser	FRG Rudi Cerne
1981	FRG Heiko Fischer	USA John Filbig	CAN Kevin Hicks
1982	FRG Leonardo Azzola	ITA Bruno Delmaestro	USA James Cygan
1983	FRG Heiko Fischer	FRG Richard Zander	CAN André Bourgeois
1984	FRG Richard Zander	USA Craig Henderson	URS Leonid Kaznakov
1985	FRG Richard Zander	USA Douglas Mattis	FRA Laurent Depouilly
1986	URS Vitali Egorov	USA Erik Larson	CAN Kurt Browning
1987	USA Todd Eldredge	USA Patrick Brault	DEN Lars Dresler
1988	USA Aren Nielsen	CAN Marcus Christensen	USA Christopher Mitchell
1989	USA Shepherd Clark	FRG Richard Zander	URS Gleb Bokii
1990	USA Michael Chack	FRA Nicolas Pétorin	URS Vladimir Petrenko
1991	USA Ryan Hunka	FRA Nicolas Pétorin	URS Vladimir Petrenko
1992	TPE David Liu	RUS Igor Pashkevich	FRA Axel Médéric
1993	CAN Jeffrey Langdon	USA Michael Weiss	CAN Jean-François Hébert

Year	Gold	Silver	Bronze
1994	RUS Ilia Kulik	USA Shepherd Clark	RUS Alexander Abt
1995	JPN Takeshi Honda	UKR Evgeni Pliuta	JPN Yosuke Takeuchi
1996	USA Michael Weiss	JPN Yamato Tamura	RUS Igor Sinyutin
1997	USA Timothy Goebel	UKR Evgeni Pliuta	RUS Alexander Abt
1998	USA Trifun Zivanovic	UKR Yevgeny Martynov	UKR Vitali Danilchenko
1999	RUS Ilia Klimkin	UKR Vitali Danilchenko	CAN Jayson Dénommée
2000	RUS Anton Klykov	USA Derrick Delmore	UKR Dmitri Dmitrenko
2001	BLR Sergei Davydov	CAN Jeffrey Buttle	EST Margus Hernits
2002	BLR Sergei Davydov	USA Benjamin Miller	CAN Fedor Andreev
2003	CAN Nicholas Young	USA Scott Smith	USA Nicholas LaRoche
2004	CAN Marc-André Craig	RUS Alexander Kondakov	USA Christopher Toland
2005	GER Stefan Lindemann	JPN Noriyuki Kanzaki	CZE Tomáš Verner
2006	CZE Tomáš Verner	USA Parker Pennington	CAN Vaughn Chipeur
2007	CZE Michal Březina	USA Shaun Rogers	CZE Tomáš Verner
2008	JPN Nobunari Oda	CZE Michal Březina	FRA Yannick Ponsero
2009	SUI Stéphane Lambiel	RUS Ivan Tretiakov	CZE Michal Březina
2010	JPN Tatsuki Machida	RUS Konstantin Menshov	GER Peter Liebers

Year	Gold	Silver	Bronze
2011	JPN Yuzuru Hanyu	CZE Michal Březina	USA Stephen Carriere
2012	JPN Nobunari Oda	RUS Konstantin Menshov	USA Keegan Messing
2013	JPN Nobunari Oda	USA Jason Brown	CAN Jeremy Ten
2014	USA Jason Brown	CZE Michal Březina	RUS Konstantin Menshov
2015	CAN Elladj Baldé	USA Max Aaron	RUS Konstantin Menshov
2016	RUS Alexander Petrov	BEL Jorik Hendrickx	USA Grant Hochstein
2017	BEL Jorik Hendrickx	USA Alexander Johnson	SWE Alexander Majorov

Nebelhorn Trophy - PAIRS

Year	Gold	Silver	Bronze
1969	FRG Frigge Drzymalla & Michael Weingart		
1970	FRG Almut Lehmann & Herbert Wiesinger		
1971	NO PAIRS	COMPETITION	THIS YEAR
1972	USA Cozette Cady & Jack Courtney		
1973	USA Tai Babilonia & Randy Gardner	FRG Corinna Halke & Eberhard Rausch	AUT Ursula Nemec & Michael Nemec
1974	CAN Kathy Huntchinson & Jamie McGregor	CAN Candace Jones & Don Fraser	AUT Ulrike Wrbik & Richard Scharf
1975	CAN Cheri Pinner & Dennis Pinner	USA Alice Cook & William Fauver	CAN Karen Newton & Glenn Laframboise

Year	Gold	Silver	Bronze
1976	FRG Susanne Scheibe & Andreas Nischwitz	FRG Rafaela Dondoni & Mario Dondoni	JPN Natsuko Hagiwara & Sumio Murata
1977	USA Gail Hamula & Frank Sweiding	USA Sheryl Franks & Michael Botticelli	GER Susanne Scheibe & Andreas Nischwitz
1978	CAN Barbara Underhill & Paul Martini	USA Maria di Domenico & Larry Schrier	USA Tracy Prussack & Scott Prussack
1979	USA Caitlin Carruthers & Peter Carruthers	URS Zhanna Ilina & Alexander Vlassov	CAN Becky Gough & Mark Rowsom
1980	United Kingdom Susan Garland & Robert Daw	CAN Mary Jo Fedy & Tim Mills	USA Dana Graham & Paul Wylie
1981	URS Elena Valova & Oleg Vasiliev	CAN Melinda Kunhegyi & Lyndon Johnston	FRA Nathalie Tortel & Xavier Videau
1982	URS Inna Volianskaya & Valeri Spiridonov	CAN Katherina Matousek & Lloyd Eisler	USA Natalie Seybold & Wayne Seybold
1983	URS Inna Bekker & Sergei Likhanski	USA Katy Keely & Gary Kemp	CAN Laurene Collin & David Howe
1984	URS Elena Bechke & Valeri Kornienko	USA Susan Dungjen & Jason Dungjen	USA Margo Shoup & Patrick Page
1985	URS Ludmila Koblova & Andrei Kalitin	USA Maria Lako & Michael Blicharski	United Kingdom Lisa Cushley & Neil Cushley
1986	CAN Melanie Gaylor & Lee Barkell	USA Ashley Stevenson & Scott Wendland	United Kingdom Lisa Cushley & Neil Cushley
1987	CAN Michelle Menzies & Kevin Wheeler	URS Elena Kvitchenko & Rashid Kadyrkaev	CAN Twana Rose & Colin Epp

Year	Gold	Silver	Bronze
1988	CAN Cindy Landry & Lyndon Johnston	URS Ekaterina Murugova & Artem Torgashev	USA Kenna Bailey & John Denton
1989	URS Elena Leonova & Gennadi Krasnitski	URS Evgenia Shishkova & Vadim Naumov	CZE Radka Kovaříková & René Novotný
1990	CAN Stacey Ball & Kris Wirtz	URS Natalia Krestianinova & Alexei Torchinski	CAN Penny Papaioannou & Raoul LeBlanc
1991	CAN Sherry Ball & Kris Wirtz	URS Natalia Krestianinova & Alexei Torchinski	CAN Penny Papaioannou & Raoul LeBlanc
1992	RUS Svetlana Titkova & Oleg Makhutov	CAN Tiina Muur & Cory Watson	CAN Jodeyne Higgins & Sean Rice
1993	CAN Caroline Haddad & Jean-Sébastien Fecteau	LAT Elena Berezhnaya & Oleg Shliakhov	USA Stephanie Stiegler & Lance Travis
1994	CAN Marie-Claude Savard-Gagnon & Luc Bradet	FRA Line Haddad & Sylvain Privé	FRA Sarah Abitbol & Stéphane Bernadis
1995	USA Shelby Lyons & Brian Wells	UKR Olena Bilousivska & Serhiy Potalov	KAZ Marina Khalturina & Andrei Krukov
1996	USA Danielle Hartsell & Steve Hartsell	RUS Olga Semkina & Andrei Chuvilaev	CAN Samanta Marchant & Chad Hawse
1997	UKR Evgenia Filonenko & Igor Marchenko	UKR Olena Bilousivska & Stanislav Morozov	USA Natalie Vlandis & Jered Guzman
1998	USA Laura Handy & Paul Binnebose	CAN Jacinthe Larivière & Lenny Faustino	RUS Milica Brozovich & Anton Nimenko
1999	UKR Aliona Savchenko & Stanislav Morozov	CAN Jacinthe Larivière & Lenny Faustino	UKR Julia Obertas & Dmitri Palamarchuk

Year	Gold	Silver	Bronze
2000	CAN Valérie Marcoux & Bruno Marcotte	USA Amanda Magarian & Jered Guzman	USA Stephanie Kalesavich & Aaron Parchem
2001	CAN Jacinthe Larivière & Lenny Faustino	CAN Valerie Saurette & Jean-Sébastien Fecteau	USA Laura Handy & Jonathon Hunt
2002	CAN Valérie Marcoux & Craig Buntin	RUS Julia Obertas & Alexei Sokolov	USA Kathryn Orscher & Garrett Lucash
2003	CAN Utako Wakamatsu & Jean Sebastian Fecteau	CAN Pascale Bergeron & Robert Davison	USA Laura Handy & Jeremy Allen
2004	USA Marcy Hinzmann & Aaron Parchem	CAN Pascale Bergeron & Robert Davison	GER Aliona Savchenko & Robin Szolkowy
2005	GER Aliona Savchenko & Robin Szolkowy	CAN Meagan Duhamel & Ryan Arnold	USA Marcy Hinzmann & Aaron Parchem
2006	USA Brooke Castile & Benjamin Okolski	USA Julia Vlassov & Drew Meekins	SWE Angelika Pylkina & Niklas Hogner
2007	GER Aliona Savchenko & Robin Szolkowy	CAN Meagan Duhamel & Craig Buntin	USA Amanda Evora & Mark Ladwig
2008	GER Aliona Savchenko & Robin Szolkowy	RUS Maria Mukhortova & Maxim Trankov	UKR Tatiana Volosozhar & Stanislav Morozov
2009	GER Aliona Savchenko & Robin Szolkowy	UKR Tatiana Volosozhar & Stanislav Morozov	CAN Anabelle Langlois & Cody Hay
2010	RUS Vera Bazarova & Yuri Larionov	ITA Stefania Berton & Ondřej Hotárek	CAN Meagan Duhamel & Eric Radford
2011	RUS Tatiana Volosozhar & Maxim Trankov	RUS Vera Bazarova & Yuri Larionov	USA Caydee Denney & John Coughlin

Year	Gold	Silver	Bronze
2012	RUS Tatiana Volosozhar & Maxim Trankov	USA Caydee Denney & John Coughlin	FRA Vanessa James & Morgan Ciprès
2013	RUS Tatiana Volosozhar & Maxim Trankov	GER Maylin Wende & Daniel Wende	GER Mari Vartmann & Aaron Van Cleave
2014	RUS Yuko Kavaguti & Alexander Smirnov	RUS Evgenia Tarasova & Vladimir Morozov	USA Alexa Scimeca & Chris Knierim
2015	RUS Tatiana Volosozhar & Maxim Trankov	USA Alexa Scimeca & Chris Knierim	FRA Vanessa James & Morgan Ciprès
2016	GER Aliona Savchenko / & Bruno Massot	CAN Lubov Ilyushechkina & Dylan Moscovitch	GER Mari Vartmann & Ruben Blommaert
2017	RUS Evgenia Tarasova & Vladimir Morozov	GER Aliona Savchenko & Bruno Massot	AUS Ekaterina Alexandrovskaya & Harley Windsor

Nebelhorn Trophy - LADIES

Year	Gold	Silver	Bronze
1969	CZE Ľudmila Bezáková		
1970	GBR Rita Pokorski		
1971	USA Dorothy Hamill		
1972	USA Wendy Burge		
1973	USA Kath Malmberg	USA Linda Fratianne	FRG Gerti Schanderl
1974	USA Priscilla Hill	USA Barbara Smith	FRG Petra Wagner
1975	USA Lisa-Marie Allen	FRG Petra Wagner	FRG Dagmar Lurz
1976	FRG Garnet Ostermeier	USA Carrie Rugh	CAN Deborah Albright

Year	Gold	Silver	Bronze
1977	JPN Reiko Kobayashi	USA Sandy Lenz	FRG Karin Riediger
1978	USA Editha Dotson	FRG Corinna Tanski	CAN Janet Morrissey
1979	USA Lynn Smith	USA Jackie Farrell	FRG Karin Riediger
1980	USA Vikki de Vries	United Kingdom Alison Southwood	CAN Elizabeth Manley
1981	FRG Cornelia Tesch	USA Kristy Hogan	USA Stephanie Anderson
1982	FRG Manuela Ruben	USA Kelley Webster	URS Natalia Ovchinnikova
1983	USA Staci McMullin	CAN Barbara Butler	ITA Karin Telser
1984	USA Debi Thomas	JPN Juri Ozawa	USA Sara MacInnes
1985	FRG Cornelia Tesch	USA Tracey Damigella	United Kingdom Joanne Conway
1986	USA Holly Cook	FRG Cornelia Renner	SUI Claudia Villiger
1987	CAN Shannon Allison	FRG Carola Wolff	CAN Lindsay Fedosoff
1988	USA Tonia Kwiatkowski	CAN Josée Chouinard	FRG Patricia Neske
1989	USA Kyoko Ina	FRA Surya Bonaly	JPN Junko Yaginuma
1990	FRA Surya Bonaly	FRG Marina Kielmann	URS Maria Butyrskaya
1991	JPN Kumiko Koiwai	FRG Marina Kielmann	URS Maria Butyrskaya
1992	GER Simone Lang	JPN Kumiko Koiwai	CAN Angela Derochie
1993	RUS Irina Slutskaya	CAN Susan Humphreys	UKR Lyudmyla Ivanova
1994	RUS Irina Slutskaya	JPN Shizuka Arakawa	USA Jennifer Karl
1995	JPN Shizuka Arakawa	CZE Lenka Kulovaná	RUS Elena Ivanova
1996	GER Eva-Maria Fitze	USA Sydne Vogel	USA Karen Kwan
1997	UKR Elena Liashenko	RUS Olga Markova	RUS Nadezhda Kanaeva
1998	USA Brittney McConn	RUS Elena Ivanova	CZE Veronika Dytrtová
1999	UKR Elena Liashenko	FIN Sanna-Maija Wiksten	FIN Elina Kettunen
2000	UKR Galina Maniachenko	SUI Sarah Meier	USA Andrea Gardiner

Year	Gold	Silver	Bronze
2001	RUS Ludmila Nelidina	USA Ann Patrice McDonough	RUS Kristina Oblasova
2002	ITA Carolina Kostner	FIN Alisa Drei	RUS Ludmila Nelidina
2003	USA Jennifer Don	CAN Lesley Hawker	RUS Olga Naidenova
2004	USA Louann Donovan	FIN Alisa Drei	CAN Mira Leung
2005	RUS Elena Sokolova	FIN Alisa Drei	USA Beatrisa Liang
2006	USA Beatrisa Liang	RUS Arina Martinova	USA Katy Taylor
2007	ITA Carolina Kostner	USA Megan Williams Stewart	FIN Laura Lepistö
2008	USA Alissa Czisny	FIN Laura Lepistö	JPN Akiko Suzuki
2009	USA Alissa Czisny	FIN Kiira Korpi	CHN Liu Yan
2010	FIN Kiira Korpi	SWE Viktoria Helgesson	USA Melissa Bulanhagui
2011	USA Mirai Nagasu	GEO Elene Gedevanishvili	SWE Joshi Helgesson
2012	CAN Kaetlyn Osmond	RUS Adelina Sotnikova	JPN Haruka Imai
2013	RUS Elena Radionova	JPN Miki Ando	USA Ashley Cain
2014	RUS Elizaveta Tuktamysheva	RUS Alena Leonova	USA Gracie Gold
2015	CAN Kaetlyn Osmond	RUS Alena Leonova	USA Courtney Hicks
2016	JPN Mai Mihara	RUS Elizaveta Tuktamysheva	CAN Gabrielle Daleman
2017	AUS Kailani Craine	SWE Matilda Algotsson	SUI Alexia Paganini

Nebelhorn Trophy - ICE DANCING

Year	Gold	Silver	Bronze
1970	FRG Angelika Buck & Erich Buck	GBR Kay Webster & Malcolm Taylor	
1971	FRG Angelika Buck & Erich Buck		

Year	Gold	Silver	Bronze
1972	USA Mary-Karen Campell & Johnny Johns		
1973	GBR Rosalind Druce & David Barker	Janet ? & Warren ?	Jane ? & Richard ?
1974	USA Judi Genovesi & Kent Weigle	GBR Odette Tolman & Trevor Davies	GBR Jennifer Thompson & Derek Tyers
1975	CAN Lorna Wighton & John Dowding	URS Elena Garanina & Igor Zavozin	URS Marina Zueva & Andrei Vitman
1976	URS Marina Zueva & Andrei Vitman	GBR Jayne Torvill & Christopher Dean	GBR Carol Long & Philip Stowell
1977	GBR Jayne Torvill & Christopher Dean	USA Carol Fox & Richard Dalley	GBR Wendy Sessions & Marc Reed
1978	URS Elena Garanina & Igor Zavozin	USA Kim Krohn & Barry Hagan	CAN Joanne French & John Thomas
1979	CAN Gina Aucoin & Hans-Peter Ponikau	GBR Carol Long & John Philpot	URS Tatiana Durasova & Sergei Ponomarenko
1980	GBR Wendy Sessions & Stephen Williams	FRG Birgit Goller & Peter Klisch	USA Susan Marie Dymecki & Anthony Bardin
1981	GBR Karen Roughton & Marc Reed	FRG Birgit Goller & Peter Klisch	USA Janice Kindrachuk & Blake Hobson
1982	URS Marina Klimova & Sergei Ponomarenko	CAN Isabelle Duchesnay & Paul Duchesnay	FRG Antonia Becherer & Ferdinand Becherer

Year	Gold	Silver	Bronze
1983	URS Marina Klimova & Sergei Ponomarenko	USA Eleanor DeVera & James Yorke	FRG Antonia Becherer & Ferdinand Becherer
1984	USA Lois Luciani & Russ Witherby	URS Irina Zhuk & Oleg Petrov	USA Kristan Lowery & Chip Rossbach
1985	URS Maya Usova & Alexander Zhulin	FRG Antonia Becherer & Ferdinand Becherer	FRA Doriane Bontemps & Charles Paliard
1986	FRG Antonia Becherer & Ferdinand Becherer	URS Svetlana Liapina & Gorsha Sur	CAN Michelle McDonald & Michael Farrington
1987	URS Ilona Melnichenko & Gennadi Kaskov	ITA Stefania Calegari & Pasquale Camerlengo	USA Dorothi Rodek & Robert Nardozza
1988	URS Ilona Melnichenko & Gennadi Kaskov	USA Elizabeth McLean & Ari Lieb	CAN Jacqueline Petr & Mark Janoschak
1989	FRA Isabelle Sarech & Xavier Debernis	USA Lisa Grove & Scott Myers	FRA Dominique Yvon & Frédéric Palluel
1990	CAN Isabelle Labossiere & Mitchell Gould	GBR Lisa Bradby & Alan Towers	FRA Christelle Descolis & Ludovic Deville
1991	URS Irina Lobacheva & Alexei Pospelov	GBR Lisa Bradby & Alan Towers	FRA Christelle Descolis & Ludovic Deville
1992	CAN Shae-Lynn Bourne & Victor Kraatz	RUS Olga Ganicheva & Maxim Kachanov	LTU Margarita Drobiazko & Povilas Vanagas
1993	CAN Martine Patenaude & Eric Massé	USA Rachel Mayer & Peter Breen	LTU Margarita Drobiazko & Povilas Vanagas

Year	Gold	Silver	Bronze
1994	FRA Barbara Piton & Alexandre Piton	UKR Elena Grushina & Ruslan Goncharov	CAN Chantal Lefebvre & Patrice Lauzon
1995	RUS Olga Sharutenko & Dmitri Naumkin	POL Iwona Filipowicz & Michal Szumski	FRA Agnes Jacquemard & Alexis Gayet
1996	RUS Ekaterina Svirina & Vladimir Leliukh	USA Eve Chalom & Mathew Gates	FRA Isabelle Delobel & Olivier Schoenfelder
1997	RUS Olga Sharutenko & Dmitri Naumkin	RUS Nina Ulanova & Mikhail Stifounin	BUL Albena Denkova & Maxim Staviski
1998	RUS Nina Ulanova & Mikhail Stifounin	USA Debbie Koegel & Oleg Fediukov	FRA Alia Ouabdelsselam & Benjamin Delmas
1999	USA Jamie Silverstein & Justin Pekarek	FRA Alia Ouabdelsselam & Benjamin Delmas	GER Stephanie Rauer & Thomas Rauer
2000	CAN Chantal Lefebvre & Justin Lanning	FRA Magali Sauri & Michail Stifunin	GBR Marika Humphreys & Vitali Baranov
2001	POL Sylwia Nowak & Sebastian Kolasiński	ITA Federica Faiella & Massimo Scali	RUS Anastasia Belova & Ilia Isaev
2002	ITA Federica Faiella & Massimo Scali	USA Melissa Gregory & Denis Petukhov	RUS Anastasia Belova & Ilia Isaev
2003	RUS Svetlana Kulikova & Vitali Novikov	RUS Jana Khokhlova & Sergei Novitski	USA Christie Moxley & Alexander Kirsanov
2004	USA Lydia Manon & Ryan O'Meara	CAN Martine Patinaude & Pascal Denis	GBR Phillipa Towler-Green & Phillip Poole
2005	USA Tanith Belbin & Benjamin Agosto	LTU Margarita Drobiazko & Povilas Vanagas	GER Christina Beier & William Beier

Year	Gold	Silver	Bronze
2006	GBR Sinead Kerr & John Kerr	USA Morgan Matthews & Maxim Zavozin	ISR Alexandra Zaretsky & Roman Zaretsky
2007	USA Jennifer Wester & Daniil Barantsev	GER Christina Beier & William Beier	UKR Alla Beknazarova & Vladimir Zuev
2008	USA Emily Samuelson & Evan Bates	ISR Alexandra Zaretsky & Roman Zaretsky	USA Jane Summersett & Todd Gilles
2009	USA Meryl Davis & Charlie White	ISR Alexandra Zaretski & Roman Zaretski	LTU Katherine Copely & Deividas Stagniūnas
2010	FRA Nathalie Péchalat & Fabian Bourzat	ITA Anna Cappellini & Luca Lanotte	RUS Ekaterina Riazanova & Ilia Tkachenko
2011	USA Madison Hubbell & Zachary Donohue	GER Nelli Zhiganshina & Alexander Gazsi	CAN Kharis Ralph & Asher Hill
2012	USA Madison Chock & Evan Bates	AZE Julia Zlobina & Alexei Sitnikov	GER Nelli Zhiganshina & Alexander Gazsi
2013	USA Madison Hubbell & Zachary Donohue	RUS Ksenia Monko & Kirill Khaliavin	CAN Alexandra Paul & Mitchell Islam
2014	CAN Kaitlyn Weaver & Andrew Poje	USA Madison Chock & Evan Bates	GER Nelli Zhiganshina & Alexander Gazsi
2015	USA Madison Chock & Evan Bates	CAN Alexandra Paul & Mitchell Islam	USA Anastasia Cannuscio & Colin McManus
2016	ITA Anna Cappellini & Luca Lanotte	USA Madison Chock & Evan Bates	CAN Piper Gilles & Paul Poirier
2017	GBR Penny Coomes & Nicholas Buckland	JPN Kana Muramoto & Chris Reed	GER Kavita Lorenz & Joti Polizoakis

Ondrej Nepela Memorial

The Ondrej Nepela Memorial (called the Ondrej Nepela Trophy from 2013 through 2015), is an annual competition that takes place in Slovakia that originated in 1993. It gets its name from 1972 Olympic champion Ondrej Nepela, (January 22, 1951 – February 2, 1989), a Slovak figure skater who represented Czechoslovakia. He was the 1972 men's Olympic champion, a three-time World champion (1971–73), and a five-time European champion (1969–73). Later in his career, he performed professionally and became a coach.

The competition has taken place every year in Bratislava, capital of Slovakia, except for 2009 when it rook place in Piešťany. It was incorporated into the ISU Challenger Series in the 2014–15 season.

Ondrej Nepela Memorial - MEN

Year	Gold	Silver	Bronze
1993	ISR Michael Shmerkin	HUN Zsolt Kerekes	
1994	HUN Zsolt Kerekes		
1995	FRA Stanick Jeannette		
1996	RUS Roman Serov	AUS Anthony Liu	USA Matthew Kessinger
1997	AUS Anthony Liu	EST Alexei Kozlov	LUX Patrick Schmit
1998	FRA Laurent Tobel	CAN Jayson Dénommée	UKR Evgeni Pliuta
1999	FRA Thierry Cerez	FRA Stanick Jeannette	FRA Frédéric Dambier
2000	FRA Vincent Restencourt	UKR Dmitri Dmitrenko	GER Silvio Smalun
2001	RUS Stanislav Timchenko	SVK Róbert Kažimír	UKR Vitali Danilchenko
2002	SUI Stéphane Lambiel	GER Stefan Lindemann	SLO Gregor Urbas
2003	BUL Naiden Borichev	GER Stefan Lindemann	ITA Karel Zelenka
2004	GER Stefan Lindemann	BEL Kevin van der Perren	GBR Tristan Cousins

Year	Gold	Silver	Bronze
2005	USA Scott Smith	BEL Kevin van der Perren	CZE Tomáš Verner
2006	SLO Gregor Urbas	USA Jordan Miller	SVK Igor Macypura
2007	BEL Kevin van der Perren	USA Nicholas LaRoche	SLO Gregor Urbas
2008	JPN Kensuke Nakaniwa	ITA Paolo Bacchini	SUI Jamal Othman
2009	JPN Kensuke Nakaniwa	AUT Viktor Pfeifer	SUI Jamal Othman
2010	JPN Akio Sasaki	MON Kim Lucine	UKR Anton Kovalevski
2011	JPN Daisuke Murakami	BEL Kevin van der Perren	ITA Samuel Contesti
2012	JPN Tatsuki Machida	JPN Daisuke Murakami	CZE Tomáš Verner
2013	CZE Tomáš Verner	JPN Takahito Mura	GER Peter Liebers
2014	USA Stephen Carriere	South KOR Kim Jin-seo	RUS Gordei Gorshkov
2015	USA Jason Brown	RUS Mikhail Kolyada	RUS Gordei Gorshkov
2016	RUS Sergei Voronov	CAN Kevin Reynolds	RUS Roman Savosin
2017	RUS Mikhail Kolyada	RUS Sergei Voronov	AUS Brendan Kerry

Ondrej Nepela Memorial - PAIRS

Year	Gold	Silver	Bronze
1993 1994 1995	NO PAIRS	COMPETITION	THESE YEARS
1996	RUS Viktoria Maxiuta & Vladislav Zhovnirsky	USA Naomi Grabow & Benjamin Oberman	CZE Veronika Joukalová & Otto Dlabola
1997	POL Dorota Zagórska & Mariusz Siudek	CZE Kateřina Beránková & Otto Dlabola	ARM Maria Krasiltseva & Alexander Chestnikh
1998	CZE Kateřina Beránková & Otto Dlabola	SVK Oľga Beständigová & Jozef Beständig	BLR Katsjarina Danko & Henadzi Yemelyanenko

Year	Gold	Silver	Bronze
1999	RUS Viktoria Maxiuta & Vitali Dubin	*No other competitors*	*No other competitors*
2000	POL Dorota Zagórska & Mariusz Siudek	SVK Diana Riskova & Vladimir Futas	USA Jessica Miller & Jeffrey Weiss
2001	SVK Oľga Beständigová & Jozef Beständig	ITA Michela Cobisi & Ruben De Pra	CZE Michaela Krutská & Marek Sedlmajer
2002	SVK Maria Guerassimenko & Vladimir Futas	CZE Andrea Vargová & Marek Sedlmajer	*No other competitors*
2003	NO PAIRS	COMPETITION	THIS YEAR
2004	GER Aliona Savchenko & Robin Szolkowy	SVK Meliza Brozovich & Vladimir Futas	*No other competitors*
2005 2006	NO PAIRS	COMPETITION	THESE YEARS
2007	CAN Mylène Brodeur & John Mattatall	CAN Becky Cosford & Brian Shales	*No other competitors*
2008	NO PAIRS	COMPETITION	THIS YEAR
2009	GER Maylin Hausch & Daniel Wende	RUS Ekaterina Sheremeti- eva & Egor Chudin	GRE Jessica Crenshaw & Chad Tsagris
2010	NO PAIRS	COMPETITION	THIS YEAR
2011	RUS Tatiana Volosozhar & Maxim Trankov	ITA Stefania Berton & Ondřej Hotárek	RUS Lubov Iliushechkina & Nodari Maisuradze
2012	RUS Anastasia Martiusheva & Alexei Rogonov	ITA Stefania Berton & Ondřej Hotárek	ITA Nicole Della Monica & Matteo Guarise
2013	USA Gretchen Donlan & Andrew Speroff	RUS Anastasia Martiusheva & Alexei Rogonov	USA Alexa Scimeca & Chris Knierim

Year	Gold	Silver	Bronze
2014	NO PAIRS	COMPETITION	THIS YEAR
2015	RUS Ksenia Stolbova & Fedor Klimov	RUS Kristina Astakhova & Alexei Rogonov	RUS Evgenia Tarasova & Vladimir Morozov
2016	RUS Evgenia Tarasova & Vladimir Morozov	RUS Yuko Kavaguti & Alexander Smirnov	RUS Natalja Zabijako & Alexander Enbert
2017	RUS Natalja Zabijako & Alexander Enbert	RUS Kristina Astakhova & Alexei Rogonov	RUS Alisa Efimova & Alexander Korovin

Ondrej Nepela Memorial - LADIES

Year	Gold	Silver	Bronze
1993	SLO Mojca Kopač		
1994	CZE Irena Zemanová		
1995	HUN Krisztina Czakó	FRA Vanessa Gusmeroli	AUT Julia Lautowa
1996	RUS Svetlana Bukareva	BUL Tsvetelina Abrasheva	USA Angela Nikodinov
1997	POL Sabina Wojtala	SLO Mojca Kopač	RUS Tatiana Plusheva
1998	SVK Zuzana Paurova	SLO Mojca Kopač	GER Christina Reidel
1999		POL Sabina Wojtala	GER Nina Sackerer
2000	UKR Galina Maniachenko	USA Amber Corwin	POL Sabina Wojtala
2001	HUN Júlia Sebestyén	AUT Julia Lautowa	SLO Mojca Kopač
2002	ITA Carolina Kostner	SUI Sarah Meier	HUN Júlia Sebestyén
2003	UKR Galina Maniachenko	HUN Júlia Sebestyén	AUT Julia Lautowa
2004	HUN Viktória Pavuk	GBR Jenna McCorkell	SVK Zuzana Babiaková
2005	HUN Júlia Sebestyén	USA Alissa Czisny	USA Amber Corwin
2006	USA Megan Williams-Stewart	HUN Júlia Sebestyén	SVK Ivana Reitmayerová

Year	Gold	Silver	Bronze
2007	HUN Júlia Sebestyén	USA Michelle Boulos	GBR Jenna McCorkell
2008	SVK Ivana Reitmayerová	TUR Tuğba Karademir	GER Sarah Hecken
2009	JPN Mutsumi Takayama	AUT Kerstin Frank	BEL Isabelle Pieman
2010	JPN Haruka Imai	ITA Valentina Marchei	SLO Patricia Glescic
2011	FRA Maé Bérénice Méité	JPN Shoko Ishikawa	FRA Léna Marrocco
2012	GBR Jenna McCorkell	SVK Monika Simančíková	CZE Eliška Březinová
2013	JPN Haruka Imai	RUS Nikol Gosviani	USA Christina Gao
2014	ITA Roberta Rodeghiero	SWE Joshi Helgesson	USA Ashley Cain
2015	RUS Evgenia Medvedeva	RUS Anna Pogorilaya	RUS Maria Artemieva
2016	RUS Maria Sotskova	RUS Yulia Lipnitskaya	USA Mariah Bell
2017	RUS Evgenia Medvedeva	JPN Rika Hongo	RUS Elena Radionova

Ondrej Nepela Memorial - ICE DANCING

Year	Gold	Silver	Bronze
1993	FRA Marina Anissina & Gwendal Peizerat		
1994	GBR Lynn Burton & Duncan Lenard		
1995	FRA Marianne Haguenauer & Romain Haguenauer	RUS ? & Rinat Farkhoutdinov	FRA Anne Chaigneau & Olivier Chapuis
1996	HUN Kornelia Barany & Andras Rozsnik		
1997	POL Agata Błażowska & Marcin Kozubek	SVK Zuzana Merzová & Tomáš Morbacher	AUT Angelika Führing & Bruno Ellinger

Year	Gold	Silver	Bronze
1998	SVK Zuzana Merzová & Tomáš Morbacher	SVK Zuzana Ďurkovská & Marián Mesároš	*no other competitors*
1999	POL Agata Błażowska & Marcin Kozubek	CZE Kateřina Kovalová & David Szurman	FRA Nadine Lesaout & Emmanuel Huet
2000	FRA Véronique Delobel & Olivier Chapuis	GBR Pamela O'Connor & Jonathon O'Dougherty	ITA Marta Paoletti & Alessando Italiano
2001	UKR Julia Golovina & Oleg Voiko	CZE Veronika Morávková & Jiří Procházka	FRA Caroline Truong & Sylvain Longchambon
2002	UKR Julia Golovina & Oleg Voiko	CZE Veronika Morávková & Jiří Procházka	GBR Pamela O'Connor & Jonathon O'Dougherty
2003	NO ICE DANCING	COMPETITION	THIS YEAR
2004	UKR Anna Zadorozhniuk & Sergei Verbillo	GBR Phillipa Towler-Green & Phillip Poole	SVK Ivana Dlhopolčeková & Hynek Bílek
2005	UKR Alla Beknazarova & Vladimir Zuev	UZB Olga Akimova & Alexander Shakalov	CZE Kamila Hájková & David Vincour
2006	NO ICE DANCING	COMPETITION	THIS YEAR
2007	FRA Isabelle Delobel & Olivier Schoenfelder	AUT Barbora Silná & Dmitri Matsjuk	ARM Anastasia Grebenkina & Vazgen Azroyan
2008	GER Nelli Zhiganshina & Alexander Gazsi	GER Carolina Hermann & Daniel Hermann	RUS Natalia Mikhailova & Arkadi Sergeev
2009	HUN Nóra Hoffmann & Maxim Zavozin	GER Christina Beier & William Beier	CZE Kamila Hájková & David Vincour
2010	HUN Nóra Hoffmann & Maxim Zavozin	CZE Lucie Myslivečková & Matěj Novák	GER Nelli Zhiganshina & Alexander Gazsi

Year	Gold	Silver	Bronze
2011	GER Nelli Zhiganshina & Alexander Gazsi	ITA Lorenza Alessandrini & Simone Vaturi	AZE Julia Zlobina & Alexei Sitnikov
2012	CAN Kaitlyn Weaver & Andrew Poje	ITA Lorenza Alessandrini & Simone Vaturi	GBR Charlotte Aiken & Josh Whidborne
2013	GBR Penny Coomes & Nicholas Buckland	ITA Charlène Guignard & Marco Fabbri	GER Tanja Kolbe & Stefano Caruso
2014	USA Maia Shibutani & Alex Shibutani	ITA Charlène Guignard & Marco Fabbri	SVK Federica Testa & Lukáš Csölley
2015	CAN Piper Gilles & Paul Poirier	GBR Penny Coomes & Nicholas Buckland	USA Maia Shibutani & Alex Shibutani
2016	RUS Ekaterina Bobrova & Dmitri Soloviev	USA Madison Chock & Evan Bates	RUS Tiffany Zahorski & Jonathan Guerreiro
2017	RUS Ekaterina Bobrova & Dmitri Soloviev	USA Rachel Parsons & Michael Parsons	RUS Betina Popova & Sergey Mozgov

Finlandia Trophy

Held annually in Finland in Helsinki and surrounding areas, The Finlandia Trophy originated in 1995. It was incorporated into the ISU Challenger Series in the 2014–15 season.

Finlandia Trophy - MEN (starts on next page)

Year	Gold	Silver	Bronze
1995	RUS Igor Pashkevich	RUS Ilia Kulik	
1996	USA Shepherd Clark	HUN Szabolcs Vidrai	AUS Anthony Liu
1997	RUS Alexei Yagudin	RUS Oleg Tataurov	RUS Evgeni Plushenko
1998	UKR Dmitri Dmitrenko	AUS Anthony Liu	USA Damon Allen
1999	RUS Roman Serov	RUS Alexei Vasilevski	CAN Jeff Langdon
2000	RUS Evgeni Plushenko	CHN Li Yunfei	FRA Stanick Jeannette
2001	RUS Ilia Klimkin	RUS Roman Serov	ROM Gheorghe Chiper
2002	GER Andrejs Vlascenko	ROM Gheorghe Chiper	RUS Ilia Klimkin
2003	ROM Gheorghe Chiper	USA Johnny Weir	SWE Kristoffer Berntsson
2004	FRA Frédéric Dambier	ISR Roman Serov	CAN Marc-André Craig
2005	*Event cancelled*		
2006	USA Jeremy Abbott	RUS Alexander Uspenski	RUS Sergei Dobrin
2007	CZE Tomáš Verner	USA Parker Pennington	BEL Kevin van der Perren
2008	JPN Takahito Mura	USA Shaun Rogers	RUS Sergei Voronov
2009	JPN Daisuke Takahashi	RUS Sergei Voronov	USA Stephen Carriere
2010	RUS Artur Gachinski	SWE Kristoffer Berntsson	ITA Samuel Contesti
2011	JPN Takahito Mura	USA Douglas Razzano	POL Maciej Cieplucha
2012	JPN Yuzuru Hanyu	USA Richard Dornbush	ESP Javier Fernández
2013	JPN Yuzuru Hanyu	RUS Sergei Voronov	RUS Artur Gachinski
2014	RUS Sergei Voronov	USA Adam Rippon	RUS Alexander Petrov
2015	RUS Konstantin Menshov	USA Adam Rippon	RUS Sergei Voronov
2016	USA Nathan Chen	CAN Patrick Chan	RUS Maxim Kovtun
2017	CHN Jin Boyang	USA Vincent Zhou	USA Adam Rippon

Finlandia Trophy - PAIRS

Year	Gold	Silver	Bronze
1995 - 2001	NO PAIRS COMPETITION HELD THESE YEARS		
2002	UKR Tatiana Chuvaeva & Dmitri Palamarchuk	RUS Viktoria Borzenkova & Andrei Chuvilaev	USA Marcy Hinzmann & Steve Hartsell
2003	CAN Utako Wakamatsu & Jean-Sébastien Fecteau	CAN Pascale Bergeron & Robert Davison	
2004 - 2006	NO PAIRS COMPETITION HELD THESE YEARS		
2007	RUS Maria Mukhortova & Maxim Trankov	USA Andrea Best & Trevor Young	GER Mari Vartmann & Florian Just
2008- 2015	NO PAIRS COMPETITION HELD THESE YEARS		
2016	CAN Meagan Duhamel & Eric Radford	RUS Kristina Astakhova & Alexei Rogonov	GER Mari Vartmann & Ruben Blommaert
2017	CHN Cheng Peng & Yang Jin	ITA Nicole Della Monica & Matteo Guarise	RUS Ksenia Stolbova & Fedor Klimov

Finlandia Trophy - LADIES

Year	Gold	Silver	Bronze
1995	RUS Elena Ivanova	POL Zuzanna Szwed	RUS Elena Sokolova
1996	RUS Maria Butyrskaya	AZE Yulia Vorobieva	RUS Elena Sokolova
1997	RUS Irina Slutskaya	AUT Julia Lautowa	HUN Krisztina Czakó
1998	RUS Elena Sokolova	RUS Viktoria Volchkova	UKR Yulia Lavrenchuk
1999	RUS Elena Sokolova	UKR Elena Liashenko	FRA Laetitia Hubert
2000	RUS Elena Sokolova	UKR Elena Liashenko	FRA Laetitia Hubert
2001	USA Sasha Cohen	FIN Alisa Drei	RUS Viktoria Volchkova

Greg Fox

Year	Gold	Silver	Bronze
2002	FIN Susanna Pöykiö	RUS Tatiana Basova	FIN Alisa Drei
2003	FIN Susanna Pöykiö	FIN Alisa Drei	AUS Miriam Manzano
2004	FIN Susanna Pöykiö	FIN Alisa Drei	FIN Elina Kettunen
2005	*Event cancelled*		
2006	FIN Kiira Korpi	FIN Susanna Pöykiö	HUN Júlia Sebestyén
2007	FIN Jenni Vähämaa	FIN Susanna Pöykiö	ITA Carolina Kostner
2008	JPN Akiko Suzuki	FIN Laura Lepistö	SUI Sarah Meier
2009	RUS Alena Leonova	FIN Laura Lepistö	FIN Kiira Korpi
2010	JPN Akiko Suzuki	FIN Kiira Korpi	RUS Alena Leonova
2011	RUS Sofia Biryukova	EST Jelena Glebova	FIN Alisa Mikonsaari
2012	RUS Yulia Lipnitskaya	FIN Kiira Korpi	USA Mirai Nagasu
2013	RUS Yulia Lipnitskaya	JPN Akiko Suzuki	RUS Elizaveta Tuktamysheva
2014	RUS Elizaveta Tuktamysheva	USA Samantha Cesario	JPN Rika Hongo
2015	JPN Rika Hongo	RUS Yulia Lipnitskaya	SWE Joshi Helgesson
2016	CAN Kaetlyn Osmond	JPN Mao Asada	RUS Anna Pogorilaya
2017	RUS Maria Sotskova	ITA Carolina Kostner	RUS Elizaveta Tuktamysheva

Finlandia Trophy - ICE DANCING

Year	Gold	Silver	Bronze
1995	POL Sylwia Nowak & Sebastian Kolasiński	KAZ Elizaveta Stekolnikova & Dmitri Kazarlyga	
1996	RUS Anna Semenovich & Vladimir Fedorov	RUS Ekaterina Svirina & Vladimir Leliukh	POL Iwona Filipowicz & Michal Szumski

Year	Gold	Silver	Bronze
1997	RUS Anna Semenovich & Vladimir Fedorov	RUS Ekaterina Davydova & Roman Kostomarov	POL Iwona Filipowicz & Michal Szumski
1998	BUL Albena Denkova & Maxim Staviski	RUS Oksana Potdykova & Denis Petukhov	AUT Angelika Führing & Bruno Ellinger
1999	BUL Albena Denkova & Maxim Staviski	ITA Federica Faiella & Luciano Milo	RUS Oksana Potdykova & Denis Petukhov
2000	BUL Albena Denkova & Maxim Staviski	RUS Natalia Romaniuta & Daniil Barantsev	GBR Marika Humphreys & Vitaliy Baranov
2002	NO ICE DANCING	COMPETITION	THIS YEAR
2003	BUL Albena Denkova & Maxim Staviski	RUS Oksana Domnina & Maxim Shabalin	GBR Pamela O'Connor & Jonathon O'Dougherty
2004-2007	NO ICE DANCING	COMPETITION	THESE YEARS
2008	GBR Sinead Kerr & John Kerr	RUS Anastasia Platonova & Alexander Grachev	RUS Kristina Gorshkova & Vitali Butikov
2009	GBR Sinead Kerr & John Kerr	RUS Anastasia Platonova & Alexander Grachev	UKR Alla Beknazarova & Vladimir Zuev
2010	FRA Nathalie Péchalat & Fabian Bourzat	HUN Nóra Hoffmann & Maxim Zavozin	RUS Kristina Gorshkova & Vitali Butikov
2011	CAN Tessa Virtue & Scott Moir	USA Maia Shibutani & Alex Shibutani	USA Madison Chock & Evan Bates
2012	RUS Ekaterina Bobrova & Dmitri Soloviev	ITA Anna Cappellini & Luca Lanotte	USA Madison Hubbell & Zachary Donohue
2013	CAN Tessa Virtue & Scott Moir	USA Madison Chock & Evan Bates	POL Justyna Plutowska & Peter Gerber

Year	Gold	Silver	Bronze
2014	RUS Alexandra Stepanova & Ivan Bukin	GER Nelli Zhiganshina & Alexander Gazsi	USA Anastasia Cannuscio & Colin McManus
2015	CAN Kaitlyn Weaver & Andrew Poje	ISR Isabella Tobias & Ilia Tkachenko	DEN Laurence Fournier Beaudry & Nikolaj Sørensen
2016	RUS Alexandra Stepanova & Ivan Bukin	USA Madison Hubbell & Zachary Donohue	RUS Tiffany Zahorski & Jonathan Guerreiro
2017	FRA Gabriella Papadakis & Guillaume Cizeron	RUS Alexandra Stepanova & Ivan Bukin	DEN Laurence Fournier Beaudry & Nikolaj Sørensen

Four Continents Figure Skating Championships

After 1948, when the European Championships changed their rules to *only* allow skaters representing European countries to compete, there was no competition specifically geared towards non-European skaters. (Although there was a biennial competition called the North American Figure Skating Championships, that existed up until 1971, that allowed for American-Canadian competition). It took almost fifty years, but the situation was rectified in 1999 with the creation of the Four Continents Figure Skating Championships. Open to skaters from Africa, the Americas, Asia and Oceania, the event serves as a counterpoint to the long-running European Figure Skating Championships. Since its inception, four countries, (Canada, China, Japan, and the United States), have prevailed, winning the large majority of medals. But as new figure skating talents emerge all over the world, that may very well change.

Four Continents Figure Skating Championships - MEN

Year	Location	Gold	Silver	Bronze
1999	CAN Halifax	JPN Takeshi Honda	CHN Li Chengjiang	CAN Elvis Stojko
2000	JPN Osaka	CAN Elvis Stojko	CHN Li Chengjiang	CHN Zhang Min
2001	USA Salt Lake City	CHN Li Chengjiang	JPN Takeshi Honda	USA Michael Weiss
2002	KOR Jeonju	CAN Jeffrey Buttle	JPN Takeshi Honda	CHN Gao Song
2003	CHN Beijing	JPN Takeshi Honda	CHN Zhang Min	CHN Li Chengjiang
2004	CAN Hamilton	CAN Jeffrey Buttle	CAN Emanuel Sandhu	USA Evan Lysacek

Year	Location	Gold	Silver	Bronze
2005	KOR Gangneung	USA Evan Lysacek	CHN Li Chengjiang	JPN Daisuke Takahashi
2006	USA Colorado Springs	JPN Nobunari Oda	CAN Christopher Mabee	USA Matthew Savoie
2007	USA Colorado Springs	USA Evan Lysacek	CAN Jeffrey Buttle	USA Jeremy Abbott
2008	KOR Goyang	JPN Daisuke Takahashi	CAN Jeffrey Buttle	USA Evan Lysacek
2009	CAN Vancouver	CAN Patrick Chan	USA Evan Lysacek	JPN Takahiko Kozuka
2010	KOR Jeonju	USA Adam Rippon	JPN Tatsuki Machida	CAN Kevin Reynolds
2011	TPE Taipei	JPN Daisuke Takahashi	JPN Yuzuru Hanyu	USA Jeremy Abbott
2012	USA Colorado Springs	CAN Patrick Chan	JPN Daisuke Takahashi	USA Ross Miner
2013	JPN Osaka	CAN Kevin Reynolds	JPN Yuzuru Hanyu	CHN Yan Han
2014	TPE Taipei	JPN Takahito Mura	JPN Takahiko Kozuka	CHN Song Nan
2015	KOR Seoul	KAZ Denis Ten	USA Joshua Farris	CHN Yan Han
2016	TPE Taipei	CAN Patrick Chan	CHN Jin Boyang	CHN Yan Han

Four Continents Figure Skating Championships - PAIRS

Year	Location	Gold	Silver	Bronze
1999	CAN Halifax	CHN Shen Xue & Zhao Hongbo	CAN Kristy Sargeant & Kris Wirtz	USA Danielle Hartsell & Steve Hartsell
2000	JPN Osaka	CAN Jamie Salé & David Pelletier	USA Kyoko Ina & John Zimmerman	USA Tiffany Scott & Philip Dulebohn
2001	USA Salt Lake City	CAN Jamie Salé & David Pelletier	CHN Shen Xue & Zhao Hongbo	USA Kyoko Ina & John Zimmerman
2002	KOR Jeonju	CHN Pang Qing & Tong Jian	CAN Anabelle Langlois & Patrice Archetto	CHN Zhang Dan & Zhang Hao
2003	CHN Beijing	CHN Shen Xue & Zhao Hongbo	CHN Pang Qing & Tong Jian	CHN Zhang Dan & Zhang Hao
2004	CAN Hamilton	CHN Pang Qing & Tong Jian	CHN Zhang Dan & Zhang Hao	CAN Valérie Marcoux & Craig Buntin
2005	KOR Gangneung	CHN Zhang Dan & Zhang Hao	CHN Pang Qing & Tong Jian	USA Kathryn Orscher & Garrett Lucash
2006	USA Colorado Springs	USA Rena Inoue & John Baldwin	CAN Utako Wakamatsu & Jean-Sébastien Fecteau	CAN Elizabeth Putnam & Sean Wirtz
2007	USA Colorado Springs	CHN Shen Xue & Zhao Hongbo	CHN Pang Qing & Tong Jian	USA Rena Inoue & John Baldwin

Greg Fox

Year	Location	Gold	Silver	Bronze
2008	KOR Goyang	CHN Pang Qing & Tong Jian	CHN Zhang Dan & Zhang Hao	USA Brooke Castile & Benjamin Okolski
2009	CAN Vancouver	CHN Pang Qing & Tong Jian	CAN Jessica Dubé & Bryce Davison	CHN Zhang Dan & Zhang Hao
2010	KOR Jeonju	CHN Zhang Dan & Zhang Hao	USA Keauna McLaughlin & Rockne Brubaker	CAN Meagan Duhamel & Craig Buntin
2011	TPE Taipei	CHN Pang Qing & Tong Jian	CAN Meagan Duhamel & Eric Radford	CAN Paige Lawrence & Rudi Swiegers
2012	USA Colorado Springs	CHN Sui Wenjing & Han Cong	USA Caydee Denney & John Coughlin	USA Mary Beth Marley & Rockne Brubaker
2013	JPN Osaka	CAN Meagan Duhamel & Eric Radford	CAN Kirsten Moore-Towers & Dylan Moscovitch	USA Marissa Castelli & Simon Shnapir
2014	TPE Taipei	CHN Sui Wenjing & Han Cong	USA Tarah Kayne & Daniel O'Shea	USA Alexa Scimeca & Chris Knierim
2015	KOR Seoul	CAN Meagan Duhamel & Eric Radford	CHN Peng Cheng & Zhang Hao	CHN Pang Qing & Tong Jian
2016	TPE Taipei	CHN Sui Wenjing & Han Cong	USA Alexa Scimeca & Chris Knierim	CHN Yu Xiaoyu & Jin Yang

Above: **Ashley Wagner**, American ladies figure skater, won the gold medal at Four Continents in 2012. She was a silver medallist at World Championships in 2016. She has also won a variety of gold, silver & bronze medals at various Grand Prix competitions over the years, including gold at Skate America twice, gold at Trophée Éric Bompard twice, and gold at Skate Canada once. Additionally, she won a bronze medal in the Team event at the 2014 Olympics in Sochi.

Four Continents Figure Skating Championships - LADIES

Year	Location	Gold	Silver	Bronze
1999	CAN Halifax	UZB Tatiana Malinina	USA Amber Corwin	USA Angela Nikodinov
2000	JPN Osaka	USA Angela Nikodinov	USA Stacey Pensgen	CAN Annie Bellemare
2001	USA Salt Lake City	JPN Fumie Suguri	USA Angela Nikodinov	JPN Yoshie Onda
2002	KOR Jeonju	USA Jennifer Kirk	JPN Shizuka Arakawa	JPN Yoshie Onda
2003	CHN Beijing	JPN Fumie Suguri	JPN Shizuka Arakawa	JPN Yukari Nakano
2004	CAN Hamilton	JPN Yukina Ota	CAN Cynthia Phaneuf	USA Amber Corwin
2005	KOR Gangneung	JPN Fumie Suguri	JPN Yoshie Onda	USA Jennifer Kirk
2006	USA Colorado Springs	USA Katy Taylor	JPN Yukari Nakano	USA Beatrisa Liang
2007	USA Colorado Springs	USA Kimmie Meissner	USA Emily Hughes	CAN Joannie Rochette
2008	KOR Goyang	JPN Mao Asada	CAN Joannie Rochette	JPN Miki Ando
2009	CAN Vancouver	KOR Kim Yuna	CAN Joannie Rochette	JPN Mao Asada
2010	KOR Jeonju	JPN Mao Asada	JPN Akiko Suzuki	USA Caroline Zhang
2011	TPE Taipei	JPN Miki Ando	JPN Mao Asada	USA Mirai Nagasu
2012	USA Colorado Springs	USA Ashley Wagner	JPN Mao Asada	USA Caroline Zhang
2013	JPN Osaka	JPN Mao Asada	JPN Akiko Suzuki	JPN Kanako Murakami
2014	TPE Taipei	JPN Kanako Murakami	JPN Satoko Miyahara	CHN Li Zijun
2015	KOR Seoul	USA Polina Edmunds	JPN Satoko Miyahara	JPN Rika Hongo
2016	TPE Taipei	JPN Satoko Miyahara	USA Mirai Nagasu	JPN Rika Hongo

Four Continents Figure Skating Championships - ICE DANCING

Year	Location	Gold	Silver	Bronze
1999	CAN Halifax	CAN Shae-Lynn Bourne & Victor Kraatz	CAN Chantal Lefebvre & Michel Brunet	USA Naomi Lang & Peter Tchernyshev
2000	JPN Osaka	USA Naomi Lang & Peter Tchernyshev	CAN Marie-France Dubreuil & Patrice Lauzon	USA Jamie Silverstein & Justin Pekarek
2001	USA Salt Lake City	CAN Shae-Lynn Bourne & Victor Kraatz	USA Naomi Lang & Peter Tchernyshev	CAN Marie-France Dubreuil & Patrice Lauzon
2002	KOR Jeonju	USA Naomi Lang & Peter Tchernyshev	USA Tanith Belbin & Benjamin Agosto	CAN Megan Wing & Aaron Lowe
2003	CHN Beijing	CAN Shae-Lynn Bourne & Victor Kraatz	USA Tanith Belbin & Benjamin Agosto	USA Naomi Lang & Peter Tchernyshev
2004	CAN Hamilton	USA Tanith Belbin & Benjamin Agosto	CAN Marie-France Dubreuil & Patrice Lauzon	CAN Megan Wing & Aaron Lowe
2005	KOR Gangneung	USA Tanith Belbin & Benjamin Agosto	USA Melissa Gregory & Denis Petukhov	USA Lydia Manon & Ryan O'Meara
2006	USA Colorado Springs	USA Tanith Belbin & Benjamin Agosto	USA Morgan Matthews & Maxim Zavozin	CAN Tessa Virtue & Scott Moir
2007	USA Colorado Springs	CAN Marie-France Dubreuil & Patrice Lauzon	USA Tanith Belbin & Benjamin Agosto	CAN Tessa Virtue & Scott Moir

Greg Fox

Year	Location	Gold	Silver	Bronze
2008	KOR Goyang	CAN Tessa Virtue & Scott Moir	USA Meryl Davis & Charlie White	USA Kimberly Navarro & Brent Bommentre
2009	CAN Vancouver	USA Meryl Davis & Charlie White	CAN Tessa Virtue & Scott Moir	USA Emily Samuelson & Evan Bates
2010	KOR Jeonju	CAN Kaitlyn Weaver & Andrew Poje	CAN Allie Hann-McCurdy & Michael Coreno	USA Madison Hubbell & Keiffer Hubbell
2011	TPE Taipei	USA Meryl Davis & Charlie White	USA Maia Shibutani & Alex Shibutani	CAN Vanessa Crone & Paul Poirier
2012	USA Colorado Springs	CAN Tessa Virtue & Scott Moir	USA Meryl Davis & Charlie White	CAN Kaitlyn Weaver & Andrew Poje
2013	JPN Osaka	USA Meryl Davis & Charlie White	CAN Tessa Virtue & Scott Moir	USA Madison Chock & Evan Bates
2014	TPE Taipei	USA Madison Hubbell & Zachary Donohue	CAN Piper Gilles & Paul Poirier	USA Alexandra Aldridge & Daniel Eaton
2015	KOR Seoul	CAN Kaitlyn Weaver & Andrew Poje	USA Madison Chock & Evan Bates	USA Maia Shibutani & Alex Shibutani
2016	TPE Taipei	USA Maia Shibutani & Alex Shibutani	USA Madison Chock & Evan Bates	CAN Kaitlyn Weaver & Andrew Poje

WORLD FIGURE SKATING CHAMPIONSHIPS

Greg Fox

Left: **Lily Kronberger** of Hungary won bronze in 1906. (Which happened to be the first World Championships to include a separate ladies competition). She was awarded the bronze again in 1907 and then, for the following four years, from 1908-1911, she would be the gold medal World Champion, (Hungary's first world champion athlete). She also was Hungary's National Champion for 3 years in a row, from 1908-1910...competing against men and women in what was a co-ed competition! On top of all that, she holds the distinction of being the first skater to use musical accompaniment for her long program.

Right: **Gillis Grafström**, Swedish men's figure skater, won gold in the World Championships in 1922, 1924, and 1929. He also won the gold medal in 3 Olympics, 1920, 1924, & 1928, as well as the silver in 1932, (despite having an on-ice collision with a photographer during the competition!). Earlier in his career, he was the Swedish National Champion for 3 years in a row, from 1917-1919.

The World Figure Skating Championships were first held way back in 1896, making them the second longest running figure skating competition in the world, (the oldest being the European Figure Skating Championships, dating back to 1891). Created by the then-newly established ISU, the first event in 1896 took place in St. Petersburg, Russia and featured four competitors. All male for the first few years, (figure skating competition, at the time, was considered a male sport), the gender barrier was broken in 1902 in London when Madge Syers entered the competition to compete against the men, (and wound up taking the silver medal). Ladies and pairs events would be added in the next decade, although initially, those events were held separately from the men's competition. It would take until 1930 for all three events to occur at the same locale, in New York City, (which also happened to be the first World Figure Skating Championships to take place outside of Europe). In 1952, ice dancing was officially given its own event. In 1991, compulsory figures were eliminated as a component of the competition.

World Figure Skating Championships - MEN

Year	Location	Gold	Silver	Bronze
1896	RUS St. Petersburg	GER Gilbert Fuchs	AUT Gustav Hügel	RUS Georg Sanders
1897	SWE Stockholm	AUT Gustav Hügel	SWE Ulrich Salchow	NOR Johan Lefstad
1898	GBR London	SWE Henning Grenander	AUT Gustav Hügel	GER Gilbert Fuchs
1899	SWI Davos	AUT Gustav Hügel	SWE Ulrich Salchow	GBR Edgar Syers
1900	SWI Davos	AUT Gustav Hügel	SWE Ulrich Salchow	*no other competitors*

Greg Fox

Year	Location	Gold	Silver	Bronze
1901	SWE Stockholm	SWE Ulrich Salchow	GER Gilbert Fuchs	*no other competitors*
1902	GBR London	SWE Ulrich Salchow	GBR Madge Syers	GER Martin Gordan
1903	RUS St. Petersburg	SWE Ulrich Salchow	RUS Nicolai Panin Kolomenkin	AUT Max Bohatsch
1904	GER Berlin	SWE Ulrich Salchow	GER Heinrich Burger	GER Martin Gordan
1905	SWE Stockholm	SWE Ulrich Salchow	AUT Max Bohatsch	SWE Per Thorén
1906	GER Munich	GER Gilbert Fuchs	GER Heinrich Burger	SWE Bror Meyer
1907	AUT-HUN Vienna	SWE Ulrich Salchow	AUT Max Bohatsch	GER Gilbert Fuchs
1908	AUT-HUN Troppau	SWE Ulrich Salchow	GER Gilbert Fuchs	GER Heinrich Burger
1909	SWE Stockholm	SWE Ulrich Salchow	SWE Per Thorén	AUT Ernest Herz
1910	SWI Davos	SWE Ulrich Salchow	GER Werner Rittberger	HUN Andor Szende
1911	GER Berlin	SWE Ulrich Salchow	GER Werner Rittberger	AUT Fritz Kachler
1912	GBR Manchester	AUT Fritz Kachler	GER Werner Rittberger	HUN Andor Szende
1913	AUT-HUN Vienna	AUT Fritz Kachler	AUT Willy Böckl	HUN Andor Szende
1914	RUS Helsinki	SWE Gösta Sandahl	AUT Fritz Kachler	AUT Willy Böckl
1915-1921	NOT HELD DUE TO W.W. 1			
1922	SWE Stockholm	SWE Gillis Grafström	AUT Fritz Kachler	AUT Willy Böckl
1923	AUT Vienna	AUT Fritz Kachler	AUT Willy Böckl	SWE Gösta Sandahl

Year	Location	Gold	Silver	Bronze
1924	GBR Manchester	SWE Gillis Grafström	AUT Willy Böckl	AUT Ernst Oppacher
1925	AUT Vienna	AUT Willy Böckl	AUT Fritz Kachler	AUT Otto Preißecker
1926	GER Berlin	AUT Willy Böckl	AUT Otto Preißecker	GBR John Page
1927	SWI Davos	AUT Willy Böckl	AUT Otto Preißecker	AUT Karl Schäfer
1928	GER Berlin	AUT Willy Böckl	AUT Karl Schäfer	AUT Hugo Distler
1929	GBR London	SWE Gillis Grafström	AUT Karl Schäfer	AUT Ludwig Wrede
1930	USA New York City	AUT Karl Schäfer	USA Roger Turner	SWI Georges Gautschi
1931	GER Berlin	AUT Karl Schäfer	USA Roger Turner	GER Ernst Baier
1932	CAN Montreal	AUT Karl Schäfer	CAN Montgomery Wilson	GER Ernst Baier
1933	SWI Zürich	AUT Karl Schäfer	GER Ernst Baier	FIN Marcus Nikkanen
1934	SWE Stockholm	AUT Karl Schäfer	GER Ernst Baier	AUT Erich Erdös
1935	HUN Budapest	AUT Karl Schäfer	GBR Jack Dunn	HUN Dénes Pataky
1936	FRA Paris	AUT Karl Schäfer	GBR Graham Sharp	AUT Felix Kaspar
1937	AUT Vienna	AUT Felix Kaspar	GBR Graham Sharp	HUN Elemér Terták

Year	Location	Gold	Silver	Bronze
1938	GER Berlin	AUT Felix Kaspar	GBR Graham Sharp	AUT Herbert Alward
1939	HUN Budapest	GBR Graham Sharp	GBR Freddie Tomlins	GER Horst Faber
1940 -1946		**NOT HELD DUE TO W.W. 2**		
1947	SWE Stockholm	SWI Hans Gerschwiler	USA Dick Button	GBR Arthur Apfel
1948	SWI Davos	USA Dick Button	SWI Hans Gerschwiler	HUN Ede Király
1949	FRA Paris	USA Dick Button	HUN Ede Király	AUT Edi Rada
1950	GBR London	USA Dick Button	HUN Ede Király	USA Hayes Alan Jenkins
1951	ITA Milan	USA Dick Button	USA James Grogan	AUT Helmut Seibt
1952	FRA Paris	USA Dick Button	USA James Grogan	USA Hayes Alan Jenkins
1953	SWI Davos	USA Hayes Alan Jenkins	USA James Grogan	ITA Carlo Fassi
1954	NOR Oslo	USA Hayes Alan Jenkins	USA James Grogan	FRA Alain Giletti
1955	AUT Vienna	USA Hayes Alan Jenkins	USA Ronnie Robertson	USA David Jenkins
1956	GDR Garmisch-Partenkirchen	USA Hayes Alan Jenkins	USA Ronnie Robertson	USA David Jenkins
1957	USA Colorado Springs	USA David Jenkins	USA Tim Brown	CAN Charles Snelling
1958	FRA Paris	USA David Jenkins	USA Tim Brown	FRA Alain Giletti
1959	USA Colorado Springs	USA David Jenkins	CAN Donald Jackson	USA Tim Brown
1960	CAN Vancouver	FRA Alain Giletti	CAN Donald Jackson	FRA Alain Calmat
1961		**CANCELLED AFTER THE SABENA FLIGHT 548 CRASH**		
1962	CZE Prague	CAN Donald Jackson	CZE Karol Divín	FRA Alain Calmat
1963	ITA Cortina d'Ampezzo	CAN Donald McPherson	FRA Alain Calmat	GER Manfred Schnelldorfer

Year	Location	Gold	Silver	Bronze
1964	GDR Dortmund	GER Manfred Schnelldorfer	FRA Alain Calmat	CZE Karol Divín
1965	USA Colorado Springs	FRA Alain Calmat	USA Scott Allen	CAN Donald Knight
1966	SWI Davos	AUT Emmerich Danzer	AUT Wolfgang Schwarz	USA Gary Visconti
1967	AUT Vienna	AUT Emmerich Danzer	AUT Wolfgang Schwarz	USA Gary Visconti
1968	SWI Geneva	AUT Emmerich Danzer	USA Tim Wood	FRA Patrick Péra
1969	USA Colorado Springs	USA Tim Wood	CZE Ondrej Nepela	FRA Patrick Péra
1970	YUG Ljubljana	USA Tim Wood	CZE Ondrej Nepela	GDR Günter Zöller
1971	FRA Lyon	CZE Ondrej Nepela	FRA Patrick Péra	SOV Sergei Chetverukhin
1972	CAN Calgary	CZE Ondrej Nepela	SOV Sergei Chetverukhin	SOV Vladimir Kovalev
1973	CZE Bratislava	CZE Ondrej Nepela	SOV Sergei Chetverukhin	GDR Jan Hoffmann
1974	GDR Munich	GDR Jan Hoffmann	SOV Sergei Volkov	CAN Toller Cranston
1975	USA Colorado Springs	SOV Sergei Volkov	SOV Vladimir Kovalev	GBR John Curry
1976	SWE Gothenburg	GBR John Curry	SOV Vladimir Kovalev	GDR Jan Hoffmann
1977	JPN Tokyo	SOV Vladimir Kovalev	GDR Jan Hoffmann	JPN Minoru Sano
1978	CAN Ottawa	USA Charles Tickner	GDR Jan Hoffmann	GBR Robin Cousins
1979	AUT Vienna	SOV Vladimir Kovalev	GBR Robin Cousins	GDR Jan Hoffmann
1980	GDR Dortmund	GDR Jan Hoffmann	GBR Robin Cousins	USA Charles Tickner
1981	USA Hartford	USA Scott Hamilton	USA David Santee	SOV Igor Bobrin
1982	DEN Copenhagen	USA Scott Hamilton	GER Norbert Schramm	CAN Brian Pockar

Year	Location	Gold	Silver	Bronze
1983	FIN Helsinki	USA Scott Hamilton	GER Norbert Schramm	CAN Brian Orser
1984	CAN Ottawa	USA Scott Hamilton	CAN Brian Orser	SOV Alexander Fadeev
1985	JPN Tokyo	SOV Alexander Fadeev	CAN Brian Orser	USA Brian Boitano
1986	SWI Geneva	USA Brian Boitano	CAN Brian Orser	SOV Alexander Fadeev
1987	USA Cincinnati	CAN Brian Orser	USA Brian Boitano	SOV Alexander Fadeev
1988	HUN Budapest	USA Brian Boitano	CAN Brian Orser	SOV Viktor Petrenko
1989	FRA Paris	CAN Kurt Browning	USA Christopher Bowman	POL Grzegorz Filipowski
1990	CAN Halifax	CAN Kurt Browning	SOV Viktor Petrenko	USA Christopher Bowman
1991	GER Munich	CAN Kurt Browning	SOV Viktor Petrenko	USA Todd Eldredge
1992	USA Oakland	CIS (Commonwealth of Independent States) Viktor Petrenko	CAN Kurt Browning	CAN Elvis Stojko
1993	CZE Prague	CAN Kurt Browning	CAN Elvis Stojko	RUS Alexei Urmanov
1994	JPN Chiba	CAN Elvis Stojko	FRA Philippe Candeloro	UKR Viacheslav Zagorodniuk
1995	GBR Birmingham	CAN Elvis Stojko	USA Todd Eldredge	FRA Philippe Candeloro
1996	CAN Edmonton	USA Todd Eldredge	RUS Ilia Kulik	USA Rudy Galindo
1997	SWI Lausanne	CAN Elvis Stojko	USA Todd Eldredge	RUS Alexei Yagudin
1998	USA Minneapolis	RUS Alexei Yagudin	USA Todd Eldredge	RUS Evgeni Plushenko
1999	FIN Helsinki	RUS Alexei Yagudin	RUS Evgeni Plushenko	USA Michael Weiss
2000	FRA Nice	RUS Alexei Yagudin	CAN Elvis Stojko	USA Michael Weiss
2001	CAN Vancouver	RUS Evgeni Plushenko	RUS Alexei Yagudin	USA Todd Eldredge
2002	JPN Nagano	RUS Alexei Yagudin	USA Timothy Goebel	JPN Takeshi Honda

Year	Location	Gold	Silver	Bronze
2003	USA Washington, D.C.	RUS Evgeni Plushenko	USA Timothy Goebel	JPN Takeshi Honda
2004	GER Dortmund	RUS Evgeni Plushenko	FRA Brian Joubert	GER Stefan Lindemann
2005	RUS Moscow	SWI Stéphane Lambiel	CAN Jeffrey Buttle	USA Evan Lysacek
2006	CAN Calgary	SWI Stéphane Lambiel	FRA Brian Joubert	USA Evan Lysacek
2007	JPN Tokyo	FRA Brian Joubert	JPN Daisuke Takahashi	SWI Stéphane Lambiel
2008	SWE Gothenburg	CAN Jeffrey Buttle	FRA Brian Joubert	USA Johnny Weir
2009	USA Los Angeles	USA Evan Lysacek	CAN Patrick Chan	FRA Brian Joubert
2010	ITA Turin	JPN Daisuke Takahashi	CAN Patrick Chan	FRA Brian Joubert
2011	RUS Moscow	CAN Patrick Chan	JPN Takahiko Kozuka	RUS Artur Gachinski
2012	FRA Nice	CAN Patrick Chan	JPN Daisuke Takahashi	JPN Yuzuru Hanyu
2013	CAN London	CAN Patrick Chan	KAZ Denis Ten	SPA Javier Fernández
2014	JPN Saitama	JPN Yuzuru Hanyu	JPN Tatsuki Machida	SPA Javier Fernández
2015	CHN Shanghai	SPA Javier Fernández	JPN Yuzuru Hanyu	KAZ Denis Ten
2016	USA Boston	SPA Javier Fernández	JPN Yuzuru Hanyu	CHN Jin Boyang
2017	FIN Helsinki	JPN Yuzuru Hanyu	JPN Shoma Uno	CHN Jin Boyang

World Figure Skating Championships - PAIRS

Year	Location	Gold	Silver	Bronze
1908	RUS St. Petersburg	GER Anna Hübler & Heinrich Burger	GBR Phyllis Johnson & James H. Johnson	RUS Lidia Popova & A. L. Fischer
1909	SWE Stockholm	GBR Phyllis Johnson & James H. Johnson	SWE Valborg Lindahl & Nils Rosenius	SWE Gertrud Ström & Richard Johansson
1910	GER Berlin	GER Anna Hübler & Heinrich Burger	GER Ludowika Eilers & FIN Walter Jakobsson	GBR Phyllis Johnson & James H. Johnson
1911	AUT-HUN Vienna	FIN Ludowika Jakobsson-Eilers & Walter Jakobsson	*no other competitors*	*no other competitors*
1912	GBR Manchester	GBR Phyllis Johnson & James H. Johnson	FIN Ludowika Ja- kobsson-Eilers & Walter Jakobsson	NOR Alexia Schøien & Yngvar Bryn
1913	SWE Stockholm	AUT Helene Engelmann & Karl Mejstrik	FIN Ludowika Ja- kobsson-Eilers & Walter Jakobsson	AUT Christa von Szabó & Leo Horwitz
1914	SWI St. Moritz	FIN Ludowika Ja- kobsson-Eilers & Walter Jakobsson	AUT Helene Engelmann & Karl Mejstrik	AUT Christa von Szabó & Leo Horwitz
1915 -1921		NOT HELD DUE	TO W.W. 1	
1922	SWI Davos	AUT Helene Engelmann & Alfred Berger	FIN Ludowika Ja- kobsson-Eilers & Walter Jakobsson	GER Margaret Metzner & Paul Metzner

Year	Location	Gold	Silver	Bronze
1923	NOR Oslo	FIN Ludowika Jakobsson-Eilers & Walter Jakobsson	NOR Alexia Bryn-Schøien & Yngvar Bryn	SWE Elna Henrikson & Kaj af Ekström
1924	GBR Manchester	AUT Helene Engelmann & Alfred Berger	GBR Ethel Muckelt & John F. Page	SWE Elna Henrikson & Kaj af Ekström
1925	AUT Vienna	AUT Herma Szabo & Ludwig Wrede	FRA Andreé Joly-Brunet & Pierre Brunet	AUT Lilly Scholz & Otto Kaiser
1926	GER Berlin	FRA Andreé Joly-Brunet & Pierre Brunet	AUT Lilly Scholz & Otto Kaiser	AUT Herma Szabo & Ludwig Wrede
1927	AUT Vienna	AUT Herma Szabo & Ludwig Wrede	AUT Lilly Scholz & Otto Kaiser	CZE Else Hoppe & Oscar Hoppe
1928	GBR London	FRA Andreé Joly-Brunet & Pierre Brunet	AUT Lilly Scholz & Otto Kaiser	AUT Melitta Brunner & Ludwig Wrede
1929	HUN Budapest	AUT Lilly Scholz & Otto Kaiser	AUT Melitta Brunner & Ludwig Wrede	HUN Olga Orgonista & Sándor Szalay
1930	USA New York City	FRA Andreé Joly-Brunet & Pierre Brunet	AUT Melitta Brunner & Ludwig Wrede	USA Beatrix Loughran & Sherwin Badger
1931	GER Berlin	HUN Emília Rotter & László Szollás	HUN Olga Orgonista & Sándor Szalay	AUT Idi Papez & Karl Zwack
1932	CAN Montreal	FRA Andreé Joly-Brunet & Pierre Brunet	HUN Emília Rotter & László Szollás	USA Beatrix Loughran & Sherwin Badger
1933	SWE Stockholm	HUN Emília Rotter & László Szollás	AUT Idi Papez & Karl Zwack	NOR Randi Bakke-Gjertsen & Christen Christensen

Year	Location	Gold	Silver	Bronze
1934	FIN Helsinki	HUN Emília Rotter & László Szollás	AUT Idi Papez & Karl Zwack	GER Maxi Herber & Ernst Baier
1935	HUN Budapest	HUN Emília Rotter & László Szollás	AUT Ilse Pausin & Erich Pausin	HUN Lucy Gallo & Rezso Dillinger
1936	FRA Paris	GER Maxi Herber & Ernst Baier	AUT Ilse Pausin & Erich Pausin	GBR Violet Cliff & Leslie Cliff
1937	GBR London	Nazi GER Maxi Herber & Ernst Baier	AUT Ilse Pausin & Erich Pausin	GBR Violet Cliff & Leslie Cliff
1938	GER Berlin , GER	GER Maxi Herber & Ernst Baier	AUT Ilse Pausin & Erich Pausin	GER Ilse Koch & Gunther Noack
1939	HUN Budapest	GER Maxi Herber & Ernst Baier	GER Ilse Pausin & Erich Pausin	GER Ilse Koch & Gunther Noack
1940 -1946	NOT HELD DUE TO W.W. 2			
1947	SWE Stockholm	BEL Micheline Lannoy & Pierre Baugniet	USA Karol Kennedy & Peter Kennedy	BEL Suzanne Diskeuve & Edmond Verbustel
1948	SWI Davos	BEL Micheline Lannoy & Pierre Baugniet	HUN Andrea Kékesy & Ede Király	CAN Suzanne Morrow & Wallace Diestel-meyer
1949	FRA Paris	HUN Andrea Kékesy & Ede Király	USA Karol Kennedy & Peter Kennedy	USA Ann Davies & Carleton Hoffner
1950	GBR London	USA Karol Kennedy & Peter Kennedy	GBR Jennifer Nicks & John Nicks	HUN Marianna Nagy & László Nagy
1951	ITA Milan	GDR Ria Baran & Paul Falk	USA Karol Kennedy & Peter Kennedy	GBR Jennifer Nicks & John Nicks

Year	Location	Gold	Silver	Bronze
1952	FRA Paris	GDR Ria Baran & Paul Falk	USA Karol Kennedy & Peter Kennedy	GBR Jennifer Nicks & John Nicks
1953	SWI Davos	GBR Jennifer Nicks & John Nicks	CAN Frances Dafoe & Norris Bowden	HUN Marianna Nagy & László Nagy
1954	NOR Oslo	CAN Frances Dafoe & Norris Bowden	SWI Silvia Grandjean & Michel Grandjean	AUT Sissy Schwarz & Kurt Oppelt
1955	AUT Vienna	CAN Frances Dafoe & Norris Bowden	AUT Sissy Schwarz & Kurt Oppelt	HUN Marianna Nagy & László Nagy
1956	GDR Garmisch-Partenkirchen	AUT Sissy Schwarz & Kurt Oppelt	CAN Frances Dafoe & Norris Bowden	GDR Marika Kilius & Franz Ningel
1957	USA Colorado Springs	CAN Barbara Wagner & Robert Paul	GDR Marika Kilius & Franz Ningel	CAN Maria Jelinek & Otto Jelinek
1958	FRA Paris	CAN Barbara Wagner & Robert Paul	CZE Věra Suchánková & Zdeněk Doležal	CAN Maria Jelinek & Otto Jelinek
1959	USA Colorado Springs	CAN Barbara Wagner & Robert Paul	GDR Marika Kilius & Hans-Jürgen Bäumler	USA Nancy Ludington & Ronald Ludington
1960	CAN Vancouver	CAN Barbara Wagner & Robert Paul	CAN Maria Jelinek & Otto Jelinek	GDR Marika Kilius & Hans-Jürgen Bäumler
1961		CANCELLED AFTER THE SABENA FLIGHT 548 CRASH		
1962	CZE Prague	CAN Maria Jelinek & Otto Jelinek	SOV Liudmila Belousova & Oleg Protopopov	GDR Margret Göbl & Franz Ningel

Year	Location	Gold	Silver	Bronze
1963	ITA Cortina d'Ampezzo	GDR Marika Kilius & Hans-Jürgen Bäumler	SOV Liudmila Belousova & Oleg Protopopov	SOV Tatiana Zhuk & Alexander Gavrilov
1964	GDR Dortmund	GDR Marika Kilius & Hans-Jürgen Bäumler	SOV Liudmila Belousova & Oleg Protopopov	CAN Debbi Wilkes & Guy Revell
1965	USA Colorado Springs	SOV Liudmila Belousova & Oleg Protopopov	USA Vivian Joseph & Ronald Joseph	SOV Tatiana Zhuk & Alexander Gorelik
1966	SWI Davos	SOV Liudmila Belousova & Oleg Protopopov	SOV Tatiana Zhuk & Alexander Gorelik	USA Cynthia Kauffman & Ronald Kauffman
1967	AUT Vienna	SOV Liudmila Belousova & Oleg Protopopov	GDR Margot Glockshuber & Wolfgang Danne	USA Cynthia Kauffman & Ronald Kauffman
1968	SWI Geneva	SOV Liudmila Belousova & Oleg Protopopov	SOV Tatiana Zhuk & Alexander Gorelik	USA Cynthia Kauffman & Ronald Kauffman
1969	USA Colorado Springs	SOV Irina Rodnina & Alexei Ulanov	SOV Tamara Moskvina & Alexei Mishin	SOV Liudmila Belousova & Oleg Protopopov
1970	YUG Ljubljana	SOV Irina Rodnina & Alexei Ulanov	SOV Liudmila Smirnova & Andrei Suraikin	GDR Heidemarie Steiner & Heinz-Ulrich Walther
1971	FRA Lyon	SOV Irina Rodnina & Alexei Ulanov	SOV Liudmila Smirnova & Andrei Suraikin	USA JoJo Starbuck & Kenneth Shelley
1972	CAN Calgary	SOV Irina Rodnina & Alexei Ulanov	SOV Liudmila Smirnova & Andrei Suraikin	USA JoJo Starbuck & Kenneth Shelley

Year	Location	Gold	Silver	Bronze
1973	CZE Bratislava	SOV Irina Rodnina & Alexander Zaitsev	SOV Liudmila Smirnova & Alexei Ulanov	GDR Manuela Groß & Uwe Kagelmann
1974	GDR Munich	SOV Irina Rodnina & Alexander Zaitsev	SOV Liudmila Smirnova & Alexei Ulanov	GDR Romy Kermer & Rolf Österreich
1975	USA Colorado Springs	SOV Irina Rodnina & Alexander Zaitsev	GDR Romy Kermer & Rolf Österreich	GDR Manuela Groß & Uwe Kagelmann
1976	SWE Gothenburg	SOV Irina Rodnina & Alexander Zaitsev	GDR Romy Kermer & Rolf Österreich	SOV Irina Vorobieva & Alexander Vlasov
1977	JPN Tokyo	SOV Irina Rodnina & Alexander Zaitsev	SOV Irina Vorobieva & Alexander Vlasov	USA Tai Babilonia & Randy Gardner
1978	CAN Ottawa	SOV Irina Rodnina & Alexander Zaitsev	GDR Manuela Mager & Uwe Bewersdorf	USA Tai Babilonia & Randy Gardner
1979	AUT Vienna	USA Tai Babilonia & Randy Gardner	SOV Marina Cherkasova & Sergei Shakhrai	GDR Sabine Baeß & Tassilo Thierbach
1980	GDR Dortmund	SOV Marina Cherkasova & Sergei Shakhrai	GDR Manuela Mager & Uwe Bewersdorf	SOV Marina Pestova & Stanislav Leonovich
1981	USA Hartford	SOV Irina Vorobieva & Igor Lisovski	GDR Sabine Baeß & Tassilo Thierbach	GDR Christina Riegel & Andreas Nischwitz
1982	DEN Copenhagen	GDR Sabine Baeß & Tassilo Thierbach	SOV Marina Pestova & Stanislav Leonovich	USA Caitlin Carruthers & Peter Carruthers
1983	FIN Helsinki	SOV Elena Valova & Oleg Vasiliev	GDR Sabine Baeß & Tassilo Thierbach	CAN Barbara Underhill & Paul Martini

Year	Location	Gold	Silver	Bronze
1984	CAN Ottawa	CAN Barbara Underhill & Paul Martini	SOV Elena Valova & Oleg Vasiliev	GDR Sabine Baeß & Tassilo Thierbach
1985	JPN Tokyo	SOV Elena Valova & Oleg Vasiliev	SOV Larisa Selezneva & Oleg Makarov	CAN Katherina Matousek & Lloyd Eisler
1986	SWI Geneva	SOV Ekaterina Gordeeva & Sergei Grinkov	SOV Elena Valova & Oleg Vasiliev	CAN Cynthia Coull & Mark Rowsom
1987	USA Cincinnati	SOV Ekaterina Gordeeva & Sergei Grinkov	SOV Elena Valova & Oleg Vasiliev	USA Jill Watson & Peter Oppegard
1988	HUN Budapest	SOV Elena Valova & Oleg Vasiliev	SOV Ekaterina Gordeeva & Sergei Grinkov	SOV Larisa Selezneva & Oleg Makarov
1989	FRA Paris	SOV Ekaterina Gordeeva & Sergei Grinkov	CAN Cindy Landry & Lyndon Johnston	SOV Elena Bechke & Denis Petrov
1990	CAN Halifax	SOV Ekaterina Gordeeva & Sergei Grinkov	CAN Isabelle Brasseur & Lloyd Eisler	SOV Natalia Mishkutenok & Artur Dmitriev
1991	GER Munich	SOV Natalia Mishkutenok & Artur Dmitriev	CAN Isabelle Brasseur & Lloyd Eisler	USA Natasha Kuchiki & Todd Sand
1992	USA Oakland	CIS (Commonwealth of Independent States) Natalia Mishkutenok & Artur Dmitriev	CZE Radka Kovaříková & René Novotný	CAN Isabelle Brasseur & Lloyd Eisler
1993	CZE Prague	CAN Isabelle Brasseur & Lloyd Eisler	GER Mandy Wötzel & Ingo Steuer	RUS Evgenia Shishkova & Vadim Naumov
1994	JPN Chiba	RUS Evgenia Shishkova & Vadim Naumov	CAN Isabelle Brasseur & Lloyd Eisler	RUS Marina Eltsova & Andrei Bushkov

Year	Location	Gold	Silver	Bronze
1995	GBR Birmingham	CZE Radka Kovaříková & René Novotný	RUS Evgenia Shishkova & Vadim Naumov	USA Jenni Meno & Todd Sand
1996	CAN Edmonton	RUS Marina Eltsova & Andrei Bushkov	GER Mandy Wötzel & Ingo Steuer	USA Jenni Meno & Todd Sand
1997	SWI Lausanne	GER Mandy Wötzel & Ingo Steuer	RUS Marina Eltsova & Andrei Bushkov	RUS Oksana Kazakova & Artur Dmitriev
1998	USA Minneapolis	RUS Elena Berezhnaya & Anton Sikharulidze	USA Jenni Meno & Todd Sand	GER Peggy Schwarz & Mirko Müller
1999	FIN Helsinki	RUS Elena Berezhnaya & Anton Sikharulidze	CHN Shen Xue & Zhao Hongbo	POL Dorota Zagórska & Mariusz Siudek
2000	FRA Nice	RUS Maria Petrova & Alexei Tikhonov	CHN Shen Xue & Zhao Hongbo	FRA Sarah Abitbol & Stéphane Bernadis
2001	CAN Vancouver	CAN Jamie Salé & David Pelletier	RUS Elena Berezhnaya & Anton Sikharulidze	CHN Shen Xue & Zhao Hongbo
2002	JPN Nagano	CHN Shen Xue & Zhao Hongbo	RUS Tatiana Totmianina & Maxim Marinin	USA Kyoko Ina & John Zimmerman
2003	USA Washington D.C	CHN Shen Xue & Zhao Hongbo	RUS Tatiana Totmianina & Maxim Marinin	RUS Maria Petrova & Alexei Tikhonov
2004	GER Dortmund	RUS Tatiana Totmianina & Maxim Marinin	CHN Shen Xue & Zhao Hongbo	CHN Pang Qing & Tong Jian
2005	RUS Moscow	RUS Tatiana Totmianina & Maxim Marinin	RUS Maria Petrova & Alexei Tikhonov	CHN Zhang Dan & Zhang Hao

Year	Location	Gold	Silver	Bronze
2006	CAN Calgary	CHN Pang Qing & Tong Jian	CHN Zhang Dan & Zhang Hao	RUS Maria Petrova & Alexei Tikhonov
2007	JPN Tokyo	CHN Shen Xue & Zhao Hongbo	CHN Pang Qing & Tong Jian	GER Aliona Savchenko & Robin Szolkowy
2008	SWE Gothenburg	GER Aliona Savchenko & Robin Szolkowy	CHN Zhang Dan & Zhang Hao	CAN Jessica Dubé & Bryce Davison
2009	USA Los Angeles	GER Aliona Savchenko & Robin Szolkowy	CHN Zhang Dan & Zhang Hao	RUS Yuko Kavaguti & Alexander Smirnov
2010	ITA Turin	CHN Pang Qing & Tong Jian	GER Aliona Savchenko & Robin Szolkowy	RUS Yuko Kavaguti & Alexander Smirnov
2011	RUS Moscow	GER Aliona Savchenko & Robin Szolkowy	RUS Tatiana Volosozhar & Maxim Trankov	CHN Pang Qing & Tong Jian
2012	FRA Nice	GER Aliona Savchenko & Robin Szolkowy	RUS Tatiana Volosozhar & Maxim Trankov	JPN Narumi Takahashi & Mervin Tran
2013	CAN London	RUS Tatiana Volosozhar & Maxim Trankov	GER Aliona Savchenko & Robin Szolkowy	CAN Meagan Duhamel & Eric Radford
2014	JPN Saitama	GER Aliona Savchenko & Robin Szolkowy	RUS Ksenia Stolbova & Fedor Klimov	CAN Meagan Duhamel & Eric Radford
2015	CHN Shanghai	CAN Meagan Duhamel & Eric Radford	CHN Sui Wenjing & Han Cong	CHN Pang Qing & Tong Jian
2016	USA Boston	CAN Meagan Duhamel & Eric Radford	CHN Sui Wenjing & Han Cong	GER Aliona Savchenko & Bruno Massot
2017	FIN Helsinki	CHN Sui Wenjing & Han Cong	GER Aliona Savchenko & Bruno Massot	RUS Evgenia Tarasova & Vladimir Morozov

World Figure Skating Championships - LADIES

Year	Location	Gold	Silver	Bronze
1906	SWI Davos	GBR Madge Syers	AUT Jenny Herz	HUN Lily Kronberger
1907	AUT-HUN Vienna	GBR Madge Syers	AUT Jenny Herz	HUN Lily Kronberger
1908	AUT-HUN Troppau	HUN Lily Kronberger	GER Elsa Rendschmidt	*no other competitors*
1909	AUT-HUN Budapest	HUN Lily Kronberger	*no other competitors*	*no other competitors*
1910	GER Berlin	HUN Lily Kronberger	GER Elsa Rendschmidt	*no other competitors*
1911	AUT-HUN Vienna	HUN Lily Kronberger	HUN Opika von Méray Horváth	GER Ludowika Jakobsson-Eilers
1912	SWI Davos	HUN Opika von Méray Horváth	GBR Dorothy Greenhough-Smith	GBR Phyllis Johnson
1913	SWE Stockholm	HUN Opika von Méray Horváth	GBR Phyllis Johnson	SWE Svea Norén
1914	SWI St. Moritz	HUN Opika von Méray Horváth	AUT Angela Hanka	GBR Phyllis Johnson
1915-1921	**NOT HELD DUE**	**TO W.W. 1**		
1922	SWE Stockholm	AUT Herma Szabo	SWE Svea Norén	NOR Margot Moe
1923	AUT Vienna	AUT Herma Szabo	AUT Gisela Reichmann	SWE Svea Norén
1924	NOR Oslo	AUT Herma Szabo	GER Ellen Brockhöft	USA Beatrix Loughran
1925	SWI Davos	AUT Herma Szabo	GER Ellen Brockhöft	GER Elisabeth Böckel
1926	SWE Stockholm	AUT Herma Szabo	NOR Sonja Henie	GBR Kathleen Shaw
1927	NOR Oslo	NOR Sonja Henie	AUT Herma Szabo	NOR Karen Simensen
1928	GBR London	NOR Sonja Henie	USA Maribel Vinson	AUT Fritzi Burger
1929	HUN Budapest	NOR Sonja Henie	AUT Fritzi Burger	AUT Melitta Brunner
1930	USA NY City	NOR Sonja Henie	CAN Cecil Smith	USA Maribel Vinson
1931	GER Berlin	NOR Sonja Henie	AUT Hilde Holovsky	AUT Fritzi Burger

Greg Fox

Year	Location	Gold	Silver	Bronze
1932	CAN Montreal	NOR Sonja Henie	AUT Fritzi Burger	CAN Constance Wilson-Samuel
1933	SWE Stockholm	NOR Sonja Henie	SWE Vivi-Anne Hultén	AUT Hilde Holovsky
1934	NOR Oslo	NOR Sonja Henie	GBR Megan Taylor	AUT Liselotte Landbeck
1935	AUT Vienna	NOR Sonja Henie	GBR Cecilia Colledge	SWE Vivi-Anne Hultén
1936	FRA Paris	NOR Sonja Henie	GBR Megan Taylor	SWE Vivi-Anne Hultén
1937	GBR London	GBR Cecilia Colledge	GBR Megan Taylor	SWE Vivi-Anne Hultén
1938	SWE Stockholm	GBR Megan Taylor	GBR Cecilia Colledge	USA Hedy Stenuf
1939	CZE Prague	GBR Megan Taylor	USA Hedy Stenuf	GBR Daphne Walker
1940-1946	NOT HELD DUE TO W.W. 2			
1947	SWE Stockholm	CAN Barbara Ann Scott	GBR Daphne Walker	USA Gretchen Merrill
1948	SWI Davos	CAN Barbara Ann Scott	AUT Eva Pawlik	CZE Jiřína Nekolová
1949	FRA Paris	CZE Alena Vrzáňová	USA Yvonne Sherman	GBR Jeannette Altwegg
1950	GBR London	CZE Alena Vrzáňová	GBR Jeannette Altwegg	USA Yvonne Sherman
1951	ITA Milan	GBR Jeannette Altwegg	FRA Jacqueline du Bief	USA Sonya Klopfer
1952	FRA Paris	FRA Jacqueline du Bief	USA Sonya Klopfer	USA Virginia Baxter
1953	SWI Davos	USA Tenley Albright	GDR Gundi Busch	GBR Valda Osborn
1954	NOR Oslo	GDR Gundi Busch	USA Tenley Albright	GBR Erica Batchelor
1955	AUT Vienna	USA Tenley Albright	USA Carol Heiss	AUT Hanna Eigel
1956	GDR Garmisch-Partenkirchen	USA Carol Heiss	USA Tenley Albright	AUT Ingrid Wendl
1957	USA Colorado Springs	USA Carol Heiss	AUT Hanna Eigel	AUT Ingrid Wendl
1958	FRA Paris	USA Carol Heiss	AUT Ingrid Wendl	AUT Hanna Walter
1959	USA Colorado Springs	USA Carol Heiss	AUT Hanna Walter	NED Sjoukje Dijkstra
1960	CAN Vancouver	USA Carol Heiss	NED Sjoukje Dijkstra	USA Barbara Ann Roles

Year	Location	Gold	Silver	Bronze
1961	CANCELLED AFTER THE SABENA FLIGHT 548 CRASH			
1962	CZE Prague	NED Sjoukje Dijkstra	CAN Wendy Griner	AUT Regine Heitzer
1963	ITA Cortina d'Ampezzo	NED Sjoukje Dijkstra	AUT Regine Heitzer	FRA Nicole Hassler
1964	GDR Dortmund	NED Sjoukje Dijkstra	AUT Regine Heitzer	CAN Petra Burka
1965	USA Colorado Springs	CAN Petra Burka	AUT Regine Heitzer	USA Peggy Fleming
1966	SWI Davos	USA Peggy Fleming	GDR Gabriele Seyfert	CAN Petra Burka
1967	AUT Vienna	USA Peggy Fleming	GDR Gabriele Seyfert	CZE Hana Mašková
1968	SWI Geneva	USA Peggy Fleming	GDR Gabriele Seyfert	CZE Hana Mašková
1969	USA Colorado Springs	GDR Gabriele Seyfert	AUT Trixi Schuba	HUN Zsuzsa Almássy
1970	YUG Ljubljana	GDR Gabriele Seyfert	AUT Trixi Schuba	USA Julie Lynn Holmes
1971	FRA Lyon	AUT Trixi Schuba	USA Julie Lynn Holmes	CAN Karen Magnussen
1972	CAN Calgary	AUT Trixi Schuba	CAN Karen Magnussen	USA Janet Lynn
1973	CZE Bratislava	CAN Karen Magnussen	USA Janet Lynn	GDR Christine Errath
1974	GDR Munich	GDR Christine Errath	USA Dorothy Hamill	NED Dianne de Leeuw
1975	USA Colorado Springs	NED Dianne de Leeuw	USA Dorothy Hamill	GDR Christine Errath
1976	SWE Gothenburg	USA Dorothy Hamill	GDR Christine Errath	NED Dianne de Leeuw
1977	JPN Tokyo	USA Linda Fratianne	GDR Anett Pötzsch	GDR Dagmar Lurz
1978	CAN Ottawa	GDR Anett Pötzsch	USA Linda Fratianne	ITA Susanna Driano
1979	AUT Vienna	USA Linda Fratianne	GDR Anett Pötzsch	JPN Emi Watanabe
1980	GDR Dortmund	GDR Anett Pötzsch	GDR Dagmar Lurz	USA Linda Fratianne
1981	USA Hartford	SWI Denise Biellmann	USA Elaine Zayak	AUT Claudia Kristofics-Binder
1982	DEN Copenhagen	USA Elaine Zayak	GDR Katarina Witt	AUT Claudia Kristofics-Binder

Greg Fox

Year	Location	Gold	Silver	Bronze
1983	FIN Helsinki	USA Rosalynn Sumners	GDR Claudia Leistner	SOV Elena Vodorezova
1984	CAN Ottawa	GDR Katarina Witt	SOV Anna Kondrashova	USA Elaine Zayak
1985	JPN Tokyo	GDR Katarina Witt	SOV Kira Ivanova	USA Tiffany Chin
1986	SWI Geneva	USA Debi Thomas	GDR Katarina Witt	USA Tiffany Chin
1987	USA Cincinnati	GDR Katarina Witt	USA Debi Thomas	USA Caryn Kadavy
1988	HUN Budapest	GDR Katarina Witt	CAN Elizabeth Manley	USA Debi Thomas
1989	FRA Paris	JPN Midori Ito	GDR Claudia Leistner	USA Jill Trenary
1990	CAN Halifax	USA Jill Trenary	JPN Midori Ito	USA Holly Cook
1991	GER Munich	USA Kristi Yamaguchi	USA Tonya Harding	USA Nancy Kerrigan
1992	USA Oakland	USA Kristi Yamaguchi	USA Nancy Kerrigan	CHN Chen Lu
1993	CZE Prague	UKR Oksana Baiul	FRA Surya Bonaly	CHN Chen Lu
1994	JPN Chiba	JPN Yuka Sato	FRA Surya Bonaly	GER Tanja Szewczenko
1995	GBR Birmingham	CHN Chen Lu	FRA Surya Bonaly	USA Nicole Bobek
1996	CAN Edmonton	USA Michelle Kwan	CHN Chen Lu	RUS Irina Slutskaya
1997	SWI Lausanne	USA Tara Lipinski	USA Michelle Kwan	FRA Vanessa Gusmeroli
1998	USA Minneapolis	USA Michelle Kwan	RUS Irina Slutskaya	RUS Maria Butyrskaya
1999	FIN Helsinki	RUS Maria Butyrskaya	USA Michelle Kwan	RUS Julia Soldatova
2000	FRA Nice	USA Michelle Kwan	RUS Irina Slutskaya	RUS Maria Butyrskaya
2001	CAN Vancouver	USA Michelle Kwan	RUS Irina Slutskaya	USA Sarah Hughes
2002	JPN Nagano	RUS Irina Slutskaya	USA Michelle Kwan	JPN Fumie Suguri
2003	USA Washington, D.C.	USA Michelle Kwan	RUS Elena Sokolova	JPN Fumie Suguri
2004	GER Dortmund	JPN Shizuka Arakawa	USA Sasha Cohen	USA Michelle Kwan
2005	RUS Moscow	RUS Irina Slutskaya	USA Sasha Cohen	ITA Carolina Kostner

Year	Location	Gold	Silver	Bronze
2006	CAN Calgary	USA Kimmie Meissner	JPN Fumie Suguri	USA Sasha Cohen
2007	JPN Tokyo	JPN Miki Ando	JPN Mao Asada	KOR Kim Yuna
2008	SWE Gothenburg	JPN Mao Asada	ITA Carolina Kostner	KOR Kim Yuna
2009	USA Los Angeles	KOR Kim Yuna	CAN Joannie Rochette	JPN Miki Ando
2010	ITA Turin	JPN Mao Asada	KOR Kim Yuna	FIN Laura Lepistö
2011	RUS Moscow	JPN Miki Ando	KOR Kim Yuna	ITA Carolina Kostner
2012	FRA Nice	ITA Carolina Kostner	RUS Alena Leonova	JPN Akiko Suzuki
2013	CAN London	KOR Kim Yuna	ITA Carolina Kostner	JPN Mao Asada
2014	JPN Saitama	JPN Mao Asada	RUS Yulia Lipnitskaya	ITA Carolina Kostner
2015	CHN Shanghai	RUS Elizaveta Tuktamysheva	JPN Satoko Miyahara	RUS Elena Radionova
2016	USA Boston	RUS Evgenia Medvedeva	USA Ashley Wagner	RUS Anna Pogorilaya
2017	FIN Helsinki	RUS Evgenia Medvedeva	CAN Kaetlyn Osmond	CAN Gabrielle Daleman

World Figure Skating Championships - ICE DANCING

Year	Location	Gold	Silver	Bronze
1952	FRA Paris	GBR Jean Westwood & Lawrence Demmy	GBR Joan Dewhirst & John Slater	USA Carol Ann Peters & Daniel Ryan
1953	SWI Davos	GBR Jean Westwood & Lawrence Demmy	GBR Joan Dewhirst & John Slater	USA Carol Ann Peters & Daniel Ryan
1954	NOR Oslo	GBR Jean Westwood & Lawrence Demmy	GBR Nesta Davies & Paul Thomas	USA Carmel Bodel & Edward Bodel
1955	AUT Vienna	GBR Jean Westwood & Lawrence Demmy	GBR Pamela Weight & Paul Thomas	GBR Barbara Radford & Raymond Lockwood
1956	GDR Garmisch-Partenkirchen	GBR Pamela Weight & Paul Thomas	GBR June Markham & Courtney Jones	GBR Barbara Thompson & Gerard Rigby
1957	USA Colorado Springs	GBR June Markham & Courtney Jones	CAN Geraldine Fenton & William McLachlan	USA Sharon McKenzie & Bert Wright
1958	FRA Paris	GBR June Markham & Courtney Jones	CAN Geraldine Fenton & William McLachlan	USA Andree Anderson & Donald Jacoby
1959	USA Colorado Springs	GBR Doreen Denny & Courtney Jones	USA Andree Anderson & Donald Jacoby	CAN Geraldine Fenton & William McLachlan
1960	CAN Vancouver	GBR Doreen Denny & Courtney Jones	CAN Virginia Thompson & William McLachlan	FRA Christiane Guhel & Jean Paul Guhel
1961	CANCELLED AFTER THE SABENA FLIGHT 548 CRASH			

Year	Location	Gold	Silver	Bronze
1962	CZE Prague	CZE Eva Romanová & Pavel Roman	FRA Christiane Guhel & Jean Paul Guhel	CAN Virginia Thompson & William McLachlan
1963	ITA Cortina d'Ampezzo	CZE Eva Romanová & Pavel Roman	GBR Linda Shearman & Michael Phillips	CAN Paulette Doan & Kenneth Ormsby
1964	GDR Dortmund	CZE Eva Romanová & Pavel Roman	CAN Paulette Doan & Kenneth Ormsby	GBR Janet Sawbridge & David Hickinbottom
1965	USA Colorado Springs	CZE Eva Romanová & Pavel Roman	GBR Janet Sawbridge & David Hickinbottom	USA Lorna Dyer & John Carrell
1966	SWI Davos	GBR Diane Towler & Bernard Ford	USA Kristin Fortune & Dennis Sveum	USA Lorna Dyer & John Carrell
1967	AUT Vienna	GBR Diane Towler & Bernard Ford	USA Lorna Dyer & John Carrell	GBR Yvonne Suddick & Malcolm Cannon
1968	SWI Geneva	GBR Diane Towler & Bernard Ford	GBR Yvonne Suddick & Malcolm Cannon	GBR Janet Sawbridge & Jon Lane
1969	USA Colorado Springs	GBR Diane Towler & Bernard Ford	SOV Liudmila Pakhomova & Alexander Gorshkov	USA Judy Schwomeyer & James Sladky
1970	YUG Ljubljana	SOV Liudmila Pakhomova & Alexander Gorshkov	USA Judy Schwomeyer & James Sladky	GDR Angelika Buck & Erich Buck
1971	FRA Lyon	SOV Liudmila Pakhomova & Alexander Gorshkov	GDR Angelika Buck & Erich Buck	USA Judy Schwomeyer & James Sladky
1972	CAN Calgary	SOV Liudmila Pakhomova & Alexander Gorshkov	GDR Angelika Buck & Erich Buck	USA Judy Schwomeyer & James Sladky

Year	Location	Gold	Silver	Bronze
1973	CZE Bratislava	SOV Liudmila Pakhomova & Alexander Gorshkov	GDR Angelika Buck & Erich Buck	GBR Hilary Green & Glyn Watts
1974	GDR Munich	SOV Liudmila Pakhomova & Alexander Gorshkov	GBR Hilary Green & Glyn Watts	SOV Natalia Linichuk & Gennadi Karponosov
1975	USA Colorado Springs	SOV Irina Moiseeva & Andrei Minenkov	USA Colleen O'Connor & James Millns	GBR Hilary Green & Glyn Watts
1976	SWE Gothenburg	SOV Liudmila Pakhomova & Alexander Gorshkov	SOV Irina Moiseeva & Andrei Minenkov	USA Colleen O'Connor & James Millns
1977	JPN Tokyo	SOV Irina Moiseeva & Andrei Minenkov	GBR Janet Thompson & Warren Maxwell	SOV Natalia Linichuk & Gennadi Karponosov
1978	CAN Ottawa	SOV Natalia Linichuk & Gennadi Karponosov	SOV Irina Moiseeva & Andrei Minenkov	HUN Krisztina Regőczy & András Sallay
1979	AUT Vienna	SOV Natalia Linichuk & Gennadi Karponosov	HUN Krisztina Regőczy & András Sallay	SOV Irina Moiseeva & Andrei Minenkov
1980	GDR Dortmund	HUN Krisztina Regőczy & András Sallay	SOV Natalia Linichuk & Gennadi Karponosov	SOV Irina Moiseeva & Andrei Minenkov
1981	USA Hartford	GBR Jayne Torvill & Christopher Dean	SOV Irina Moiseeva & Andrei Minenkov	SOV Natalia Bestemianova & Andrei Bukin
1982	DEN Copenhagen	GBR Jayne Torvill & Christopher Dean	SOV Natalia Bestemianova & Andrei Bukin	SOV Irina Moiseeva & Andrei Minenkov

Year	Location	Gold	Silver	Bronze
1983	FIN Helsinki	GBR Jayne Torvill & Christopher Dean	SOV Natalia Bestemianova & Andrei Bukin	USA Judy Blumberg & Michael Seibert
1984	CAN Ottawa	GBR Jayne Torvill & Christopher Dean	SOV Natalia Bestemianova & Andrei Bukin	USA Judy Blumberg & Michael Seibert
1985	JPN Tokyo	SOV Natalia Bestemianova & Andrei Bukin	SOV Marina Klimova & Sergei Ponomarenko	USA Judy Blumberg & Michael Seibert
1986	SWI Geneva	SOV Natalia Bestemianova & Andrei Bukin	SOV Marina Klimova & Sergei Ponomarenko	CAN Tracy Wilson & Robert McCall
1987	USA Cincinnati	SOV Natalia Bestemianova & Andrei Bukin	SOV Marina Klimova & Sergei Ponomarenko	CAN Tracy Wilson & Robert McCall
1988	HUN Budapest	SOV Natalia Bestemianova & Andrei Bukin	SOV Marina Klimova & Sergei Ponomarenko	CAN Tracy Wilson & Robert McCall
1989	FRA Paris	SOV Marina Klimova & Sergei Ponomarenko	SOV Maya Usova & Alexander Zhulin	FRA Isabelle Duchesnay & Paul Duchesnay
1990	CAN Halifax	SOV Marina Klimova & Sergei Ponomarenko	FRA Isabelle Duchesnay & Paul Duchesnay	SOV Maya Usova & Alexander Zhulin

Greg Fox

Year	Location	Gold	Silver	Bronze
1991	GER Munich	FRA Isabelle Duchesnay & Paul Duchesnay	SOV Marina Klimova & Sergei Ponomarenko	SOV Maya Usova & Alexander Zhulin
1992	USA Oakland	CIS (Commonwealth of Independent States) Marina Klimova & Sergei Ponomarenko	CIS (Commonwealth of Independent States) Maya Usova & Alexander Zhulin	CIS (Commonwealth of Independent States) Pasha Grishuk & Evgeni Platov
1993	CZE Prague	RUS Maya Usova & Alexander Zhulin	RUS Pasha Grishuk & Evgeni Platov	RUS Anjelika Krylova & Vladimir Fedorov
1994	JPN Chiba	RUS Oksana Grishuk & Evgeni Platov	FRA Sophie Moniotte & Pascal Lavanchy	FIN Susanna Rahkamo & Petri Kokko
1995	GBR Birmingham	RUS Oksana Grishuk & Evgeni Platov	FIN Susanna Rahkamo & Petri Kokko	FRA Sophie Moniotte & Pascal Lavanchy
1996	CAN Edmonton	RUS Oksana Grishuk & Evgeni Platov	RUS Anjelika Krylova & Oleg Ovsyannikov	CAN Shae-Lynn Bourne & Victor Kraatz
1997	SWI Lausanne	RUS Oksana Grishuk Evgeni Platov	RUS Anjelika Krylova Oleg Ovsyannikov	CAN Shae-Lynn Bourne Victor Kraatz
1998	USA Minneapolis	RUS Anjelika Krylova & Oleg Ovsyannikov	FRA Marina Anissina & Gwendal Peizerat	CAN Shae-Lynn Bourne & Victor Kraatz
1999	FIN Helsinki	RUS Anjelika Krylova & Oleg Ovsyannikov	FRA Marina Anissina & Gwendal Peizerat	CAN Shae-Lynn Bourne & Victor Kraatz
2000	FRA Nice	FRA Marina Anissina & Gwendal Peizerat	ITA Barbara Fusar-Poli & Maurizio Margaglio	LIT Margarita Drobiazko & Povilas Vanagas
2001	CAN Vancouver	ITA Barbara Fusar-Poli & Maurizio Margaglio	FRA Marina Anissina & Gwendal Peizerat	RUS Irina Lobacheva & Ilia Averbukh

Year	Location	Gold	Silver	Bronze
2002	JPN Nagano	RUS Irina Lobacheva & Ilia Averbukh	CAN Shae-Lynn Bourne & Victor Kraatz	Israel Galit Chait & Sergei Sakhnovski
2003	USA Washington D.C.	CAN Shae-Lynn Bourne & Victor Kraatz	RUS Irina Lobacheva & Ilia Averbukh	BUL Albena Denkova & Maxim Staviski
2004	GER Dortmund	RUS Tatiana Navka & Roman Kostomarov	BUL Albena Denkova & Maxim Staviski	GER Kati Winkler & René Lohse
2005	RUS Moscow	RUS Tatiana Navka & Roman Kostomarov	USA Tanith Belbin & Benjamin Agosto	UKR Elena Grushina & Ruslan Goncharov
2006	CAN Calgary	BUL Albena Denkova & Maxim Staviski	CAN Marie-FRA Dubreuil & Patrice Lauzon	USA Tanith Belbin & Benjamin Agosto
2007	JPN Tokyo	BUL Albena Denkova & Maxim Staviski	CAN Marie-FRA Dubreuil & Patrice Lauzon	USA Tanith Belbin & Benjamin Agosto
2008	SWE Gothenburg	FRA Isabelle Delobel & Olivier Schoenfelder	CAN Tessa Virtue & Scott Moir	RUS Jana Khokhlova & Sergei Novitski
2009	USA Los Angeles	RUS Oksana Domnina & Maxim Shabalin	USA Tanith Belbin & Benjamin Agosto	CAN Tessa Virtue & Scott Moir
2010	ITA Turin	CAN Tessa Virtue & Scott Moir	USA Meryl Davis & Charlie White	ITA Federica Faiella & Massimo Scali
2011	RUS Moscow	USA Meryl Davis & Charlie White	CAN Tessa Virtue & Scott Moir	USA Maia Shibutani & Alex Shibutani
2012	FRA Nice	CAN Tessa Virtue & Scott Moir	USA Meryl Davis & Charlie White	FRA Nathalie Péchalat & Fabian Bourzat

Year	Location	Gold	Silver	Bronze
2013	CAN London	USA Meryl Davis & Charlie White	CAN Tessa Virtue & Scott Moir	RUS Ekaterina Bobrova & Dmitri Soloviev
2014	JPN Saitama	ITA Anna Cappellini & Luca Lanotte	CAN Kaitlyn Weaver & Andrew Poje	FRA Nathalie Péchalat & Fabian Bourzat
2015	CHN Shanghai	FRA Gabriella Papadakis & Guillaume Cizeron	USA Madison Chock & Evan Bates	CAN Kaitlyn Weaver & Andrew Poje
2016	USA Boston	FRA Gabriella Papadakis & Guillaume Cizeron	USA Maia Shibutani & Alex Shibutani	USA Madison Chock & Evan Bates
2017	FIN Helsinki	CAN Tessa Virtue & Scott Moir	FRA Gabriella Papadakis & Guillaume Cizeron	USA Maia Shibutani & Alex Shibutani

World Junior Championships

Originating in 1976, the ISU-sanctioned World Junior Figure Skating Championships is the most significant competition event for junior skaters, (those older than the age of 13 and younger than 19, except for male pairs and figure skaters, who must be younger than 21). Originally held in the spring, the event switched to being held in November or December in 1980. However, in 2000, the event switched back to being held in the spring again.

World Junior Figure Skating Championships - MEN

Year	Location	Gold	Silver	Bronze
1976	FRA Megève	USA Mark Cockerell	JPN Takashi Mura	CAN Brian Pockar
1977	FRA Megève	CAN Daniel Beland	GBR Mark Pepperday	SUI Richard Furrer
1978	FRA Megève	CAN Dennis Coi	URS Vladimir Kotin	USA Brian Boitano
1979	GER Augsburg	URS Vitali Egorov	USA Bobby Beauchamp	URS Alexander Fadeev
1980	FRA Megève	URS Alexander Fadeev	URS Vitali Egorov	GDR Falko Kirsten
1981	CAN London, Ontario	USA Paul Wylie	URS Yuri Bureiko	USA Scott Williams
1982	GER Oberstdorf	USA Scott Williams	USA Paul Guerrero	GDR Alexander König
1983	YUG Sarajevo	USA Christopher Bowman	FRA Philippe Roncoli	GDR Nils Köpp

Greg Fox

Year	Location	Gold	Silver	Bronze
1984	JPN Sapporo	URS Viktor Petrenko	CAN Marc Ferland	USA Tom Cierniak
1985	USA Colorado Springs	USA Erik Larson	URS Vladimir Petrenko	USA Rudy Galindo
1986	YUG Sarajevo	URS Vladimir Petrenko	USA Rudy Galindo	URS Yuriy Tsymbalyuk
1987	CAN Kitchener	USA Rudy Galindo	USA Todd Eldredge	URS Yuriy Tsymbalyuk
1988	AUS Brisbane	USA Todd Eldredge	URS Viacheslav Zagorodniuk	URS Yuriy Tsymbalyuk
1989	YUG Sarajevo	URS Viacheslav Zagorodniuk	USA Shepherd Clark	JPN Masakazu Kagiyama
1990	USA Colorado Springs	URS Igor Pashkevich	URS Alexei Urmanov	USA John Baldwin Jr.
1991	HUN Budapest	URS Vasili Eremenko	URS Alexander Abt	FRA Nicolas Pétorin
1992	CAN Hull	URS Dmitri Dmitrenko	URS Konstantin Kostin	USA Damon Allen
1993	KOR Seoul	UKR Evgeni Pliuta	USA Michael Weiss	RUS Ilia Kulik
1994	USA Colorado Springs	USA Michael Weiss	JPN Naoki Shigematsu	USA Jere Michael
1995	HUN Budapest	RUS Ilia Kulik	FRA Thierry Cerez	JPN Seiichi Suzuki
1996	AUS Brisbane	RUS Alexei Yagudin	JPN Takeshi Honda	CHN Guo Zhengxin
1997	KOR Seoul	RUS Evgeni Plushenko	USA Timothy Goebel	CHN Guo Zhengxin
1998	CAN Saint John	USA Derrick Delmore	RUS Sergei Davydov	CHN Li Yunfei
1999	CRO Zagreb	RUS Ilia Klimkin	FRA Vincent Restencourt	JPN Yosuke Takeuchi
2000	GER Oberstdorf	GER Stefan Lindemann	FRA Vincent Restencourt	USA Matthew Savoie
2001	BUL Sofia	USA Johnny Weir	USA Evan Lysacek	FRA Vincent Restencourt

Year	Location	Gold	Silver	Bronze
2002	NOR Hamar	JPN Daisuke Takahashi	BEL Kevin van der Perren	RUS Stanislav Timchenko
2003	CZE Ostrava	RUS Alexander Shubin	USA Evan Lysacek	FRA Alban Préaubert
2004	NED The Hague	RUS Andrei Griazev	USA Evan Lysacek	USA Jordan Brauninger
2005	CAN Kitchener	JPN Nobunari Oda	FRA Yannick Ponsero	RUS Sergei Dobrin
2006	SLO Ljubljana	JPN Takahiko Kozuka	RUS Sergei Voronov	FRA Yannick Ponsero
2007	GER Oberstdorf	USA Stephen Carriere	CAN Patrick Chan	RUS Sergei Voronov
2008	BUL Sofia	USA Adam Rippon	RUS Artem Borodulin	CHN Guan Jinlin
2009	BUL Sofia	USA Adam Rippon	CZE Michal Březina	RUS Artem Grigoriev
2010	NED The Hague	JPN Yuzuru Hanyu	CHN Song Nan	RUS Artur Gachinski
2011	KOR Gangneung	CAN Andrei Rogozine	JPN Keiji Tanaka	SWE Alexander Majorov
2012	BLR Minsk	CHN Yan Han	USA Joshua Farris	USA Jason Brown
2013	ITA Milan	USA Joshua Farris	USA Jason Brown	USA Shotaro Omori
2014	BUL Sofia	CAN Nam Nguyen	RUS Adian Pitkeev	USA Nathan Chen
2015	EST Tallinn	JPN Shoma Uno	CHN Jin Boyang	JPN Sota Yamamoto
2016	HUN Debrecen	ISR Daniel Samohin	CAN Nicolas Nadeau	USA Tomoki Hiwatashi
2017	TPE Taipei	USA Vincent Zhou	RUS Dmitri Aliev	RUS Alexander Samarin

World Junior Figure Skating Championships - PAIRS

Year	Location	Gold	Silver	Bronze
1976	FRA Megève	CAN Sherri Baier & Robin Cowan	USA Lorene Mitchell & Donald Mitchell	AUS Elizabeth Cain & Peter Cain
1977	FRA Megève	CAN Josée France & Paul Mills	RSA Elga Balk & Gavin MacPherson	*no other competitors*
1978	FRA Megève	CAN Barbara Underhill & Paul Martini	CZE Jana Blahová & Ludek Feno	USA Beth Flora & Ken Flora
1979	FRG Augsburg	URS Veronika Pershina & Marat Akbarov	URS Larisa Selezneva & Oleg Makarov	CAN Lori Baier & Lloyd Eisler
1980	FRA Megève	URS Larisa Selezneva & Oleg Makarov	URS Marina Nikitiuk & Rashid Kadyrkaev	FRA Kathia Dubec & Xavier Douillard
1981	CAN London, Ontario	URS Larisa Selezneva & Oleg Makarov	CAN Lorri Baier & Lloyd Eisler	URS Marina Nikitiuk & Rashid Kadyrkaev
1982	FRG Oberstdorf	URS Marina Avstriyskaya & Yuri Kvashnin	URS Inna Bekker & Sergei Likhanski	GDR Babette Preussler & Torsten Ohlow
1983	YUG Sarajevo	URS Marina Avstriyskaya & Yuri Kvashnin	GDR Peggy Seidel & Ralf Seifert	URS Inna Bekker & Sergei Likhanski
1984	JPN Sapporo	GDR Manuela Landgraf & Ingo Steuer	USA Susan Dungjen & Jason Dungjen	URS Olga Neizvestnaya & Sergei Khudiakov
1985	USA Colorado Springs	URS Ekaterina Gordeeva & Sergei Grinkov	URS Irina Mironenko & Dmitri Shkidchenko	URS Elena Gud & Evgeni Koltun

Year	Location	Gold	Silver	Bronze
1986	YUG Sarajevo	URS Elena Leonova & Gennadi Krasnitski	URS Irina Mironenko & Dmitri Shkidchenko	URS Ekaterina Murugova & Artem Torgashev
1987	CAN Kitchener	URS Elena Leonova & Gennadi Krasnitski	URS Ekaterina Murugova & Artem Torgashev	USA Kristi Yamaguchi & Rudy Galindo
1988	AUS Brisbane	USA Kristi Yamaguchi & Rudy Galindo	URS Evgenia Chernyshova & Dmitri Sukhanov	URS Yulia Liashenko & Andrei Bushkov
1989	YUG Sarajevo	URS Evgenia Chernyshova & Dmitri Sukhanov	GDR Angela Caspari & Marno Kreft	URS Irina Saifutdinova & Alexei Tikhonov
1990	USA Colorado Springs	URS Natalia Krestianinova & Alexei Torchinski	URS Svetlana Pristav & Viacheslav Tkachenko	USA Jennifer Heurlin & John Frederiksen
1991	HUN Budapest	URS Natalia Krestianinova & Alexei Torchinski	URS Svetlana Pristav & Viacheslav Tkachenko	USA Jennifer Heurlin & John Frederiksen
1992	CAN Hull	URS Natalia Krestianinova & Alexei Torchinski	CAN Caroline Haddad & Jean-Sebastien Fecteau	URS Svetlana Pristav & Viacheslav Tkachenko
1993	KOR Seoul	RUS Inga Korshunova & Dmitri Saveliev	RUS Maria Petrova & Anton Sikharulidze	CAN Isabelle Coulombe & Bruno Marcotte
1994	USA Colorado Springs	RUS Maria Petrova & Anton Sikharulidze	CAN Caroline Haddad & Jean-Sebastien Fecteau	UKR Galina Maniachenko & Evgeni Zhigurski

Year	Location	Gold	Silver	Bronze
1995	HUN Budapest	RUS Maria Petrova & Anton Sikharulidze	USA Danielle Hartsell & Steve Hartsell	UKR Evgenia Filonenko & Igor Marchenko
1996	AUS Brisbane	RUS Victoria Maxiuta & Vladislav Zhovnirski	UKR Evgenia Filonenko & Igor Marchenko	USA Danielle Hartsell & Steve Hartsell
1997	KOR Seoul	USA Danielle Hartsell & Steve Hartsell	RUS Maria Petrova & Teimuraz Pulin	RUS Victoria Maxiuta & Vladislav Zhovnirski
1998	CAN Saint John	UKR Julia Obertas & Dmytro Palamarchuk	RUS Svetlana Nikolaeva & Alexei Sokolov	RUS Victoria Maxiuta & Vladislav Zhovnirski
1999	CRO Zagreb	UKR Julia Obertas & Dmytro Palamarchuk	USA Laura Handy & Paul Binnebose	RUS Victoria Maxiuta & Vladislav Zhovnirski
2000	GER Oberstdorf	UKR Aliona Savchenko & Stanislav Morozov	UKR Julia Obertas & Dmitri Palamarchuk	RUS Julia Shapiro & Alexei Sokolov
2001	BUL Sofia	CHN Zhang Dan & Zhang Hao	JPN Yuko Kawaguchi & Alexander Markuntsov	USA Kristen Roth & Michael McPherson
2002	NOR Hamar	RUS Elena Riabchuk & Stanislav Zakarov	RUS Julia Karbovskaya & Sergei Slavnov	CHN Ding Yang & Ren Zhongfei
2003	CZE Ostrava	CHN Zhang Dan & Zhang Hao	CHN Ding Yang & Ren Zhongfei	USA Jennifer Don & Jonathon Hunt
2004	NED The Hague	RUS Natalia Shestakova & Pavel Lebedev	CAN Jessica Dube & Bryce Davison	RUS Maria Mukhortova & Maxim Trankov
2005	CAN Kitchener	RUS Maria Mukhortova & Maxim Trankov	CAN Jessica Dubé & Bryce Davison	RUS Tatiana Kokoreva & Egor Golovkin
2006	SLO Ljubljana	USA Julia Vlassov & Drew Meekins	USA Kendra Moyle & Andy Seitz	RUS Ksenia Krasilnikova & Konstantin Bezmaternikh

Year	Location	Gold	Silver	Bronze
2007	GER Oberstdorf	USA Keauna McLaughlin & Rockne Brubaker	RUS Vera Bazarova & Yuri Larionov	RUS Ksenia Krasilnikova & Konstantin Bezmaternikh
2008	BUL Sofia	RUS Ksenia Krasilnikova & Konstantin Bezmaternikh	RUS Lubov Iliushechkina & Nodari Maisuradze	CHN Dong Huibo & Wu Yiming
2009	BUL Sofia	RUS Lubov Iliushechkina & Nodari Maisuradze	RUS Anastasia Martiusheva & Alexei Rogonov	USA Marissa Castelli & Simon Shnapir
2010	NED The Hague	CHN Sui Wenjing & Han Cong	JPN Narumi Takahashi & Mervin Tran	RUS Ksenia Stolbova & Fedor Klimov
2011	KOR Gangneung	CHN Sui Wenjing & Han Cong	RUS Ksenia Stolbova & Fedor Klimov	JPN Narumi Takahashi & Mervin Tran
2012	BLR Minsk	CHN Sui Wenjing & Han Cong	CHN Yu Xiaoyu & Jin Yang	RUS Vasilisa Davankova & Andrei Deputat
2013	ITA Milan	USA Haven Denney & Brandon Frazier	CAN Margaret Purdy & Michael Marinaro	RUS Lina Fedorova & Maxim Miroshkin
2014	BUL Sofia	CHN Yu Xiaoyu & Jin Yang	RUS Evgenia Tarasova & Vladimir Morozov	RUS Maria Vigalova & Egor Zakroev
2015	EST Tallinn	CHN Yu Xiaoyu & Jin Yang	CAN Julianne Séguin & Charlie Bilodeau	RUS Lina Fedorova & Maxim Miroshkin
2016	HUN Debrecen	CZE Anna Dušková & Martin Bidař	RUS Anastasia Mishina & Vladislav Mirzoev	RUS Ekaterina Borisova & Dmitry Sopot
2017	TPE Taipei	AUS Ekaterina Alexandrovskaya & Harley Windsor	RUS Aleksandra Boikova & Dmitrii Kozlovskii	CHN Gao Yumeng & Xie Zhong

Greg Fox

World Junior Figure Skating Championships - LADIES

Year	Location	Gold	Silver	Bronze
1976	FRA Megève	USA Suzie Brasher	FRG Garnet Ostermeier	GBR Tracey Solomons
1977	FRA Megève	CAN Carolyn Skoczen	AUT Christa Jorda	SUI Corine Wyrsch
1978	FRA Megève	USA Jill Sawyer	URS Kira Ivanova	FRG Petra Ernert
1979	GER Augsburg	USA Elaine Zayak	FRG Manuela Ruben	USA Jacki Farrell
1980	FRA Megève	USA Rosalynn Sumners	CAN Kay Thomson	GDR Carola Paul
1981	CAN London, Ontario	USA Tiffany Chin	URS Marina Serova	URS Anna Antonova
1982	GER Oberstdorf	GDR Janina Wirth	FRG Cornelia Tesch	CAN Elizabeth Manley
1983	YUG Sarajevo	GDR Simone Koch	GDR Karin Hendschke	AUT Parthena Sarafidis
1984	JPN Sapporo	GDR Karin Hendschke	GDR Simone Koch	JPN Midori Ito
1985	USA Colorado Springs	URS Tatiana Andreeva	FRG Susanne Becher	URS Natalia Gorbenko
1986	YUG Sarajevo	URS Natalia Gorbenko	FRG Susanne Becher	CAN Linda Florkevich
1987	CAN Kitchener	USA Cindy Bortz	FRG Susanne Becher	CAN Shannon Allison
1988	AUS Brisbane	USA Kristi Yamaguchi	JPN Junko Yaginuma	JPN Yukiko Kashihara
1989	YUG Sarajevo	USA Jessica Mills	JPN Junko Yaginuma	FRA Surya Bonaly
1990	USA Colorado Springs	JPN Yuka Sato	FRA Surya Bonaly	GDR Tanja Krienke
1991	HUN Budapest	FRA Surya Bonaly	USA Lisa Ervin	CHN Chen Lu
1992	CAN Hull	FRA Laëtitia Hubert	USA Lisa Ervin	CHN Chen Lu
1993	KOR Seoul	JPN Kumiko Koiwai	USA Lisa Ervin	GER Tanja Szewczenko
1994	USA Colorado Springs	USA Michelle Kwan	HUN Krisztina Czakó	RUS Irina Slutskaya
1995	HUN Budapest	RUS Irina Slutskaya	RUS Elena Ivanova	HUN Krisztina Czakó
1996	AUS Brisbane	RUS Elena Ivanova	RUS Elena Pingacheva	RUS Nadezhda Kanaeva

Year	Location	Gold	Silver	Bronze
1997	KOR Seoul	USA Sydne Vogel	RUS Elena Sokolova	RUS Elena Ivanova
1998	CAN Saint John	RUS Julia Soldatova	RUS Elena Ivanova	RUS Viktoria Volchkova
1999	CRO Zagreb	RUS Daria Timoshenko	USA Sarah Hughes	RUS Viktoria Volchkova
2000	GER Oberstdorf	USA Jennifer Kirk	USA Deanna Stellato	SUI Sarah Meier
2001	BUL Sofia	RUS Kristina Oblasova	USA Ann Patrice McDonough	FIN Susanna Pöykiö
2002	NOR Hamar	USA Ann Patrice McDonough	JPN Yukari Nakano	JPN Miki Ando
2003	CZE Ostrava	JPN Yukina Ota	JPN Miki Ando	ITA Carolina Kostner
2004	NED The Hague	JPN Miki Ando	USA Kimmie Meissner	USA Katy Taylor
2005	CAN Kitchener	JPN Mao Asada	KOR Kim Yuna	USA Emily Hughes
2006	SLO Ljubljana	KOR Kim Yuna	JPN Mao Asada	USA Christine Zukowski
2007	GER Oberstdorf	USA Caroline Zhang	USA Mirai Nagasu	USA Ashley Wagner
2008	BUL Sofia	USA Rachael Flatt	USA Caroline Zhang	USA Mirai Nagasu
2009	BUL Sofia	RUS Alena Leonova	USA Caroline Zhang	USA Ashley Wagner
2010	NED The Hague	JPN Kanako Murakami	USA Agnes Zawadzki	RUS Polina Agafonova
2011	KOR Gangneung	RUS Adelina Sotnikova	RUS Elizaveta Tuktamysheva	USA Agnes Zawadzki
2012	BLR Minsk	RUS Yulia Lipnitskaya	USA Gracie Gold	RUS Adelina Sotnikova
2013	ITA Milan	RUS Elena Radionova	RUS Yulia Lipnitskaya	RUS Anna Pogorilaya
2014	BUL Sofia	RUS Elena Radionova	RUS Serafima Sakhanovich	RUS Evgenia Medvedeva
2015	EST Tallinn	RUS Evgenia Medvedeva	RUS Serafima Sakhanovich	JPN Wakaba Higuchi
2016	HUN Debrecen	JPN Marin Honda	RUS Maria Sotskova	JPN Wakaba Higuchi
2017	TPE Taipei	RUS Alina Zagitova	JPN Marin Honda	JPN Kaori Sakamoto

World Junior Figure Skating Championships - ICE DANCING

Year	Location	Gold	Silver	Bronze
1976	FRA Megève	GBR Kathryn Winter & Nicholas Slater	GBR Denise Best & David Dagnell	FRA Martine Olivier & Yves Tarayre
1977	FRA Megève	GBR Wendy Sessions & Mark Reed	GBR Karen Barber & Kim Spreyer	CAN Marie McNeil & Robert McCall
1978	FRA Megève	URS Tatiana Durasova & Sergei Ponomarenko	CAN Kelly Johnson & Kris Barber	FRA Nathalie Hervé & Pierre Husarek
1979	FRG Augsburg	URS Tatiana Durasova & Sergei Ponomarenko	URS Elena Batanova & Andrei Antonov	CAN Kelly Johnson & Kris Barber
1980	FRA Megève	URS Elena Batanova & Alexei Soloviev	HUN Judit Péterfy & Csaba Bálint	USA Renée Roca & Andrew Ouellette
1981	CAN London, Ontario	URS Elena Batanova & Alexei Soloviev	URS Natalia Annenko & Vadim Karkachev	CAN Karyn Garossino & Rodney Garossino
1982	FRG Oberstdorf	URS Natalia Annenko & Vadim Karkachev	URS Tatiana Gladkova & Igor Shpilband	USA Lynda Malek & Alexander Miller
1983	YUG Sarajevo	URS Tatiana Gladkova & Igor Shpilband	URS Elena Novikova & Oleg Bliakhman	USA Christina Yatsuhashi & Keith Yatsuhashi
1984	JPN Sapporo	URS Elena Krykanova & Evgeni Platov	USA Christina Yatsuhashi & Keith Yatsuhashi	URS Svetlana Liapina & Georgi Sur
1985	USA Colorado Springs	URS Elena Krykanova & Evgeni Platov	URS Svetlana Liapina & Georgi Sur	FRA Doriane Bontemps & Charles Paliard

Year	Location	Gold	Silver	Bronze
1986	YUG Sarajevo	URS Elena Krykanova & Evgeni Platov	URS Svetlana Serkeli & Andrei Zharkov	FRA Corinne Paliard & Didier Courtois
1987	CAN Kitchener	URS Ilona Melnichenko & Gennadi Kaskov	URS Oksana Grishuk & Alexander Chichkov	CAN Catherine Pal & Donald Godfrey
1988	AUS Brisbane	URS Oksana Grishuk & Alexander Chichkov	URS Irina Antsiferova & Maxim Sevastianov	URS Maria Orlova & Oleg Ovsyannikov
1989	YUG Sarajevo	URS Angelika Kirkhmaier & Dmitri Lagutin	URS Liudmila Berezova & Vladimir Fedorov	FRA Marina Morel & Gwendal Peizerat
1990	USA Colorado Springs	URS Marina Anissina & Ilia Averbukh	URS Elena Kustarova & Sergei Romashkin	CAN Marie-France Dubreuil & Bruno Yvars
1991	HUN Budapest	URS Aliki Stergiadu & Yuri Razguliaiev	FRA Marina Morel & Gwendal Peizerat	URS Elena Kustarova & Sergei Romashkin
1992	CAN Hull	URS Marina Anissina & Ilia Averbukh	URS Yaroslava Nechaeva & Yuri Chesnichenko	CAN Amelie Dion & Alexandre Alain
1993	KOR Seoul	RUS Ekaterina Svirina & Sergei Sakhnovski	POL Sylwia Nowak & Sebastian Kolasiński	FRA Bérangère Nau & Luc Monéger
1994	USA Colorado Springs	POL Sylwia Nowak & Sebastian Kolasiński	RUS Ekaterina Svirina & Sergei Sakhnovski	FRA Agnes Jacquemard & Alexis Gayet
1995	HUN Budapest	RUS Olga Sharutenko & Dmitri Naumkin	FRA Stéphanie Guardia & Franck Laporte	POL Iwona Filipowicz & Michał Szumski
1996	AUS Brisbane	RUS Ekaterina Davydova & Roman Kostomarov	FRA Isabelle Delobel & Olivier Schoenfelder	UKR Natalia Gudina & Vitali Kurkudym
1997	KOR Seoul	RUS Nina Ulanova & Mikhail Stifounin	RUS Oksana Potdykova & Denis Petukhov	POL Agata Błażowska & Marcin Kozubek

Year	Location	Gold	Silver	Bronze
1998	CAN Saint John	USA Jessica Joseph & Charles Butler Jr.	ITA Federica Faiella & Luciano Milo	RUS Oksana Potdykova & Denis Petukhov
1999	CRO Zagreb	USA Jamie Silverstein & Justin Pekarek	ITA Federica Faiella & Luciano Milo	RUS Natalia Romaniuta & Daniil Barantsev
2000	GER Oberstdorf	RUS Natalia Romaniuta & Daniil Barantsev	USA Emilie Nussear & Brandon Forsyth	USA Tanith Belbin & Benjamin Agosto
2001	BUL Sofia	RUS Natalia Romaniuta & Daniil Barantsev	USA Tanith Belbin & Benjamin Agosto	RUS Elena Khaliavina & Maxim Shabalin
2002	NOR Hamar	USA Tanith Belbin & Benjamin Agosto	RUS Elena Khaliavina & Maxim Shabalin	RUS Elena Romanovskaya & Alexander Grachev
2003	CZE Ostrava	RUS Oksana Domnina & Maxim Shabalin	HUN Nóra Hoffmann & Attila Elek	RUS Elena Romanovskaya & Alexander Grachev
2004	NED The Hague	RUS Elena Romanovskaya & Alexander Grachev	HUN Nóra Hoffmann & Attila Elek	USA Morgan Matthews & Maxim Zavozin
2005	CAN Kitchener	USA Morgan Matthews & Maxim Zavozin	CAN Tessa Virtue & Scott Moir	RUS Anastasia Gorshkova & Ilia Tkachenko
2006	SLO Ljubljana	CAN Tessa Virtue & Scott Moir	RUS Natalia Mikhailova & Arkadi Sergeev	USA Meryl Davis & Charlie White
2007	GER Oberstdorf	RUS Ekaterina Bobrova & Dmitri Soloviev	EST Grethe Grünberg & Kristjan Rand	CAN Kaitlyn Weaver & Andrew Poje

Year	Location	Gold	Silver	Bronze
2008	BUL Sofia	USA Emily Samuelson & Evan Bates	CAN Vanessa Crone & Paul Poirier	RUS Kristina Gorshkova & Vitali Butikov
2009	BUL Sofia	USA Madison Chock & Greg Zuerlein	USA Maia Shibutani & Alex Shibutani	RUS Ekaterina Riazanova & Jonathan Guerreiro
2010	NED The Hague	RUS Elena Ilinykh & Nikita Katsalapov	CAN Alexandra Paul & Mitchell Islam	RUS Ksenia Monko & Kirill Khaliavin
2011	KOR Gangneung	RUS Ksenia Monko & Kirill Khaliavin	RUS Ekaterina Pushkash & Jonathan Guerreiro	USA Charlotte Lichtman & Dean Copely
2012	BLR Minsk	RUS Victoria Sinitsina & Ruslan Zhiganshin	RUS Alexandra Stepanova & Ivan Bukin	USA Alexandra Aldridge & Daniel Eaton
2013	ITA Milan	RUS Alexandra Stepanova & Ivan Bukin	FRA Gabriella Papadakis & Guillaume Cizeron	USA Alexandra Aldridge & Daniel Eaton
2014	BUL Sofia	USA Kaitlin Hawayek & Jean-Luc Baker	RUS Anna Yanovskaya & Sergey Mozgov	CAN Madeline Edwards & Zhao Kai Pang
2015	EST Tallinn	RUS Anna Yanovskaya & Sergei Mozgov	USA Lorraine McNamara & Quinn Carpenter	UKR Oleksandra Nazarova & Maksym Nikitin
2016	HUN Debrecen	USA Lorraine McNamara & Quinn Carpenter	USA Rachel Parsons & Michael Parsons	RUS Alla Loboda & Pavel Drozd
2017	TPE Taipei	USA Rachel Parsons & Michael Parsons	RUS Alla Loboda & Pavel Drozd	USA Christina Carreira & Anthony Ponomarenko

Greg Fox

Above: **Dorothy Hamill** and **Brian Boitano**, two American figure skating superstars who both won Olympic gold medals, (Hamill at Innsbruck, Austria in 1976, and Boitano at Calgary, Alberta, Canada in 1988). While both were accomplished skaters already, (Hamill a 3-time US National Champion, and Boitano a 4-time US National Champion and 1-time World Champion), it would be their Olympic gold medal performances that turned them into household names. Additionally, they would each go on to win a World Championship title, (a first for Hamill), immediately after their Olympic wins.

For many people, Olympic figure skating may possibly be the only figure skating they're familiar with, as the TV and media coverage of the Olympic games is enormous. While figure skating has its own set of prestigious competitions that take place every year, (as we've seen in this book), the once-every-4-years Olympic event seems to be the pinnacle competition for many fans, (and skaters, too). And winning an Olympic medal, especially the gold, all but insures that a figure skater will become a household name and have a lifetime of accolades connected with that. It also just so happens that some of the most dramatic, (and infamous), events in figure skating history have taken place at the Olympics: the battle of the Brians and the dueling Carmens, (both 1988)... Nancy & Tonya, (1994)... the Canadian pairs skating judging scandal, (2002).

Figure skating at the Olympics actually predates the Winter Olympics. Figure skating was first introduced at the 1908 Summer Olympics in London, (before there even *was* a separate Winter Olympics event). By the time of the first Winter Olympics in 1924, (held at Chamonix, France), three figure skating events were on the program: men's singles, ladies' singles, and pairs. (A one-time only event called "special figures" was included in the 1908 Olympics, which involved the tracing of even more elaborate figures on the ice than those traced in what was then a standard part of the singles competition). Ice dancing officially was added to the program in 1976. And in 2014, an all-new Team Event was added, which involved a team from each competing country comprised of one men's singles skater, one ladies' singles skater, one pair and one ice dancing couple.

Will a new set of figure skating stars emerge at the next Winter Olympics? (As of this writing, the next one is scheduled only months away, in February, 2018, in PyeongChang, South Korea). I think you can pretty much count on it. And for those of us who have been faithfully following the various figure skating competitions through the years, those Olympic "new stars" may be, to us, skaters that we've already come to know and love, and we can smile and say, "Yeah, I knew them back when they skated in their first Nebelhorn..."

The Olympics - MEN

Games	Gold	Silver	Bronze
1908 London	Ulrich Salchow SWE	Richard Johansson SWE	Per Thorén SWE
1912 Stockholm	Figure Skating not included in the Olympic program		
1920 Antwerp	Gillis Grafström SWE	Andreas Krogh NOR	Martin Stixrud NOR
1924 Chamonix	Gillis Grafström SWE	Willy Böckl AUT	Georges Gautschi SUI
1928 St. Moritz	Gillis Grafström SWE	Willy Böckl AUT	Robert van Zeebroeck BEL
1932 Lake Placid	Karl Schäfer AUT	Gillis Grafström SWE	Montgomery Wilson CAN
1936 Garmisch-Partenkirchen	Karl Schäfer AUT	Ernst Baier GER	Felix Kaspar AUT
1948 St. Moritz	Dick Button USA	Hans Gerschwiler SUI	Edi Rada AUT
1952 Oslo	Dick Button USA	Helmut Seibt AUT	James Grogan USA
1956 Cortina d'Ampezzo	Hayes Alan Jenkins USA	Ronnie Robertson USA	David Jenkins USA
1960 Squaw Valley	David Jenkins USA	Karol Divín TCH	Donald Jackson CAN
1964 Innsbruck	Manfred Schnelldorfer EUA	Alain Calmat FRA	Scott Allen USA
1968 Grenoble	Wolfgang Schwarz AUT	Timothy Wood USA	Patrick Péra FRA
1972 Sapporo	Ondrej Nepela TCH	Sergei Chetverukhin URS	Patrick Péra FRA
1976 Innsbruck	John Curry GBR	Vladimir Kovalev URS	Toller Cranston CAN
1980 Lake Placid	Robin Cousins GBR	Jan Hoffmann GDR	Charles Tickner USA
1984 Sarajevo	Scott Hamilton USA	Brian Orser CAN	Jozef Sabovčík TCH
1988 Calgary	Brian Boitano USA	Brian Orser CAN	Viktor Petrenko URS

Opposite Page: **Richard Johansson**, 4x Swedish National Champion men's figure skater, won the silver medal at the 1908 Olympics.

Games	Gold	Silver	Bronze
1992 Albertville	Viktor Petrenko EUN	Paul Wylie USA	Petr Barna TCH
1994 Lillehammer	Alexei Urmanov RUS	Elvis Stojko CAN	Philippe Candeloro FRA
1998 Nagano	Ilia Kulik RUS	Elvis Stojko CAN	Philippe Candeloro FRA
2002 Salt Lake City	Alexei Yagudin RUS	Evgeni Plushenko RUS	Timothy Goebel USA
2006 Torino	Evgeni Plushenko RUS	Stéphane Lambiel SUI	Jeffrey Buttle CAN
2010 Vancouver	Evan Lysacek USA	Evgeni Plushenko RUS	Daisuke Takahashi JPN
2014 Sochi	Yuzuru Hanyu JPN	Patrick Chan CAN	Denis Ten KAZ

The Olympics - MEN's SPECIAL FIGURES

Games	Gold	Silver	Bronze
1908 London	Nikolai Panin RUS	Arthur Cumming GBR	Geoffrey Hall-Say GBR

Greg Fox

The Olympics - PAIRS

Games	Gold	Silver	Bronze
1908 London	Anna Hübler & Heinrich Burger GER	Phyllis Johnson & James H. Johnson GBR	Madge Syers & Edgar Syers GBR
1912 Stockholm	*Figure Skating not included in the Olympic program*		
1920 Antwerp	Ludowika Jakobsson & Walter Jakobsson FIN	Alexia Bry & Yngvar Bryn NOR	Phyllis Johnson & Basil Williams GBR
1924 Chamonix	Helene Engelmann & Alfred Berger AUT	Ludowika Jakobsson & Walter Jakobsson FIN	Andrée Joly & Pierre Brunet FRA
1928 St. Moritz	Andrée Joly & Pierre Brunet FRA	Lilly Scholz & Otto Kaiser AUT	Melitta Brunner & Ludwig Wrede AUT
1932 Lake Placid	Andrée Brunet & Pierre Brunet FRA	Beatrix Loughran & Sherwin Badger USA	Emília Rotter & László Szollás HUN
1936 Garmisch-Partenkirchen	Maxi Herber & Ernst Baier GER	Ilse Pausin & Erik Pausin AUT	Emília Rotter & László Szollás HUN
1948 St. Moritz	Micheline Lannoy & Pierre Baugniet BEL	Andrea Kékesy & Ede Király HUN	Suzanne Morrow & Wallace Diestelmeyer CAN
1952 Oslo	Ria Falk & Paul Falk GER	Karol Kennedy & Peter Kennedy USA	Marianna Nagy & László Nagy HUN
1956 Cortina d'Ampezzo	Sissy Schwarz & Kurt Oppelt AUT	Frances Dafoe & Norris Bowden CAN	Marianna Nagy & László Nagy HUN
1960 Squaw Valley	Barbara Wagner & Robert Paul CAN	Marika Kilius & Hans-Jürgen Bäumler EUA	Nancy Ludington & Ronald Ludington USA
1964 Innsbruck	Ludmila Belousova & Oleg Protopopov URS	Marika Kilius & Hans-Jürgen Bäumler EUA Debbi Wilkes & Guy Revell CAN *	Vivian Joseph & Ronald Joseph USA

* The silver medal in 1964 is shared by both of these pairs teams

Games	Gold	Silver	Bronze
1968 Grenoble	Ludmila Belousova & Oleg Protopopov URS	Tatyana Zhuk & Aleksandr Gorelik URS	Margot Glockshuber & Wolfgang Danne FRG
1972 Sapporo	Irina Rodnina & Alexei Ulanov URS	Lyudmila Smirnova & Andrei Suraikin URS	Manuela Groß & Uwe Kagelmann GDR
1976 Innsbruck	Irina Rodnina & Alexander Zaitsev URS	Romy Kermer & Rolf Österreich GDR	Manuela Groß & Uwe Kagelmann GDR
1980 Lake Placid	Irina Rodnina & Alexander Zaitsev URS	Marina Cherkasova & Sergei Shakhrai URS	Manuela Mager & Uwe Bewersdorf GDR
1984 Sarajevo	Elena Valova & Oleg Vasiliev URS	Kitty Carruthers & Peter Carruthers USA	Larisa Selezneva & Oleg Makarov URS
1988 Calgary	Ekaterina Gordeeva & Sergei Grinkov URS	Elena Valova & Oleg Vasiliev URS	Jill Watson & Peter Oppegard USA
1992 Albertville	Natalia Mishkutenok & Artur Dmitriev EUN	Elena Bechke & Denis Petrov EUN	Isabelle Brasseur & Lloyd Eisler CAN
1994 Lillehammer	Ekaterina Gordeeva & Sergei Grinkov RUS	Natalia Mishkutenok & Artur Dmitriev RUS	Isabelle Brasseur & Lloyd Eisler CAN
1998 Nagano	Oksana Kazakova & Artur Dmitriev RUS	Elena Berezhnaya & Anton Sikharulidze RUS	Mandy Wötzel & Ingo Steuer GER
2002 Salt Lake City	Jamie Salé & David Pelletier CAN and Elena Berezhnaya & Anton Sikharulidze RUS	*None awarded ** (see pages 26-28 in this book for the details of the judging scandal that led to this decision).*	Shen Xue & Zhao Hongbo CHN

Greg Fox

Games	Gold	Silver	Bronze
2006 Torino	Tatiana Totmianina & Maxim Marinin RUS	Zhang Dan & Zhang Hao CHN	Shen Xue & Zhao Hongbo CHN
2010 Vancouver	Shen Xue & Zhao Hongbo CHN	Pang Qing & Tong Jian CHN	Aliona Savchenko & Robin Szolkowy GER
2014 Sochi	Tatiana Volosozhar & Maxim Trankov RUS	Ksenia Stolbova & Fedor Klimov RUS	Aliona Savchenko & Robin Szolkowy GER

The Olympics - LADIES

Games	Gold	Silver	Bronze
1908 London	Madge Syers GBR	Elsa Rendschmidt GER	Dorothy Greenhough Smith GBR
1912 Stockholm	*Figure Skating not included in the Olympic program*		
1920 Antwerp	Magda Julin SWE	Svea Norén SWE	Theresa Weld USA
1924 Chamonix	Herma Szabo AUT	Beatrix Loughran USA	Ethel Muckelt GBR
1928 St. Moritz	Sonja Henie NOR	Fritzi Burger AUT	Beatrix Loughran USA
1932 Lake Placid	Sonja Henie NOR	Fritzi Burger AUT	Maribel Vinson USA
1936 Garmisch-Partenkirchen	Sonja Henie NOR	Cecilia Colledge GBR	Vivi-Anne Hultén SWE
1948 St. Moritz	Barbara Ann Scott CAN	Eva Pawlik AUT	Jeannette Altwegg GBR
1952 Oslo	Jeannette Altwegg GBR	Tenley Albright USA	Jacqueline du Bief FRA
1956 Cortina d'Ampezzo	Tenley Albright USA	Carol Heiss USA	Ingrid Wendl AUT
1960 Squaw Valley	Carol Heiss USA	Sjoukje Dijkstra NED	Barbara Roles USA
1964 Innsbruck	Sjoukje Dijkstra NED	Regine Heitzer AUT	Petra Burka CAN
1968 Grenoble	Peggy Fleming USA	Gabriele Seyfert GDR	Hana Mašková TCH
1972 Sapporo	Beatrix Schuba AUT	Karen Magnussen CAN	Janet Lynn USA
1976 Innsbruck	Dorothy Hamill USA	Dianne de Leeuw NED	Christine Errath GDR
1980 Lake Placid	Anett Pötzsch GDR	Linda Fratianne USA	Dagmar Lurz FRG
1984 Sarajevo	Katarina Witt GDR	Rosalynn Sumners USA	Kira Ivanova URS
1988 Calgary	Katarina Witt GDR	Elizabeth Manley CAN	Debi Thomas USA

Greg Fox

Games	Gold	Silver	Bronze
1992 Albertville	Kristi Yamaguchi USA	Midori Ito JPN	Nancy Kerrigan USA
1994 Lillehammer	Oksana Baiul UKR	Nancy Kerrigan USA	Chen Lu CHN
1998 Nagano	Tara Lipinski USA	Michelle Kwan USA	Chen Lu CHN
2002 Salt Lake City	Sarah Hughes USA	Irina Slutskaya RUS	Michelle Kwan USA
2006 Torino	Shizuka Arakawa JPN	Sasha Cohen USA	Irina Slutskaya RUS
2010 Vancouver	Kim Yuna KOR	Mao Asada JPN	Joannie Rochette CAN
2014 Sochi	Adelina Sotnikova RUS	Kim Yuna KOR	Carolina Kostner ITA

The Olympics - TEAM TROPHY

Games	Gold	Silver	Bronze
2014 Sochi	RUS Evgeni Plushenko Yulia Lipnitskaya Ksenia Stolbova Fedor Klimov Elena Ilinykh Nikita Katsalapov Tatiana Volosozhar Maxim Trankov Ekaterina Bobrova Dmitri Soloviev	CAN Kevin Reynolds Kaetlyn Osmond Kirsten Moore-Towers Dylan Moscovitch Tessa Virtue Scott Moir Patrick Chan Meagan Duhamel Eric Radford	USA Jason Brown Gracie Gold Marissa Castelli Simon Shnapir Meryl Davis Charlie White Jeremy Abbott Ashley Wagner

The Olympics - ICE DANCING

Games	Gold	Silver	Bronze
1976 Innsbruck	Lyudmila Pakhomova & Aleksandr Gorshkov URS	Irina Moiseyeva & Andrei Minenkov URS	Colleen O'Connor & James Millns USA
1980 Lake Placid	Natalia Linichuk & Gennadi Karponossov URS	Krisztina Regőczy & András Sallay HUN	Irina Moiseyeva & Andrei Minenkov URS
1984 Sarajevo	Jayne Torvill & Christopher Dean GBR	Natalia Bestemianova & Andrei Bukin URS	Marina Klimova & Sergei Ponomarenko URS
1988 Calgary	Natalia Bestemianova & Andrei Bukin URS	Marina Klimova & Sergei Ponomarenko URS	Tracy Wilson & Robert McCall CAN
1992 Albertville	Marina Klimova & Sergei Ponomarenko EUN	Isabelle Duchesnay & Paul Duchesnay FRA	Maya Usova & Alexander Zhulin EUN
1994 Lillehammer	Oksana Grishuk & Evgeny Platov RUS	Maya Usova & Alexander Zhulin RUS	Jayne Torvill & Christopher Dean GBR
1998 Nagano	Oksana Grishuk & Evgeny Platov RUS	Anjelika Krylova & Oleg Ovsyannikov RUS	Marina Anissina & Gwendal Peizerat FRA
2002 Salt Lake City	Marina Anissina & Gwendal Peizerat FRA	Irina Lobacheva & Ilia Averbukh RUS	Barbara Fusar-Poli & Maurizio Margaglio ITA
2006 Torino	Tatiana Navka & Roman Kostomarov RUS	Tanith Belbin & Benjamin Agosto USA	Elena Grushina & Ruslan Goncharov UKR
2010 Vancouver	Tessa Virtue & Scott Moir CAN	Meryl Davis & Charlie White USA	Oksana Domnina & Maxim Shabalin RUS
2014 Sochi	Meryl Davis & Charlie White USA	Tessa Virtue & Scott Moir CAN	Elena Ilinykh & Nikita Katsalapov RUS

Greg Fox

SOME FIGURE SKATING WEBSITES TO CHECK OUT:

SKATE GUARD

A figure skating history blog. Rummaging deep into the archives to bring you the stories you don't always get to hear!

http://skateguard1.blogspot.ca/

The ultimate archive of figure skating's fascinating & fabulous history. Researched, written & organized by Ryan Stevens.

Facebook - http://www.facebook.com/SkateGuard
Twitter - http://twitter.com/SkateGuardBlog
Pinterest - http://www.pinterest.com/SkateGuard

SOME OTHER FIGURE SKATING RESOURCES ONLINE:

- US Figure Skating - http://www.usfigureskating.org/
- Skate Canada - https://skatecanada.ca/
- National Ice Skating Association of Great Britain - http://www.iceskating.org.uk/
- Ice Skating Australia - http://www.isa.org.au/
- Fédération Français des Sports de Glace (French Federation of Ice Sports) - https://ffsg.org/
- Deutsche Eislauf-Union (German Ice Skating Union) - http://www.eislauf-union.de/
- Federazione Italiana Sport del Ghiaccio (Italian Ice Sports Federation) - http://www.fisg.it/
- International Skating Union (ISU) - http://www.isu.org/

♥ Links of Love ♥

These aren't figure skating-related websites, but I wanted to take a moment to point out some websites of organizations that, from what I can tell, and as of this date, are doing major-league amazing work to help bring some light into this world. If you have the time and inclination, I encourage you to visit some of their websites and find out more about them for yourself.

- www.doctorswithoutborders.org   **Doctors Without Borders**, (Médecins Sans Frontières), Providing emergency medical care around the world in desperate situations.
- www.oxfamamerica.org   **Oxfam** is an international confederation of 15 organizations working in more than 90 countries worldwide to find lasting solutions to poverty and related injustice around Providing emergency medical care around the world in desperate situations.
- www.glwd.org   **God's Love We Deliver** is the tri-state area's, (NY, NJ, CT). leading provider of nutritious, individually-tailored meals to people who are too sick to shop or cook for themselves.
- www.angelfood.org   **Project Angel Food** Providing daily meals for people homebound or disabled by HIV/AIDS and other serious illnesses in Los Angeles.
- www.nrdc.org   (**National Resource Defense Council**) NRDC's mission is to safeguard the Earth: its people, its plants and animals and the natural systems on which all life depends.
- www.Care2.com (Click on Take Action/Petition Site)
- www.TheHungerSite.com (Click & Donate Free Food!)
- www.FreeRice.com (Play game & Donate Free Rice!)
- www.OutRightInternational.org   **OutRight Action International** (formerly known as the International Gay & Lesbian Human Rights Campaign) a US-based international non-governmental organization that addresses human rights violations against lesbians, gay men, bisexuals, intersex people, transgender people and people with HIV/AIDS. It is accredited by the United Nations.
- www.jflag.org   **J-FLAG's** mission is to work towards a Jamaican society in which the Human Rights and Equality of Lesbians, All-Sexuals, and Gays are guaranteed.
- www.gmhc.org   **The Gay Men's Health Crisis** (GMHC) is a NYC-based non-profit, volunteer-supported and community-based AIDS service organization that has led the United States in the fight against AIDS.
- www.whyhunger.org   **Why Hunger** (formerly World Hunger Year). Working to eradicate world hunger.
- www.TheTrevorProject.org   Focused on suicide prevention efforts among LGBTQ youth
- www.thursdayschildofli.org   A non-profit agency providing support & housing for people with hiv/aids on Long Island.
- www.VolunteerMatch.org
- www.marrow.org   (Save a life/Donate bone marrow)
- www.stjude.org   St. Jude's Children's Hospital
- www.One.org
- www.Water.org
- www.Kiva.org
- www.ata.org   **ATA** is a global leader in the effort to find a cure for tinnitus. They bring together patients, researchers, healthcare professionals, industry partners and lawmakers to develop tinnitus management tools and fund vital tinnitus research.
- www.licares.org   The mission of **Long Island Cares** – The Harry Chapin Food Bank is to bring together all available resources for the benefit of the hungry on Long Island.

ALSO AVAILABLE from SUGAR MAPLE PRESS

KYLE'S BED & BREAKFAST
by Greg Fox

The first collection of the syndicated comic strip **Kyle's B&B**, about a bed & breakfast in Northport full of drama, romance, and sheer wackiness. When this collection was first released, it became a **Lambda Literary Award Finalist** for "**Best Humor Book of the Year**"! Available now at your local bookstore, and at Amazon.com

• BLACK & WHITE •

KYLE'S BED & BREAKFAST: A Second Bowl of Serial
by Greg Fox

The B&B boys are back for more romance, drama, laughter, and pure wackiness in their second collection of adventures! Included also is a never-before-seen anywhere else 3-episode adventure that is sure to touch your heart! Available now at your local bookstore, and at Amazon.com

• BLACK & WHITE •

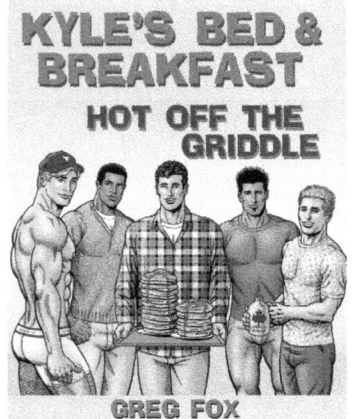

KYLE'S BED & BREAKFAST: Hot Off the Griddle
by Greg Fox

The B&B stories continue, more vibrantly than ever as this volume marks the beginning of the strip's run in FULL COLOR! Some new characters arrive to shake things up, and as always, the shenanigans continue unabated! Available now at your local bookstore, and at Amazon.com

• FULL COLOR •

KYLE'S BED & BREAKFAST: Without Reservations
by Greg Fox

And the B&B stories continue! Once again, in FULL COLOR! We meet some more new arrivals, including Rudy, Olympic figure skater Michael, and the debut of the super-popular Alabama muscle-bear himself, Drew Danvers! Not to mention, a certain couple gets engaged! Also included in this volume is an all-new, never-before published seven page story that is sure to touch your heart! Available now at your local bookstore, and at Amazon.com

• FULL COLOR •

Want to see more of the B&B guys? You can visit with them anytime, and catch up on all the romance, drama, & laughter in every new episode of **Kyle's Bed & Breakfast!**

New episodes posted every other Tuesday at:

WWW.KYLECOMICS.COM

Also, check out the **Kyle's B&B Facebook Page** at:
www.facebook.com/kylecomics

Greg Fox is the writer/illustrator of several comic strips, including "An Angel's Story" and the nationally syndicated comic strip "Kyle's Bed & Breakfast", of which 4 collections have been published. His work was also included in the #1 New York Times bestselling graphic anthology "Love is Love", (DC Comics/IDW), in 2017, and he has done work for several other comic book companies. He is the editor of "The Sugar Maple Press Anthology of Nature Poems". He received a B.A. from Geneseo College in upstate New York. He currently resides in Northport, Long Island, New York. His work can be viewed online at:
www.kylecomics.com

He can be reached at: gregfox727@gmail.com

Greg Fox would like to thank:

- His mother, Eleanor Fox, whose love infuses **An Angel's Story**, **Kyle's Bed &Breakfast**, and his other work.
- Aunt Sheila, for her light, love, laughter and inspiration
- The rest of his family...in New York, California, and elsewhere.
- His friends far and wide: from Huntington, Geneseo, Spize, Sam Ash, Northport, Book Revue, the Berndt Toast gang, and elsewhere.
- The many publications that have published his work over the years.
- All of the readers of **Kyle's B&B** and **An Angel's Story** for their tremendous love & support.
- His Patreon sustaining members, for their deep generosity.
- God, Jesus, the Holy Spirit, St. Jude, and the Angels

Thank You!

www.ingramcontent.com/pod-product-compliance
Lightning Source LLC
Chambersburg PA
CBHW060458090426
42735CB00011B/2032